W9-CSG-941

REVIVING AMERICA'S FORGOTTEN NEIGHBORHOODS

CONTEMPORARY URBAN AFFAIRS
VOLUME 13
ROUTLDGE REFERENCE LIBRARY OF SOCIAL SCIENCE
VOLUME 1404

CONTEMPORARY URBAN AFFAIRS

RICHARD BINGHAM, Series Editor

Reviving America's Forgotten Neighborhoods
An Investigation of Inner City Revitalization Efforts

Elise M. Bright

The Maxine Goodman Levin
College of Urban Affairs
at Cleveland State University

Routledge
New York and London

Published in 2003 by
Routledge
29 West 35th Street
New York, NY 10001
www.routldge-ny.com

Published in Great Britain by
Routledge
11 New Fetter Lane
London EC4P 4EE
www.routledge.co.uk

Routledge is an imprint of the Taylor & Francis Group

Copyright © 2000 by Elise M. Bright

Printed in the United States of America on acid-free paper.

All rights reserved. No part of this book may be reprinted or reproduced or utilized in any form or by any electronic, mechanical, or other means, now known or hereafter invented, including photocopying and recording, or in any information storage or retrieval system, without permission in writing from the publisher.

10 9 8 7 6 5 4 3 2 1

Library of Congress Cataloging-in-Publication Data

Bright, Elise M. (Elise Marie Bussard).
    Reviving America's forgotten neighborhoods: an investigation of inner city revitalization efforts / Elise M. Bright.
        p. cm. — (Contemporary urban affairs) (Routledge reference library of social science)
    Includes bibliographical references and index
    ISBN 0-415-94527-5 (alk. paper)
    1. Urban renewal—United States—Case studies. 2. Urban policy—United States.
I. Title. II. Series. III. Routledge reference library of social science. Contemporary urban affairs.
HT175.B73 .L69 2000
307.3'416'0973—dc21   00-061760

Dedication

This book is dedicated to all those who have not given up on improving life for America's less fortunate, in hopes that it will provide valuable guidance for your efforts. If it inspires elected and appointed officials to make the major changes in federal, state, and local policy that are needed to thoroughly revive our cities, that will be a great accomplishment. But even if it inspires only a single city manager, state housing administrator, foundation director, or federal department head to reach out, form partnerships with other governments and private parties, and start pilot programs based on the lessons learned and presented here, that will be enough to have made this research effort worthwhile.

This book is also dedicated to all those who are struggling to conduct research regarding ways to better the lives of the poor and the excluded. Your work, carried on in the face of little funding or political support, was the inspiration for my efforts.

Contents

Series Editor's Foreword

In *Reviving America's Forgotten Neighborhoods: An Investigation of Inner City Revitalization Efforts,* Elise Bright asks the question: What can be done to improve America's poorest urban neighborhoods? The book answers that question by discussing the approaches used in a variety of low income city neighborhoods that are generally recognized as having achieved some degree of successful revitalization.

The author conducted field research in a dozen cities, interviewing government officials, community groups, and neighborhood representatives. She also visited each of the revitalization projects and collected unpublished documents and plans. The cases presented here offer valuable, transferable lessons for achieving successful redevelopment.

All of the successful programs addressed the major substantive elements of safety, service, shelter, and social capital affecting low income residents' quality of life. Bright identifies a number of procedural factors necessary for successful development, including the following:

Allow area residents to take charge
Provide adequate local government services
Fully support resident-led initiatives
Keep track of temporarily obsolete, abandoned, or derelict sites (TOADS)
    and streamline procedures for their reuse
Pursue regional coordination
Involve the private sector
Insist on microplanning
Be comprehensive
Provide federal support

A combination of these factors seems to explain improvements in neighborhoods in spite of the continuing presence of the forces that created the urban devastation in the first place.

Richard D. Bingham
Cleveland State University

Preface

The poorest parts of America's metropolitan areas have been forgotten, neglected, and abused for decades. They are in dire need of revitalization. The problem has not gone unnoticed: Millions of taxpayers' dollars have been spent to combat inadequate housing, substance abuse, crime, neighborhood abandonment, and the many other symptoms of urban decline that characterize very low income residential neighborhoods. Yet data indicate that overall there has been little improvement in these symptoms, and most have even worsened since the early 1970s (Garreau, 1991; Rusk, 1993; Squires, 1994).

It is easy to become discouraged by these facts, and it is not surprising that to many, the task of revitalization seems hopeless: The problems are so enormous, so complex, so expensive to change, and so intractable that it is difficult to know where to begin.[1] Indeed, the post-1980 cutbacks in federal aid to cities and the 1990s welfare cutbacks, coupled with the lack of support for—or even discussion of—any sweeping federal initiatives, are evidence that many Americans have given up on solving the problems of poor urban neighborhoods. Yet we all would benefit from the reduced crime rates, fewer tax increases, and so on, that would result from improving these neighborhoods. Thus, conscience as well as self-interest dictate that we not give up. Surely there must be something that can be done to improve America's poorest urban neighborhoods—but what?

This book attempts to answer that question by presenting, and commenting on, the approaches used in a variety of low income city neighborhoods that are generally recognized as having achieved at least some degree of successful revitalization. By presenting cases and discussing the insights that can be gleaned from them, it is hoped that this work will prove beneficial to three types of readers. First, those now working to effect neighborhood change may find this information useful in their own efforts. One neighborhood activist summed up the opinions of many interviewees when she said, "There's very little communication among us. We have no idea what our counterparts are doing in other cities" (author's interview with Kate Monter, 1996). This book was written partly in an effort to fill that gap. Second, as discussed in greater detail in Chapter 1, the academic literature is sparse regarding descriptions or analyses of revitalization policies, plans, programs, or projects in very low income residential neighborhoods (throughout this book, references to "projects" or "efforts" should be understood to include projects, policies, plans, and programs). Thus, it is hoped that those who are conducting related research will find this to be a valuable source of information in their academic pursuits. Third, this book is aimed at those who have, or are in training to assume, positions that can influence the comprehensive web of factors that affect the success of revitalization efforts—factors that must be changed if widespread significant neighborhood improvement is ever to occur. It is hoped that these people will consider the book's conclusions when making federal, state, local, neighborhood, and private sector policies and revitalization plans. If they do, then this book will have played a small role in improving life for residents of these presently bypassed parts of the urban landscape.

NOTES

1. This hopeless feeling has been expressed to the author numerous times, both by laypersons and professionals in the field. Perhaps the malaise was best summed up by a graduate student who had just completed a tour of a very low income neighborhood for which his class was beginning development of a revitalization plan. When the class, which was gathered in a vacant lot after the tour, was asked for revitalization ideas, he immediately replied, "Bulldoze it!"

Acknowledgments

The author wishes to acknowledge the support and assistance of the National Center for the Revitalization of Central Cities (NCRCC), University of New Orleans, College of Urban and Public Affairs, and its director, Fritz Wagner, Ph.D., for help in funding and completion of field and background research. Without NCRCC support and the guidance of Fritz and his colleagues Bob Whelan, Mickey Lauria, Tim Joder and Tony Mumphrey, this research would never even have begun. Thanks also to University of Texas at Arlington graduate students David Fleger, Curvie Hawkins, Edward Owens, and Jennifer Kacines, who worked long and hard to help complete the library research, and especially to Theresa Daniel for doing extensive reading, editing, fact checking, and table making in a very short time frame. Special thanks to Richard Cole, dean, School of Urban and Public Affairs, University of Texas at Arlington, for his encouragement and support throughout this project. The cheerful helpfulness of Amy Shipper, Mia Zamora, and Marcia Franco at Garland Press was also much appreciated during the difficult process of getting the manuscript in print.

Especially deserving of thanks is my family. To my children Zack, Larissa, and Sarah, thanks for putting up with hearing "Not now, I have to write!" for so long. You could always make me laugh, and your love kept me from losing my sanity. Thanks also to my husband Neal Chisholm—your willingness to tolerate my working late at night was amazing, and your quiet encouragement, insights, and sense of humor got me through many difficult moments.

I would also like to thank the many people who took time to talk with me—the information you provided made this book possible. In Seattle, I am especially grateful to Janeen Smith, project manager, Housing Development and Rehabilitation Unit, Seattle Department of Housing and Human Services, for always taking the time to provide the latest data for me; George W.

Frost, project manager, Neighborhood Planning Office, City of Seattle, for taking me on a site visit of the area and introducing me to many other helpful people; George Rolfe, professor, University of Washington, for his insights into the development of Pike Place Market and for directing me to other parts of Seattle that could be examples of successful revitalization; Mike Usen, planner, City of Seattle, and John Burbank, director, Fremont Public Association, for information on the plans for Sand Point; and Patricia J. Chemnick (economic development manager for Southeast Effective Development), Ruby Jones (director, Unified Community Economic Development Association, Community Development Corporation); Mark Pomeroy (Housing Development and Rehabilitation Unit, Seattle Department of Housing and Human Services), Jackie Walker (director, Central Area Development Association), and assorted area residents and CDC workers, for sharing their knowledge and enthusiasm with me; Gary Hack, Don Miller and Hilda Blanco of the University of Washington suggested people to contact. In Minneapolis many thanks to Dawn Hagen, public information specialist for the Minneapolis Community Development Agency (MCDA), who gave me much printed information and arranged other meetings; Earl Pettiford, housing manager at the Minneapolis Community Development Agency, who let me take far too much of his time in interviews; Jennifer Billig, with MCDA's Neighborhood Revitalization Program; Cynthia Lee, who answered many faxed questions promptly and at length; and University of Texas at Arlington School of Urban and Public Affairs alumnus and MCDA employee Patrick Connoy, who contacted me and offered to help after reading about the research in a SUPA newsletter. In St. Paul, Principal Planner Lawrence Soderholm and Housing Administrator Gary Peltier (both with the City) deserve special thanks, as does Project Manager Sheryl Pemberton, the friendly staff of the Lowertown Redevelopment Corporation and the McKnight Foundation; Professors Ed Goetz and Judith Martin of the University of Minnesota suggested information sources and interviewees for the Twin Cities. Marshall Runkel, an aide to City Councilman Erik Sten, was a helpful guide and information source for Portland; planning director Pamela Sweet provided information on Ottawa, and York University Professor Francis Frisken gave me valuable insights into Toronto's government. In Boston, former Dudley Neighbors Inc. (DNI) Executive Director Paul Yelder deserves special mention for his time spent in interviews; Dudley Street Neighborhood Initiative (DSNI) staffer Trish Settles, local businessman Glen Lloyd and former Director Frank Sepulveda conducted an area site visit that provided much valuable information; resident and historic preservation activist Thomas Plant gave insights into the area's historic structures; Planner Michael Thomas (with the Neighborhood Planning Division, Boston Department of Neighborhood Development) deserves special recognition for returning numerous long distance phone calls to help me track down details, and former Boston Redevelopment Authority (BRA) employee Patrick McGuigan provided insights into local politics and program administration; Michelle Thompson of Cornell and Sam Bass Warner of MIT guided me to the right people for interviews and reviewing. In Pittsburgh, Manchester Citizens Corporation (MCC) Executive Director Rhonda Brandon, Bloomfield-Garfield CDC Deputy Director Aggie Brose and Executive Director Richard Swartz, PCRG Research Analyst Myron Dowell and several others, and Action Housing Director John Zimmer were very helpful, on very short notice; PCRG Administrative Assistant Diane Smith was invaluable in arranging interviews, and Dr. Sabina Dietrick of the University of Pittsburgh helped with brownfields information and contact names. In Cleveland, City Neighborhood Planner Nora McNamara along with Michael M. Sweeney (director, Delinquent Tax Department, Office of the County Treasurer) and Joseph A. Sidoti (assistant commissioner, Department of Community Development, City of Cleveland Division of Neighborhood Development) deserve special thanks for devoting so much time to interviews and to showing me around the neighborhoods; Kate Monter Durban, assistant to the director of the Cleveland Housing Network, provided valuable information; and James Kunde of SUPA and Dennis Keating of CSU helped me find the right people to contact.

Finally, I would like to thank those people whom I interviewed but whose efforts are not directly reflected in this book. The insights you provided were very helpful in guiding the research, and in corroborating the factors that appeared to be important in the larger case studies; they gave me courage to claim wider applicability for the conclusions of this book. Thanks to Kendra Proctor, policy analyst, and Patrick McGuigan, executive director of the Providence Plan; professor Hilary Silver with the University of Rhode Island; Matt Powell, former executive director of the Providence Plan Housing Corporation; Tom Deller, deputy director of the Providence Planning and Development Department; Patricia Gallagher, Chicago's Cityspace project director; Len Hopper, chief of landscape architecture, New York City Housing Authority; Planners Donald Burns and Takisia Ward with the Bronx Borough; and especially to Gail Ryan, director of Ft. Worth Habitat for Humanity, whose call for assistance started me down this path.

List of Figures and Tables

List of Abbreviations

BID	Business Improvement District
CBO	Community Based Organization
CDBG	Community Development Block Grant
CDC	Community Development Corporation
CHDO	Community Housing Development Organization
CPTED	Crime Prevention through Environmental Design
CRA	Community Reinvestment Act of 1977, as amended
DOE	U.S. Department of Energy
DHHS	U.S. Department of Health and Human Services
DOT	U.S. Department of Transportation
EDA	U.S. Department of Commerce Economic Development Administration
FDIC	Federal Deposit Insurance Corporation
FHA	Federal Housing Administration
HMDA	Home Mortgage Disclosure Act
HOW	Home Ownership Works
HUD	U.S. Department of Housing and Urban Development
LISC	Local Initiatives Support Corporation
MUD	Municipal Utility District
NRP	Neighborhood Renaissance Partnership
PDA	Public Development Authority
PID	Public Improvement District
SRO	Single Room Occupancy
TDR	Transfer of Development Rights
TIF	Tax Increment Financing
TOADS	Temporarily Obsolete, Abandoned, or Derelict Sites
UDAG	Urban Development Action Grants

URA   Urban Redevelopment Authority
UTA   University of Texas at Arlington
VA   Veterans Administration
ZBA   Zoning Board of Adjustment (or Appeals)

CHAPTER 1

Setting the Stage

The effort to answer the question posed in the Preface—What can be done to improve America's poorest urban neighborhoods?—could follow at least two logical research paths. The first approach would be deductive: A search of the literature could identify theoretical constructs regarding why some urban neighborhoods have problems and what might improve them, in hopes that deductive reasoning could then be used to apply the results to real neighborhoods. The second approach would be inductive, based on empirical knowledge: Cases of successful low income neighborhood revitalization could be studied in hopes of deriving a paradigm regarding why these problems developed and what might improve these areas. This research employs aspects of both approaches—however, for reasons explained in the following sections, the focus is on the inductive approach.

THE DEDUCTIVE APPROACH

Many Americans think they know why the slums are so filled with problems: it is the fault of the people who live there. This attitude is well-documented in numerous popular articles and in the work of William Julius Wilson (1987), who coined the term "the undeserving poor" to describe this popular perception and who presents carefully researched evidence to counter it. Research shows that low income neighborhood residents are commonly viewed as being criminals, drunks, and drug dealers who threaten good citizens in the "better" parts of town; as people who have babies in order to get more welfare money (see Anderson, 1990, for convincing evidence to the contrary); people who don't get married because they want the rest of us to be responsible for their kids (Mead, 1992; see W. J. Wilson, 1987, for an opposing view); who don't hold jobs because they'd rather live off the rest of us (Schien, 1995, documents and eloquently refutes this attitude); and who have chosen to replace American "family values" with drugs, domestic violence, and crime (see Adler, 1995, for an alternative, more realistic and compassionate view of the reasons for the prevalence of these problems).

The literature reveals that the reasons for low income neighborhood problems are far different. There are many works that suggest a wide range of possible causes for the present condition of very low income neighborhoods, ranging from globalization of the economy to a lack of "marriageable men" (in addition to those mentioned in the following paragraphs, see Downs, 1991; Fainstein, 1994; Feagin, 1978; Fuller & Fuller, 1990; Orum, 1995; Phillips, 1996; Roudebush & Well, 1980; Sands, 1994; Sawicki & Craig, 1996). Here is a brief summary of these studies.

The roots of the deterioration found in so many of America's big cities reach back to the slowing of European immigration in the early 1900s, and the ripple effect of successive waves of poorer people moving into the aging housing stock. The massive migration of African-Americans from the south in the ensuing decades (Keating, Krumholz, & Perry, 1995) coupled with housing discrimination when they arrived initiated the formation of racially segregated neighborhoods, replacing the ethnically segregated ones that had previously housed European immigrants (Whyte, 1966). There is no doubt that the quality of life in these segregated neighborhoods was far from ideal; minority neighborhoods suffered from lower levels of city service provision, school quality, and so on, than were found in their nonminority counterpart areas. But there is also no doubt that the quality of life in these minority neighborhoods then was much better than it is today, largely because, as the reader will see in Malcolm X's description of his life in Roxbury, Massachusetts (quoted in Chapter 4), these neighborhoods contained the full spectrum of economic and social groups. Until the federal government stepped in after World War II (as explained in the next paragraph), America's big cities still housed large numbers of middle class and wealthy residents. These people not only had the political clout necessary to demand adequate schools, roads, police protection, and other city services, they also provided the tax base to fund provision of these services. Even the racially segregated neighborhoods were, at least, economically integrated (Byrum, 1992; Jacobs, 1969; Whyte, 1966).

But in the 1950s and 1960s a number of well-intentioned programs were enacted into law that, although often successful in achieving their stated goals, had severe unintended adverse effects on big-city urban neighborhoods throughout the country. First, the postwar Federal Housing Administration (FHA) and Veterans Administration (VA) mortgage loan programs coupled with U.S. Department of Transportation urban highway-building programs in following years[1] energized white flight to the suburbs; soon, jobs and businesses left too (Byrum, 1992). Urban highway-building not only made living far from work a real possibility, it also displaced thousands of city residents, ruining the one advantage still held by urban neighborhoods when compared to the suburbs: quality of social life, or social capital.[2] Displacement reached new heights as the federal urban renewal program was implemented in the 1950s and 1960s, further disrupting viable neighborhoods (Gans, 1962) and accentuating the displacement and reconcentration of the urban poor in cities throughout America. In response, in the late 1960s riots broke out in poor minority urban neighborhoods across the nation, just as federal civil rights laws were passed, which began to open the suburbs to middle and upper class minorities. The 1970s and 1980s also saw the passage of tough federal environmental laws such as brownfields cleanup requirements and enhanced global communications and transportation, which facilitated not only legitimate business but also the international drug trade (Adler, 1995), and relaxation of federal economic and legal barriers to manufacturing overseas where labor was cheap, regulations few, and benefits lacking. Together these forces lured away the few manufacturing jobs that had resisted the flight to the suburbs (Blakely, 1994; Judd & Parkinson, 1990). In the 1980s the federal government delivered the final blow when it slashed its aid to cities.

The end result of all these unintended side effects of otherwise well-conceived federal policies and programs should have been entirely predictable. Nearly all those who could move out of the old urban neighborhoods did, leaving the poor (including many single mothers and their children), elderly homeowners, and the mentally ill or physically disabled behind (Baum & Burnes, 1993). Meanwhile, with political and economic power leaving, city services were cut back, and the remaining city residents were left to fill the gap with their own dwindling financial resources. Buildings and lots were abandoned, and the once-proud neighborhoods became seas of devastation. A foreign visitor summed up the result when he returned, shocked and disillusioned after spending the day working in a Dallas slum, and declared, "These places are worse than Lebanon during the war!" (author's interview with Aref Joulani, 1990).

Federal policies may have been the initiators of inner city neighborhood decline, but their effects were supported and augmented by longstanding state and local policies and laws that obstructed what efforts were made to keep urban neighborhoods vital. For example, in an effort to attract businesses, many localities loosened up zoning laws to the point of creating blight (Babcock & Weaver, 1979). State laws regarding property appraisal and tax assessment and collection fueled abandonment and decimated property values in some poor neighborhoods (Bright, 1995). City decisions regarding provision of services, infrastructure maintenance, and allocation of grant funds often penalized inner city neighborhoods (Wagner, Joder, & Mumphrey, 1995; Bright, 1996). The lack of effective state and local policies regarding growth management and intergovernmental cooperation did nothing but help to fuel the federally financed move of upper and middle class residents to the suburbs (Nelson & Milgroom, 1993). In the academic literature, these state and local laws and policies have received much less attention than the federal ones. However, the reader will see that the cases documented in this book show them to be of paramount importance. Even if no new federal initiatives are proposed, there is much that states and localities can do to undo the damage done to their poor neighborhoods.

Besides discussing reasons for decline, the academic literature offers many substantive, often divergent solutions. Mixing incomes is favored by some (Levitt, 1987; Gratz, 1994), while others believe that the existing low income population should be retained without gentrification (Gans, 1962). Some favor regional government as a solution (Rusk, 1993), while others emphasize the need for community control (Glaser, Denhardt, & Grubbs 1995); some favor housing construction (Fuller & Fuller, 1990), while others tout the importance of building social capital (Schien, 1995); some suggest universal subsidies (Wilson, 1987), while others favor programs that target the needy (Feagin, 1975). In sum, there appears to be little agreement on which are the best substantive programs[3] to improve America's low income neighborhoods.

On closer observation, however, one realizes that many of these published works are focusing on a part of the problem. To borrow an analogy from children's literature, in the folk tale about the blind men and the elephant, each visually challenged man describes an elephant based on what he felt when touching one part. Each is convinced that his description is correct, and in fact, for the part of the elephant each man touched, it is. But all the information must be combined to even approximate a description of a whole elephant.

The scholars whose works were cited previously are far from blind; they take great pains to point out the limits of their work and the importance of conducting further research into the problem at hand, and many of them see a great deal of the proverbial elephant. The point of the story is simply to suggest that there may be more agreement in the current literature than there first appears to be, since much of the work is complementary rather than contradictory; all the authors may be right. The causes of low income neighborhood decline are legion. A plethora of federal, state, regional and local government policies are cited as culprits; policies of lending institutions, insurance companies, retailers and corporations are also responsible. Likewise, a multitude of actions apparently would be needed to effect change. For example, reviving a single neighborhood may necessitate efforts designed to retain the existing population while encouraging wealthier new residents to move in; universal child care subsidies as well as targeted income subsidies; and so on. Finally, since each neighborhood is different, no single substantive combination of programs—for example, jobs for teenagers and housing rehabilitation—will work in all neighborhoods. The substantive aspects of revitalization must be tailored to each area.

Thus, it became clear that building a deductive model based on current literature was well beyond the scope of this research effort. Indeed, the problem is so complex that it seems beyond our capabilities to solve—as complex as sending a human to another star or finding a cure for AIDS. However, the deductive investigation was still used in the data analysis; not to build a comprehensive model revitalization program, but as a check on the conclusions derived from the descriptive studies. For example, if a factor was found to be important in several revitalization efforts, was it also mentioned in the literature and were theories advanced as to why? A factor that was important in the revitalization projects studied but was not mentioned very often in the literature would be less likely to be included in any paradigm that might be derived from the case material. With this in mind, we turned to evidence from the real world. Perhaps some substantive or procedural common ground would be found there.

THE INDUCTIVE APPROACH

There are case studies that focus on successful instances of commercial revitalization in low income areas (Gratz, 1995; Ford Foundation, 1973; Frieden & Sagalyn, 1992; Kotler, 1978; McNulty, Jacobson, & Penne, 1985; Wagner et al., 1995). In the 1970s, some of these were of major importance in spreading the concept of the community development corporation, while others arc now receiving attention as models for downtown redevelopment or new urbanist approaches. The proven utility of this literature gave support for the idea that an empirical study of successful residential revitalization efforts in poor neighborhoods could yield important information regarding what actions apparently succeed in achieving neighborhood revitalization.

Detailed case studies of the revitalization of poor urban residential neighborhoods are more rare than are commercial ones; there is very little empirical research regarding what has worked for the former. Apparently, either there are few successes to report, or they have not been widely publicized.[4] What documentation there is (for example, Keating, Krumholz, & Star, 1996; Medoff & Sklar, 1994; Mier, 1993; Pierce & Guskind, 1993; Rooney, 1995; Temkin & Rohe, 1996; van Vliet, 1997) lends support to the idea that case studies might provide valuable insights. Thus the research question "What can be done to improve America's poorest urban neighborhoods?" was refined to focus on the inductive approach, becoming "What, if any, lessons for achieving success might be extracted from studying apparently successful low income residential neighborhood improvement efforts?" In order to answer this question we first had to discover whether any successful revitalization efforts have occurred in these neighborhoods. If the results were positive, we would investigate how the successful revitalization was achieved and what lessons might be applicable elsewhere.

DEFINING SUCCESSFUL REVITALIZATION

In order to identify suitable projects for study, the concept of "successful revitalization" first has to be defined. This concept really necessitates two definitions: "revitalization" and "success."

The issue of what constitutes "revitalization" and how best to measure it remains unresolved in the existing literature (for example, Baker, 1995; Byrum, 1992; Varady, 1986). For the purpose of this book, "revitalization" is defined as "changes that improve the existing residents' 'quality of life.'" This necessitates a definition of "quality of life." Many scholars have attempted to define and measure quality of life (for example, Burchell & Listokin, 1981; Cole, Smith, & Taebel, 1984; Environmental Protection Agency, 1973; McNulty et al., 1985; Myers, 1988; Savageau, 1993). As discussed earlier, many scholars have also identified a wide range of problems—that is, barriers to a high quality of life—faced by residents of very low income inner city areas (for example, see Anderson, 1990; Blakely, 1994; Ferguson & Dickens, 1999; Fuller & Fuller, 1990; Gittell & Vidal, 1999; Orum, 1995; Phillips, 1996; Roudebush & Well, 1980; Sawicki & Craig, 1996; Schien, 1995; Squires, 1994; Wilson, 1987). After a thorough review of the works, the author developed a typology designed for inner city residential areas in which quality of life is reflected by the quality of neighborhood safety, services, shelter, and social capital, with a large number of more detailed items falling into each of these four broad categories. Thus "revitalization" was defined as improvement in the factors listed in Figure 1.

Next came the need to define "successful" revitalization. Statistics show that in most of the measures of safety, services, and shelter listed in Figure 1, in any large city the poorest neighborhoods rank at or near the bottom (McHarg, 1969; U.S. Bureau of the Census, 1960, 1970, 1980 and 1990). Only in the area of social capital can a case be made that low income unrevitalized neighborhoods are on a par with, or even superior to, their wealthier neighbors (Baumgartner, 1988; Gans, 1962; Whyte, 1966) prior to revitalization. Thus, measures of safety, services, and shelter correlate well with the income level of urban neighborhoods, as do some social capital measures. At least in theory, they could form a set of benchmarks for assessing the success of revitalization efforts. Note that measures of wealth (income, property values, and so on) are not included in Figure 1. This represents a deliberate decision, the reasons for which are discussed later in this chapter.

MEASURING SUCCESS

Projects that produced overall improvement in some of the measures of residents' safety, services, shelter and/or social capital (as listed in Figure 1) were considered to be at least partially successful. However, determining the extent of the improvement and whether it occurred as a direct result of the project

FIGURE 1. Factors Considered Neighborhood Quality of Life Determinants

(Lists under each factor are not comprehensive, but serve as examples of data that could be used as indicators of the factor above it.)

Safety

- Rates of violent crime and crimes against property: murder, rape, domestic violence, child abuse, arson, burglary, theft
- Rates of death, particularly for persons under 65: infant mortality, miscarriage, cancer, suicide, accidents
- Rates of alcohol and drug abuse: arrests for possession, DWI arrests, dealing arrests, treatment referrals
- Degree of exposure to environmental toxins: lead-contaminated soil, presence of brownfields, air pollution data

Services

- Adequacy of government services:
    age and size of water and sewer lines
    distance to police and fire stations
    frequency of garbage service, and large item pickup
    condition of streets and sidewalks
    presence of litter, junk, weeds
    quality of landscaping in publicly owned areas
    number and condition of parks, libraries, recreation centers, other public facilities
    frequency and types of transit service
    number of police officers per person

- Access to adequate business services:
    number, pay, and types of neighborhood employment opportunities
    distance to employment, and accessibility by transit
    number and types of retail shopping opportunities
    distance to grocery store, drug store, and other retail shopping, and accessibility by transit
    number and types of entertainment facilities (restaurant, theater)
    distance to entertainment facilities, and accessibility by transit

- Adequacy of social services:
    primary and secondary education
    private, trade, or vocational schools (cost, programs)
    colleges and universities (cost, programs, accessibility by transit)
    child care (cost, programs, vacancy rates, accessibility by transit)
    places of worship
    distance to shelters (homeless, safe houses, soup kitchens)
    emergency intervention and placement services
    programs for delivery of food and medicine
    distance to social services agencies, and accessibility by transit
    distance to medical clinic and hospital
    number of doctors per person

(continued)

FIGURE 1.   Factors Considered Neighborhood Quality of Life Determinants
          (*continued*)

Shelter

- Number and condition of housing units by type:
    range and median rent, residential property value, and vacant property value
    availability of housing for extended families, disabled residents, the homeless,
       elderly individuals, and other types of nonnuclear households

- Access to homeownership (loan availability, new construction, rehab, and so on)

- Number of abandoned, dilapidated, or derelict properties (TOADS):
    number, value and amount owed on city and private tax-delinquent property

- Level of neighborhood maintenance:
    code enforcement citations and follow-up
    litter control citations and follow-up
    number of code enforcement officers per person
    level of government and private property maintenance

Social Capital

- Presence of informal networks of people (family, friends, neighbors)

- Urban design that provides opportunities for meeting and being with a variety of
  people, discouraging crime, expressing neighborhood heritage (Crime Prevention
  through Environmental Design, path/district/node/edge/landmark analysis, murals,
  markers)

- Access to city political power; population growth

- Regular contact with people of other incomes, races, ethnicities, and education
- Presence of, and funding for, formal networks of people (Community Develop-
    ment Corporations, other community based organizations, interest groups)

proved to be no easy task. A quantitative approach was considered and
rejected, for the following reasons. First, data is only available for many of
the measures every ten years, when the Census is taken; this time frame is too
long, and/or too much at odds with project timing, to detect changes resulting
from a single neighborhood revitalization effort. Also, many of the revitalization efforts were not finished before 1990, so their effects would not yet show
in the Census. Data on other measures (for example crime rates, infant mortality rates, presence of toxic substances, unemployment, and so on) are
available at varying intervals, which may or may not prove useful with
respect to project inception, completion, and impact assessment. All the data
from all sources suffer from problems of reliability and comparability, since
they are collected in different ways and these ways change within the same
data category over time. Geographic compatibility is another issue; the data
are aggregated into geographic areas with boundaries that often do not coin-

cide with those used in other data collection efforts, and that bear little resemblance to what might be considered an impact area for a given revitalization project. Finally, data on some measures simply are not available at all, particularly baseline data (that is, data from the years before the project began). Moving to issues of data analysis, it is nearly impossible to know whether factors other than the revitalization project might account for some change in the data, and if so, how to adjust for it in the assessment. In view of all these problems, initial project selection was based on identification of the project as "successful" in the literature. Although they were located in low income areas, many of the projects initially identified in the literature as "successful" involved the replacement of low income residents with either higher income residents (for example, those who could afford luxury housing), or with non-residential uses—for example, commercial, industrial, office, or highway development (Begovich, 1995; Coffey & Kliniewski, 1988; Martz, 1995; Saltman, 1990; Schill, Nathan, & Persaud, 1983; Singer, 1989; Sutro, 1990). Those who define successful revitalization in terms of wealth (for example, increasing residents' incomes or area property values) would probably consider such projects successful. However, the definition of successful revitalization given previously is based on improvements in the quality of life of existing neighborhood residents. One cannot assume that increased neighborhood income levels or property values mean that the existing residents' quality of life has improved; in fact, numerous studies have shown that often such increases resulted from gentrification, and that by disrupting neighborhoods and displacing residents, the gentrification actually decreased the existing residents' quality of life (Gans, 1962; Gratz, 1995). Indeed, the idea that an increase in income or property value alone would indicate better quality of life has overtones of class prejudice that should make it suspect. It is important to note that the existence of poverty is not the underlying cause of neighborhood decline; the literature clearly shows (as discussed earlier in this chapter) that the real cause is its concentration. Thus, if increases in income or property values are caused by income mixing without displacement then they could be a positive indicator of success, but income or property values alone cannot show this. Therefore, a project that resulted in gentrification and displacement would not be considered successful—despite higher resulting area income and property value—unless it produced improvements in the quality of life of both the new residents and the existing low income residents. This is at least theoretically possible: Even massive relocation of low income residents could be successful, if improvements in their postrelocation quality of life were great enough to outweigh the destruction of social fabric that relocation causes and if improvements were also made as promised on the site. Unfortunately, the literature clearly shows that neither of these caveats as adhered to in the urban renewal/urban highway programs, which are the most prevalent types of projects in the United States involving massive relocation of the poor (Gruen, 1964; Caro, 1975; Phillips, 1996). There is no evidence whatsoever that this approach to successful revitalization, however possible it may be theoretically, has ever actually been achieved (Babcock, 1979; Feagin & Parker, 1990). Therefore, projects directly benefiting (rather than displacing) low-income residents were expected to be most successful, and were given priority for investigation in this study. Inadvertently, the decision to consider as successful only those projects that benefited existing residents allowed resolution of another major issue in defining successful revitalization: Should the measure of success be improvements in the neighborhood, or in the lives of its residents? As one expert put it, "[There is] confusion with respect to assertions regarding the identification of successfully revitalized neighborhoods. Is the criterion of success the social mobility of the population or the improved physical appearance of the area?" (Hornburg, 1998) Since projects that resulted in the poor moving out were not considered successful, social mobility is not a factor in this definition of success; appearance is one of many factors listed in Figure 1 as determinants of quality of life, and thus it would have some effect. Most success factors have little to do with either social mobility or appearance, however.

PROJECT SELECTION AND DATA COLLECTION

The work began with an extensive literature search designed to identify projects described as successful in low income neighborhood revitalization. In view of the common perception that revitalizing these neighborhoods is a hopeless task, it was somewhat surprising that the search produced more than 250 candidate projects. Unfortunately, the documentation itself is quite sparse: Usually, successful projects were given a few brief paragraphs in the mainstream literature. More project descriptions were found in business trade publications than in the academic planning/urban affairs/administration literature. Clearly, this is a neglected part of the field. The criteria described previously regarding gentrification and displacement of existing residents was then applied. This culled from the list slightly fewer than one hundred possibilities, most of which were in the upper Midwest and Northeast. This does not necessarily mean that these two parts of the country are doing a better job with low income neighborhoods. As Michael R. Greenberg and Frank J. Popper (1994) concluded from the results of a recent survey, "The large cities in the northeast and midwest typically reported more temporarily obsolete abandoned derelict sites (TOADS) than their southern and western counterparts. Buildings are newer in the Sunbelt, and the region's rapid economic growth has raised the value of almost any property in many areas." Since the TOADS problem is larger in these parts of the country, one would expect that these areas would also have the largest sampling of successful revitalization efforts. A questionnaire was then prepared in an effort to standardize data collection, and a site visit itinerary was developed. At this point, some projects were dropped from the survey simply for logistical reasons: Promising efforts in Atlanta, Miami, Indianapolis, and several parts of California were not included in the site visits, although the available written material was analyzed to determine if there were major inconsistencies with the conclusions expressed later in this book. The author then conducted field research in Boston, Cleveland, Chicago, Louisville, Minneapolis, New York, Pittsburgh, Portland, Providence, St. Louis, Seattle, Toronto, and Washington, DC. City staff, nonprofit group activists, and neighborhood representatives were interviewed, after relying on a series of phone calls to determine who was most familiar with the project and would therefore be interviewed. In addition to describing the area's preproject conditions, the process by which the project was carried out and the issues addressed, interviewees were asked to comment on the degree to which each project had improved the factors listed in Figure 1. Their comments resulted in some changes in the study. For example, one city was dropped after in-person interviews with local experts revealed that although tremendous improvement has been made downtown, they felt little change in the city's poor neighborhoods had actually occurred. The author also visited each project area and ranked its condition using a composite of neighborhood evaluation scales (see, for example, Burchell & Listokin, 1981) with additional factors added. Unpublished documents and copies of local plans and policies were obtained in order to identify key substantive and procedural project components. Finally, after the site visits had been made and all the other data had been collected and analyzed, the author rated each project according to the criteria listed in Figure 1. These results are discussed in Chapter 7, and summarized in Tables 7–8 of that chapter.

RESULTS

From the list of cities visited, a few clearly successful efforts emerged. Others can be viewed as partially successful. All of these cases offered valuable, transferable, lessons for achieving success. Chapters 2 through 6 explain the policies, plans, and programs implemented in Seattle, where planning has been especially important; the Twin Cities (contrasted with Portland and some Canadian cities), where a regional approach has been used and foundation support has also been very important; Boston, where a grassroots resident-based effort produced outstanding results; Pittsburgh, where residents have excelled in putting the Community Reinvestment Act to work; and Cleveland, which has reused thousands of TOADS (temporarily obsolete abandoned dilapidated sites) (see Greenberg & Popper, 1994). Other notable efforts—for example, those in Atlanta, Baltimore, New York, Chicago, Louisville, Oakland, and St. Louis—are not included simply due to lack of space: However, data from these cities also support the conclusions drawn from those efforts that are included in this book. The conclusions (Chapter 7) discuss the efforts' commonalities. For example, all of the projects included in the study achieved success by addressing a wide spectrum of the factors that affect low income residents' quality of life. But beyond the overall similarities, the cities differ from one another in that each has emphasized some factors more than others. It is clear that every case study offers its own unique set of lessons, each of which will have varying degrees of usefulness in other spheres. The author must ask for the reader's sympathy, tolerance, and understanding when digesting the details of each case. The neighborhood dynamics in each city are extremely complex, with quality of life affected by an intricate web of factors. Thus, no single chapter could possibly paint a complete picture of any urban neighborhood or revitalization effort; some omissions and inaccuracies are inevitable. Also, the way in which events, their causes, and their levels of success are viewed depends in part on one's perspective. For example, if one compares a real project to an ideal standard then it might be viewed less favorably than if it is compared to other similar projects. The author has tried to make her basis for comparison and her perspective clear, and to paint the most accurate picture possible. Hopefully, the reader will be able to overlook any minor unintentional factual errors or omissions, differences in interpretation of facts, or differing perspectives that they may find, and focus instead on the lessons these cities have to offer to us all.

NOTES

1. Massive urban highway construction is not dead, although it now poses more opportunities for neighborhood-building than threats to existing neighborhoods, as Boston's Central Artery Project shows. The Central Artery, which divides the city's downtown from the waterfront, carries almost 200,000 vehicles every day. More than 20,000 homes were torn down in the 1950s to build the north-south highway. Partly because of its characteristic massive traffic jams, the Artery is now being torn down and relocated underground; it is the largest highway project currently under construction in the United States. The $13.1 billion project, which is funded 85% by the Federal Highway Administration, is the most expensive few miles of highway ever built in the U.S. Planning was begun in 1986; construction started in 1991 and will not be finished until at least 2004, when the old highway is scheduled for demolition. This will free up 27 acres of prime property in the heart of Boston, much of which is scheduled to be retained as open space. This idea has generated much criticism from local planners; as Boston architect Jonathan Hale said, ". . . the artery fails in its plans for knitting the city back together—blowing a once-in-a-lifetime opportunity . . . [the] swath of undefined open space puts the reuse plan squarely in the anti-urban tradition of 1960s windswept plazas. We have an example in the desolate City Hall Plaza, a product of that era. If the artery planners really want to undo the old highway's lingering damage, they should be thinking of small squares, intimate parks—the kind of open space that would connect new buildings and activities with the old" (Hodges, 1998b).

Others contend that the unprecedented opportunities for city building and renewal presented by the project have not been ignored; in fact, they are a key part of the environmental impact mitigation required. The artery project's environmental manager Allan Hodges (1998b) said, "Our main objective was to mitigate the barrier created by the elevated highway. . . . All this land is publicly owned, but the city and the state have committed to public-private development partnerships where appropriate. Design guidelines have been drawn up. . . ." A total of $4.4 billion will be spent on mitigation, including the cleanup, substantial expansion, and creation of a park on Boston Harbor's Spectacle Island using some of the 13.5 million cubic yards of dirt that must be disposed of. Whether the Central Artery project becomes a landmark case of highway building that supports urban neighborhood life or becomes one more example of highway-induced devastation remains to be seen.

2. *Social capital* is perhaps the most nebulous of the four elements to define and quantify. It refers in large part to the community interactions implicit in the African proverb "It takes a village to raise a child" (a theme expanded on in Hillary Clinton's 1996 book). As writer Sylvia Paine (1995) summarized, "An area such as Nicollet Island in Minneapolis does not preserve itself without a close sense of community." This closeness is expressed in everything from block parties to neighborhood ball games; as one Nicollet resident said, "The community has its own structure, its own rules. You can't take action one hundred percent unilaterally. You have to discuss things with your neighbors or matters don't go right." Felecia Mitchell-Bute of Chicago's South Austin Community Council gave an example of one aspect of social capital situated in a rundown apartment building. "They [the female residents] had this support network, sisters and cousins who lived in the same building and raised each other's kids in spite of the fact that the building was falling in around them" (Activist Women Explore Shelter Issues, 1986). These examples are in line with the definition given by Ferguson and Dickens (1999), who defined social capital as "norms, shared understandings, trust, and other factors that make relationships feasible and productive," adding that it is one of five basic forms of community assets (the other four being physical capital, intellectual and human capital, financial capital, and political capital).

Social capital can carry a wider meaning. For example, Temkin and Rohe (1996) include in their definition "the degree to which residents feel their neighborhood is a spatially distinct place; interact with one another in the form of borrowing small items, visiting, discussing local problems, and helping each other with small tasks; work and socialize in the neighborhood; and use neighborhood facilities for worship and grocery shopping . . . [as well as] the presence and quality of neighborhood organizations, voting by residents, volunteer efforts and the degree to which those are focused on neighborhood issues, and the visibility of the neighborhood to citywide officials. . . ." (Gittell & Vidal, 1999). This definition is broader than the one summarized in Figure 1, since it includes some items that would be included under services (worship facilities, groceries), but in all other respects it is the same.

Change can threaten social capital in ways other than overt neighborhood destruction.

> South Boston . . . lost half its population between 1950 and 1990, but it stayed physically intact and maintained its ethnic character. . . . Today, the community's 31,000 residents are still mainly of Irish descent and many of the traditional

businesses have hung on. But over the last few years, the character of businesses along Broadway, South Boston's Main Street, has changed. . . . "South Boston has been discovered," says housing activist Martin Nee, who fears that the close-knit community will lose its special qualities as a result. . . . [head of the South Boston Chamber of Commerce Michael] Foley adds that rents have doubled in the past few years. "It's hard for a working class family that can only afford $800 a month to compete with three guys who make $45,000 each a year and are willing to pay $1,400 for a three-bedroom apartment." Both Nee and Foley are apprehensive about the Boston Redevelopment Authority's newly issued plan for the South Boston Seaport, an area that Mayor Thomas Menino has called the city's "growth frontier." The plan for the 1,000-acre site calls for a new convention center, 3,800 hotel rooms, and 6,400 new jobs. (Homsy, 1998)

These apprehensions reflect a perceived potential loss of neighborhood social capital as gentrification occurs.

3. By "substantive programs" I mean those directed at a particular problem such as jobs, housing, drugs, education, and so on. Figure 1 lists many of the substantive issues that influence neighborhood quality of life.

4. In view of the dearth of case material, it strikes the author as odd that there is an enormous body of anecdotal evidence on the subject. The news media often cover stories such as the welfare mother hired to work in the White House, or the paroled felon now employed by the governor. Yet building on these anecdotes to describe success beyond the level of the individual, or even to analyze individual anecdotes in hopes of identifying commonalities that might be associated with success on a larger scale, does not seem to commonly occur. Despite this lack of data, the public is quick to seize upon these anecdotes, combine them with a generous sprinkling of political rhetoric, and form strong opinions regarding what should be done about "the problem," whether the focus is crime, abandonment, joblessness, drug abuse, or any of the other urban ills that are believed to characterize low income neighborhoods. The lack of understanding of the complex nature of these problems, coupled with an aversion to learning more on the subject, is truly remarkable and makes the task of program development to achieve success even more difficult. Ways to overcome the biased views of an angry, ill-informed public in order to develop programs that build on the successes described in this and other case studies, is a topic beyond the scope of this book, which is in need of further research.

CHAPTER 2

Seattle
A Planned Approach

ROOTS OF DECLINE

The city of Seattle experienced rapid postwar growth until the 1960s, when the trend reversed. By 1980 more than 60,000 people had left the city, most choosing a suburban location. This scenario mirrors that found in large cities throughout the northern United States; unlike many snowbelt cities, however, since 1980 Seattle's low income neighborhoods have experienced an influx of new, more affluent residents while retaining the pre-existing low income population. Evidence shows that this reversal of two decades of out-migration was the result of revitalization planning and implementation efforts that are characterized by city-resident cooperation, with the local government and the voters providing extensive citywide support for resident-led microplanning, housing, and other improvements within low income neighborhoods, coupled with heavy incentives to encourage income and use mixing throughout the city.

From 1950 to 1960 Seattle's population increased by 89,496 people (19.1%), reaching its peak size in 1960 with a population of 557,000. However, this does not mean that people were choosing central city life over suburban living: Nearly all of this increase was due to annexation. By 1960, 86,079 people (15.5% of the city's population) were living in territory annexed during the previous ten years, giving Seattle the thirteenth largest numerical population increase for a city in the nation resulting from annexation during this period. Indeed, Seattle's suburban growth was even more explosive, with the population living outside the city limits rising from 153,918 in 1950 to 307,022 in 1960 (U.S. Bureau of the Census, 1950 and 1960). Table 1 shows more of the details.

Annexation slowed after 1960, and population within Seattle's city limits began to decline: By 1980, more than 60,000 people had left. As is the case in

Table 1: Population Change in Seattle Area, 1950 through 1990

	City of Seattle	King County	Seattle-Tacoma CMSA*	CMSA Area Outside Seattle
1950	467,504	732,992	1,008,868	541,364
1960	557,087	935,014	1,428,803	871,716
1970	530,831	1,156,633	1,832,896	1,302,065
1980	493,846	1,269,749	2,093,112	1,599,266
1990	516,259	1,507,319	2,559,164	2,042,905

Source: U.S. Bureau of the Census, 1950–1990
*Consolidated Metropolitan Statistical Area

many of America's cities, this exodus was at least in part due to a massive migration to the suburbs. During the same time period, the population of Seattle's suburbs continued to grow, adding more than 700,000 people to the urban area. Although Seattle has not undergone the magnitude of population and employment losses experienced by some cities in the upper Midwest and Northeast, between 1960 and 1980, low income areas in need of revitalization developed as the population shifted.

Unlike the large snowbelt cities, since 1980 the city of Seattle has witnessed a reversal in the post-1960 population loss trend. Table 1 illustrates that although suburban growth continued unabated from 1980 to 1990 (another quarter million new residents arrived in the city's suburbs), the city also experienced residential growth, rising from a low of 493,846 in 1980 to 516,259 in 1990. The city population is expected to reach 590,000 by the year 2010 (Seattle Planning Department, 1993b).

SIGNS OF CHANGE

What caused the post-1980 reversal of the previous twenty-year trend of out-migration from the city of Seattle? Doubtless, part of the explanation lies in the recent exodus of California residents, many of whom moved to the Pacific Northwest, causing property values regionwide to rise and cities in many parts of the region to experience in-migration. Thus, unlike the situation in many northeastern cities, Seattle's low income areas are not saddled with large amounts of idle property which have fallen into government hands due to property tax delinquency. In Seattle, demand is sufficient to ensure that the vast majority of delinquent properties are resold at the annual tax auctions. "There is no place where property is unsaleable," City Planner George Frost said. Property values are rising, and there are many homes over $125,000 throughout the city. But the prosperity has not affected all parts of the city equally. If it had not been for the proactive planning and funding efforts undertaken by the residents and the city that helped make neighborhoods attractive to residents who might otherwise have chosen a suburban location, Seattle's low income neighborhoods would have been bypassed. What techniques were utilized to effect this change?

Citywide Support for Neighborhood-Based Planning

Seattle's power base lies not in political parties but in community councils. As Professor George Rolfe explained, "These are populist (neither liberal nor conservative), interest-based, grassroots, issue-oriented neighborhood groups, which form coalitions that come and go" (author's interview with Rolfe, 1996). Besides the community councils, there are many long-established, active Community Development Corporations (CDCs) in the neighborhoods (CDC projects have been funded by Local Initiatives Support Corporation [LISC],[1] Boeing, churches, and the city). Thus it is not surprising to find Seattle's revitalization successes rooted in a planning and implementation process which has been active at the neighborhood level, with citywide support, for many years.

Neighborhood Plans. Central and Southeast Seattle are the lowest income parts of the city. Within these larger areas lie the I-90 Redevelopment Area and the neighborhood commonly known as Judkins-Rejected (which the neighborhood community council now refers to as Judkins Park), which includes the I-90 tunnel and overlaps with much of the I-90 Redevelopment Area. Not surprisingly, there have been a host of plans and projects developed for these neighborhoods, beginning in 1958 with the first Central Area Plan and the Yesler-Atlantic Urban Renewal Plan, which focused on a smaller area which included Judkins-Rejected. The Renewal Plan resulted in the designation of the city's first urban renewal area, the demolition of 200 homes along with relocation of the existing residents, and the city's acquisition of more than 40 acres of property in the vicinity of I-90 and the Judkins-Rejected neighborhood for redevelopment. "The major shortcoming of the clearance program was that it failed to recognize that existing financial policies coupled with neglect had destroyed the real estate market for inner-city land . . . clearance was begun before there was a demonstrated demand for raw land and before there were specific redevelopment proposals," according to the 1976 Atlantic Neighborhood Improvement Plan which covered areas served by the Rejected, Judkins, and Jackson Place Community councils. This plan was developed in response to the failure of the urban renewal program, and was designed to attract a single, large developer to plan, develop, and build new housing. The 1978 Judkins-Rejected Redevelopment Plan, covering the southern portion of the Yesler-Atlantic neighborhood, focused on single family housing development and allowed a portion of the area to be declared "blighted."

Yet despite this extensive planning effort, the neighborhoods continued to deteriorate. Reasons for this are explored in the following sections on I-90 and its surrounding vicinity.

More recently, the planning activity focused on preparation of five year, implementation-oriented Action Plans. Neighborhood community councils, CDCs, and residents desiring assistance in revitalization have been spearheading this planning activity for many years in the city's low income neighborhoods. SEED (Southeast Effective Development, Inc., a CDC) Economic Development Manager Pat Chemnick described the Action Planning process in Southeast Seattle as follows: "The community and SEED wrote the Action Plan for this area in 1990. Every year, the city and SEED convene citizens groups to review and update the plan. Then the responses go to the mayor, who circulates them to the city departments and says, 'What are you doing about this?' and they respond. Then the community organizations review the responses and push for more" (in an interview with the author, 1996). Similar planning processes have been operating throughout the city, with coordination, specialized knowledge, and implementation assistance provided by city staff.

In the Central area, community-sponsored and led Action Plan development took place from 1991 through 1993. The plan contains goals and strategies to address issues of business and economic development, housing, land use, youth development (including empowerment, employment, services, and education) and community capacity building and related implementation strategies. In early 1995, CAAP-IT (Central Area Action Plan–Implementation Team), a team composed of neighborhood residents, community council, and CDC representatives, "was established to serve as a catalyst to facilitate comprehensive community empowerment and develop new initiatives to spur broad community development in the Central Area" (author's interview with Central Area Development Association (CADA) Director Jackie Walker, 1996). The team is responsible for ensuring that the Central Area Action Plan, which was completed in 1993, is implemented. CAAP-IT provides communication and facilitation among the various groups and individuals involved, providing a neutral forum for discussion of issues and working to build cooperation and trust.

"Planning for the Central neighborhood has been resident-led and city-supported," according to the city's I-90 Project Manager Janeen Smith (in an interview with the author, 1996). The Central Action Plan was developed as the result of a 1991 initiative introduced by Mayor Norm Rice, Neighborhood Seattle, which was designed to develop strategies for assisting those neighborhoods in greatest need of assistance, namely Southeast and Central. The following year the City obtained a $750,000 HUD economic revitalization grant for use in implementing the Central Area Action Plan and related economic revitalization efforts in the area. Each year, the Plan is updated and implementation is supervised by CAAP-IT, with City funding; the City made

$75,000 in Community Development Block Grant (CDBG) funds available for CAAP-IT support in 1995 alone. Many activities have been completed, including an inventory of vacant and "underdeveloped" property, a housing maintenance repair survey to determine the condition of area housing, planning for urban villages (see the next section), applying for a street utilities grant, and implementing job creation and business development programs (Central Area Development Association, 1996). A detailed example from the I-90 Redevelopment Area (one part of the Central area) is given later in this chapter.

Urban Villages: A New Approach. The adoption of a new citywide comprehensive plan in the mid-1990s marked the beginning of a new approach to neighborhood planning in Seattle based on the idea that growth should be concentrated in "urban villages." As explained in the new plan, "Urban Villages are characterized by mixed and/or adjacent commercial and residential uses which lend themselves to neighborhood ownership, pedestrian friendliness and human scale, but which also produce sufficient urban vitality to attract visitors from other parts of the city" (Seattle Planning Department, 1993b). There are four categories of these villages: Urban Centers (and Urban Center Villages within them), Hub Urban Villages, Residential Urban Villages, and Neighborhood Villages, with Urban Centers designated for the most intense development (with intensity measured in terms of specific targeted numbers of dwelling units and/or jobs per acre), and Neighborhood Villages for the least intense development. The system will be implemented via "permit metering," which sets a maximum amount of growth permitted each year for each specific village within each of the four types. All parts of the city not designated for development as one of the villages are classified as Urban Neighborhoods, in which city policy will be "maintaining existing conditions;" new development will be directed away from these areas and toward the villages by means of restrictive zoning and utilities control rather than permit metering.

The three examples described in the following sections fall into the hierarchy as follows:

1. Central and Southeast
2. Downtown
3. Sand Point

Central and Southeast: One area, known as Rainier/I-90, has been designated as a "Potential Residential Hub Urban Village," meaning that the area "lacks the critical mass of employment and housing characteristics of a Hub Urban Village, and will require a major transformation involving substantial public investment over an extended period of time in order to function in that capacity" (Seattle Planning Department, 1993b). This area is included in the

South Atlantic Street Neighborhood Plan as well as the geographically larger Southeast Action Plan.

An area immediately to the west, identified as Beacon Hill, is designated as a "Potential Residential Urban Village," meaning that the area lacks many characteristics of a fully developed residential Urban Village but would be a desirable location in which to increase the intensity of residential development in the future. A Neighborhood Plan is already underway for the Beacon Hill area; additionally, the Southeast Action Plan proposes two village locations that are not part of the city's plan.

Another "Potential Residential Urban Village" has been designated at 23rd at Union, and an area around 23rd at Jackson has been designated as an "Evolving Residential Urban Village," meaning that the area "already has sufficient amenities and public infrastructure to support growth." The previously begun Central Area Action Plan covers both of these areas.

Most of the Central and Southeast areas fall into the "Urban Neighborhoods" category, in which city policy will be "maintaining existing conditions." In view of the relatively low quality of life offered by these areas, this designation may not be good news for area residents.

Downtown: The Pike Place and Pioneer Square neighborhoods fall into two designated "Urban Center Villages" (Retail Core/Office Core/Central Harborfront and Pioneer Square/Kingdome, respectively) within the larger Downtown Urban Center, which is one of five areas citywide that are designated as suitable for this highest intensity category of growth.

Sand Point: This area now falls into the "Urban Neighborhoods" category, a designation that is somewhat ironic in view of the extensive plans for the site's development.

The urban village approach now being pursued by Seattle planners takes a more citywide view than did the Action Plan efforts, so it is not surprising that the issue of how the new approach will mesh with Action Plans is still a matter of debate. According to the new comprehensive plan, neighborhood planning will now be directed at "Urban Centers and Urban Villages included as priority areas for public investments during Phase I of the Comprehensive Plan" (Seattle Planning Department, 1993b). The state's Growth Management Act requires consistency between these approaches. Therefore, if a recently developed neighborhood plan already exists that includes an area now identified as an Urban Center or Village and is judged to be consistent with the new comprehensive plan, its land use proposals will be adopted. If there is an inconsistent plan or a plan still under development, city planners will work with neighborhood residents and business owners to obtain consistency; if no recent plan exists, the city will initiate neighborhood planning efforts. Many neighborhoods objected to the urban village approach because they feared that the process would be more city-driven, moving away from the community-based approach embodied in the Action Plans. So the City

Council offered the opportunity for the "villages" to plan for themselves, with the city providing technical assistance and funding. Under this city-run Neighborhood Planning program, in general, neighborhood organizations contract with the city to do urban village plans (often with the help of consultants). The Central area got more than one contract because it contains more than one village. Funding comes from city sources (the Office of the Mayor), not federal funds. "This concerted effort at revitalization, which includes a wide variety of activities including service provision, is different from the earlier approach, which focused on housing rehab alone," according to Central and Southeast Neighborhood Planner George Frost (in an interview with the author, 1996). Frost's job is evidence of the commitment that the city has made to integrate Urban Village planning with Seattle's ongoing neighborhood and action plans: Although Frost is a city employee, he acts as a community organizer and facilitator for the Central Action Plan area and works with many community-based organizations that are involved heavily with plan implementation. These include the Central Area Development Association, the Southeast Effective Development Corporation, the United Community Economic Development Association, the Delridge CDC, and the Midtown-Commons Economic Development Association. The city's desire to work closely with area residents is shown by the assignment of Frost and other planners to specific neighborhoods, and the opening of satellite offices in the neighborhoods themselves.

Although the relationship between the city and low-income neighborhood residents has improved, there is still antagonism. Frost and his counterparts hope that as residents work more closely with them, the residents will realize that it is the residents themselves who are still in control of the planning process and the antagonism will be replaced with a greater level of trust.

Citywide Support for Implementation

The most notable citywide support for neighborhood revitalization has come in the arena of implementation, particularly with respect to mixed-use neighborhoods and mixed income housing. The Urban Village planning strategy places heavy emphasis on mixed use, and this has been reflected in city zoning changes. "Land use policy changes have increased the land area available for multifamily housing development, thereby expanding the capacity for new multifamily units. These changes have resulted in the inclusion of residential uses in commercial zones. . . . Currently, mixed-use housing is allowed outright in the majority of commercial zones." This policy has been particularly effective in the Downtown Urban Center, where four neighborhoods have been designated as residential. Over 1,000 new housing units have been built in these four neighborhoods since 1991, and another 6,000 are "in the planning, permitting or development stage" (Seattle Department of Housing and Human Services, 1996).

The second area in which citywide support has been remarkable is that of improving the stock of affordable housing. According to a recent publication, "The City of Seattle is nationally recognized as a leader in providing low income housing. The City's commitment includes the allocation of millions of local tax dollars and public funds to the preservation and development of affordable housing" (Seattle Department of Housing and Human Services, 1996). The reduction in federal aid for housing, which occurred in the early 1980s, "required the City to assume a greater role in funding low income housing. . . . The magnitude of the unmet housing need in the City of Seattle is overwhelming. The City has over 60,000 households that are in need of assistance with the cost of housing—about one quarter of the total number of households in the city" (Seattle Planning Department, 1993b). Seattle residents and elected officials have responded actively to this problem for more than a decade. In 1981, Seattle voters passed a $48.1 million senior housing bond issue, and in 1986 they provided neighborhood revitalization assistance, passing a $49.9 million low income housing property tax levy. They repeated this public-spirited performance in November 1995 by approving another $59 million for use in providing low income housing. Five percent of the levy is for low income new home ownership; the rest is divided between rehabilitation of single family and multifamily units, and construction of new multifamily housing. Plans of each bond issue call for 1,300 new units to be built with each bond issue, for people making less than 50% of the median income.

Local elected officials have backed up the voters by contributing several million dollars for publicly owned low income housing from Real Estate Excise Tax revenues, which are available to fund "public facilities and infrastructure" (Seattle Planning Department, 1993b), by lobbying for changes in state-mandated property valuation techniques that are harmful to low income areas,[2] and by making a wide variety of assistance available to the nonprofit agencies and developers (more than $5 million in 1996 alone) (Seattle Department of Housing and Human Services, 1996). Over the years, officials have also appropriated a total of about $10 million from the general fund, established a Multifamily Code Enforcement Fund to assist owners in making code-related improvements, modified codes to increase housing affordability,[3] established a Growth-related Housing Fund,[4] and investigated the use of Community Redevelopment Financing (CRF), transfer of development rights and density bonuses as tools to increase the provision of affordable housing[5] (Seattle Department of Housing and Human Services, 1996).

The City's efforts to ensure adequate provision of low income housing have been reinforced by a variety of related actions. First, in keeping with this book's definition of what constitutes a successful program, with a few exceptions, "The City will not assist projects which result in the permanent displacement of low-income tenants" (Seattle Department of Housing and Human Services, 1996). Additionally, housing built with public assistance is reserved for occupancy by low income people for at least the term of the deferred payment loan, which is 40 years with extensions encouraged. This is enforced via covenants, which require loan repayment with penalties and interest if the use changes before the time period is up. Leveraging of locally provided funds to obtain federal grant money or state Housing Trust Fund allocations is also strongly encouraged. Developers must notify community residents early in the project planning process and work closely with the community throughout the project's development.

There are three programs available: Small Families (for new construction and rehab of single or multifamily housing with at least two bedrooms, for families with children), Downtown Preservation (for renovation of existing, occupied buildings in the Downtown Urban Center, which includes the Pike Place and Pioneer Square areas) and Special Needs (for homeless housing, either single-family group homes or multifamily). Funds from all of these may be used in mixed income and mixed use projects, as long as the proportion of funds utilized from these programs does not exceed the proportion of project space devoted to low income housing.

Neighborhood residents and the city government have not acted alone. In addition to the city, the state is the biggest partner, appropriating funds that are used by the City Department of Housing and Human Services (DHHS) to provide 40- to 75-year deferred loans[6] to nonprofit developers to build housing, mainly multifamily. Federal HOME funds, McKinney Act funds (for special populations) and Section 8 funds are also important, especially in financing rehab. LISC is another important player: The city has a joint predevelopment fund with LISC which also acts as a consultant to the city. Finally, the participation of nonprofit developers is essential. The Capitol Hill Improvement Project, the Plymouth Housing Group, and the Low Income Housing Institute (which acts as a consultant for other small groups) are important local nonprofit housing developers. They find sites for new housing but mainly focus on rehab, and utilize federal low income housing tax credits to make provision of this housing financially feasible (author's interview with city staff member Mark Pomerantz, 1996).

The difference between the Action Plan approach and the Urban Village–based approach is very clear when one examines the way that funds are now allocated. Whereas previously the focus was on upgrading the Central and Southeast neighborhoods, a priority of the Urban Village approach to neighborhood planning is income and use mixing throughout the city. The guidelines for approval of these funding allocations reflect that primary goal. First, income mixing within projects for the mixed income component of the Small Family Program is assured by limiting funds to apartment or townhouse projects that include no more than 35 percent of the total units for low income occupancy (about $600,000 was available under this program in 1996). Income mixing within blocks is assured by a policy, applicable to all three programs (exceptions include projects in the Downtown area, and mixed income or Section 8 voucher projects), that "limits the proportion of subsidized rental housing in a Census block group to no more than 30 percent of the total existing units"[7] (Seattle Department of Housing and Human Services, 1996). Projects that would cause this percentage to be exceeded will not be approved.

But the most innovative aspect of the program is its heavy emphasis on dispersing low income housing throughout the city. "Projects that include low-income units in mixed-income and/or mixed-use configurations to disperse low-income housing as much as possible" (Seattle Department of Housing and Human Services, 1996) have a higher priority for funding, as will "sites in neighborhoods where less City low-income housing dollars have been spent," housing for low income small families which features "innovative design and flexible configurations," and housing which includes some, but not all, units for the homeless. The city has gone so far as to specify priority, prohibited and special objectives in areas. "Priority Areas," are areas which are defined as sections with low concentrations of subsidized housing and which include all of the city's middle and high income neighborhoods. Sand Point, described later in this chapter, is located in one of these. Perhaps its status as a Priority Area for low income housing overrode its designation as an Urban Neighborhood in which development would not be encouraged. "Prohibited Areas" in which subsidized housing is not allowed, are areas which are quite geographically specific but generally include those areas which already have plenty of low income housing along with areas within a quarter mile of any of Seattle's three public housing projects (referred to as "garden communities" by city staff). "Special Objectives Areas" (SOAs), are defined as areas that "need attention for specific housing issues." Within these SOAs, "Impact Areas" are designated based on high poverty levels, a weak housing market, poor housing conditions and high crime rates. Downtown (in which all types of subsidized housing are encouraged without restriction), the Central and Southeast areas are all SOAs, and also contain Impact Areas.

The Central and Southeast SOA restrictions reflect the city's intention to disperse low income housing to other parts of town, while stabilizing, increasing home ownership, and bringing middle and high income residents back to Central and Southeast. Given these goals, it is understandable that city housing assistance in the Central area is limited to projects that focus on home ownership for moderately low income people (50-80% of median), home repair assistance for existing homeowners, and rental rehab assistance for housing for very low income people (below 50% of median). Both conversion and new construction of low income rental housing is prohibited. Within the I-90 Impact Area, the city has developed two special programs to help tenants in state-owned housing buy their homes and to attract higher income residents to build on vacant land (Seattle Department of Housing and Human Services, 1996). This focus has worried area residents and CDC staff, who foresee less support for moderately low rental rehab and new construction as the dispersal policies take hold; it remains to be seen whether differences can be worked out.

Like the Central SOA, a few blocks in Southeast SOA Impact Areas will receive special concentrated efforts at revitalization; also like the Central SOA, new construction of subsidized rental housing is prohibited. But the Southeast fares better in the city housing funding structure because some additional goals have been established for this area, including the development of mixed income multifamily communities, owner rehab assistance, and rental acquisition/rehab assistance. In the Rainier Valley Impact Area, acquisition and rehab of small projects is prohibited but rehab of projects with more than five units into mixed income developments is encouraged, with city subsidies possible even for market rate units.

RESULTS

The three widely varying examples discussed below illustrate the range of revitalization efforts that have occurred. Grassroots efforts in the Central neighborhood area have achieved success in turning an area around that was devastated by highway construction. In the downtown area, deteriorating structures such as those in Pioneer Square and the Pike Place Market were slated for clearance as part of the urban renewal program; unlike many other urban downtown areas which experienced similar problems, by choosing to preserve Pioneer Square and Pike Place the city was able to successfully reuse these properties for commercial and mixed income residential use, creating major tourist attractions in the process. Finally, the 1995 closing of the Sand Point Naval Station provided a parcel of unused land in a wealthier area, which the city has chosen to reuse in part as a housing site for very low income people.

Action Plans and Housing: Seattle's Central Neighborhood

The I-90 Area. The I-90 Redevelopment Project area is a rare example of revitalization using government-owned land in Seattle's low income residential areas; as SEED Economic Development Manager Pat Chemnick said, "There is no useable abandoned public land in all of southeast and east central Seattle except for the I-90 right of way in the Judkins area" (interview with the author, 1996).

In the 1940s the federal government dug a tunnel for I-90, acquiring considerable land in the process. Anticipation of I-90 expansion began to cause neighborhood decline in Judkins-Rejected in the 1950s, when Federal "war housing" (World War II) along Martin Luther King (MLK) Jr. Way was torn down and the Colman school was vacated. These properties were left vacant for years. In the 1960s, a north-south freeway was also planned, following the route of the current MLK Jr. Way, with major interchanges with I-90 in the Judkins-Rejected area. By the late 1960s people in the Judkins area had been unable to obtain home mortgages for over a decade, so finally the state began buying these homes too. Further acquisition was stopped by an injunction in the late 1970s by freeway opponents. This north-south freeway (the R. H. Thomson Expressway) was dropped from the City's comprehensive plan in the 1970s due to citizen opposition, and the I-90 expansion plans were reduced in scope; thus, some properties which had been acquired were no longer needed (Seattle Department of Community Development, 1976). When the I-90 expansion was finished, with certain exceptions where the State sold the property at auction, the surplus I-90 property was sold to and through the City, in accordance with a December 1976 Memorandum Agreement with the State of Washington Department of Transportation (Seattle, City of, et al., 1976). The current plans for the I-90 area date back to the late 1970s and the 1980s (Seattle Department of Community Development, 1989); they are now in the implementation phase, as illustrated by the following projects.

In response to community demands for a project that would "heal the wound" of I-90 (Smith, 1997), in the 1976 Memorandum Agreement all affected governments agreed to "provision for a full lid tying affected Seattle neighborhoods together. The lid shall be constructed to permit park and/or two story residential or business construction (not industrial uses) to take place on top of the highway between the Mt. Baker tunnel and 23rd Avenue South." But lawsuits held up its implementation until 1984 and the project was not completed until the early 1990s. The 44-acre lid is now a large grassy park over the top of the freeway. Opinion is divided on the healing effect of this project. Some believe that it formed another barrier to neighborhood cohesion (author interview with University of Washington professor George Rolfe, 1996), but many others view it as a valuable asset (Smith, 1997).

The long-vacated Colman School was actually sitting on top of the tunnel so the state took ownership, evicting the African-American squatters who were occupying the building. A group of Moslems is trying to obtain approval for opening a school, the African American Academy, along with an African-American Heritage Center in the building. The state has provided a new Colman school north of the freeway.

Successful revitalization of the I-90 Redevelopment Area has been more problematic. By 1980, two-thirds of the land area was vacant. Further, more than half the area's property was owned by government agencies: the Washington State DOT, which acquired 18 parcels by 1980 and owned or leased nearly 200 parcels (30.9 acres) by 1989; the Seattle Housing Authority, which in 1980 owned more than a block; and King County, which owned three parcels. "There are no plans for developing any of these properties. There has been no rebuilding within the past 15 years. Many vacant lots are overgrown with tall grass and show long years of neglect. Properties listed for sale have been withdrawn for lack of interest" (Seattle, City of, 1980). In 1980, several city ordinances were passed establishing the area as a Redevelopment Area and authorizing the city to buy some of these parcels using CDBG funds, but many state properties were not actually made available until 1990 so the redevelopment project "never went anywhere" (Smith, 1997). Despite this, by 1989 plans for the area's development had expanded to include "the construction of low-density middle income single-family and town house development as the highest priority. Development will occur in phases . . . through at least 1995. Ultimately, between 374 and 661 new housing units will be built on 50 separate sites" (Seattle Department of Community Development, 1989).

This would have been the city's largest housing development in decades; but unfortunately, the plan has not been implemented smoothly. Private developers were not interested in the area, so in 1990 the city turned the job of residential construction over to HomeSight, a private nonprofit developer financed largely with federal and private foundation grants, and the city also made $1.5 million of its own money plus CDBG funds available to HomeSight for assistance to low and moderate income first-time buyers. An internal city reorganization that split authority for the project exacerbated the problems as the city was responsible for purchasing land from the Washington State DOT for use by HomeSight, and the state was slow in conveying properties. "People in central Seattle neighborhoods flanking Interstate 90 are voicing increasing rage over broken promises. They're angry that the city hasn't delivered on pledges to build hundreds of affordable houses, the key to bringing the neighborhoods back to life," a 1994 article reported, adding that only 13 of the planned 374–661 new units had been built and 14 rehabbed (Merritt & Goldsmith, 1994a). Critics charge that city resources have been spent on downtown projects (a symphony hall, library, and Seattle Commons, a large downtown-area park) at the expense of the neighborhood, but city officials cite problems in obtaining title to the state-owned land. The state wanted "fair market value," which city staff viewed as anything but fair. "The state's appraisals of many properties threatens to put the cost of housing out of reach for HomeSight's low and moderate income clients. HomeSight is obviously having trouble marketing property at prices people can afford," said the city's housing director Earl Richardson (Merritt & Goldsmith, 1994a). Eventually the state negotiated a lower price with the city for some vacant parcels, but the time delay still added to development costs.

HomeSight worked with HUD and FHA to get the appraisals raised high enough to cover the actual costs of new construction; previous appraisals were based on nearby dilapidated areas. HomeSight also obtained a Nehemiah

Housing Opportunity Program grant. Nehemiah provides $15,000 equity loans at 0% interest. Average home cost is around $125,000 (not including closing costs) which is covered by a $90,000 mortgage and $35,000 in housing assistance (the $15,000 Nehemiah mortgage plus City and/or State development assistance). This down payment assistance is provided in the form of the deferred, subordinated loans described earlier in this chapter. First mortgage money through banks comes from tax-exempt bond proceeds (see the description earlier in this chapter) which were authorized several times by voters citywide.

HomeSight director Dorothy Lingyel cited state policies as the primary factor that has hampered her efforts, explaining that the state paralyzed development in the neighborhoods for more than a decade (while the freeway expansion project was being pursued), so it should sell its properties as cheaply as possible in order to enhance revitalization efforts. "I see this as war reparations. How can anybody look at this area and say they haven't screwed up?" she asked, adding that developers are hard-pressed to keep house prices under $120,000. "They're not going to want to keep working with us because they can't make any money," she said (Merritt & Goldsmith, 1994b).

Smith expressed a different view. "I consider the I-90 Redevelopment Project a qualified success, thanks largely to HomeSight, but it took a VERY long time. Factors inhibiting the revitalization effort include:

1. prolonged uncertainty about the final freeway right-of-way, including entrance and exit ramps, which delayed transfer of land;
2. market conditions (local and national) unfavorable to residential development when land was first offered; and
3. inability or unwillingness of the City to offer significant incentives to redevelopers (for example, infrastructure improvements, land price discounts, expedited permit processing)" (Smith, 1997).

Southeast and Central Seattle beyond the I-90 Area. The implementation focus in Seattle's low income neighborhoods has been mainly on rehab. According to Chemnick, "There have been hundreds, if not thousands, of units rehabbed" (1997). HomeSight has built 200–300 units of single-family and duplex housing in the area over the past four years. Part of HomeSight's success is due to its emphasis on home ownership. Through mid-1996, 55 owner-occupied homes were completed, of which 29 are in the I-90 area; the rest are in other parts of central and southeast Seattle, mainly the Yesler-Atlantic urban renewal area. Within a few years it is hoped that the area will have improved sufficiently so that HomeSight's role will decrease and revitalization will proceed through the private market.

Racial mixing is an important goal that has largely been achieved. For example, both the Judkins-Rejected and the Central neighborhoods are about

50% African-American, 40% European-American, and 10% Asian-American (Chemnick, 1997; Smith, 1997). Southeast Seattle has "maintained ethnic diversity over several decades. . . . we discovered that the Southeast is indeed genuinely diverse" (Gordon, Ulberg, & Locke, 1996). HomeSight pushes hard to use minority contractors, and its projects are also well integrated, both racially and with respect to income. Only 40% of HomeSight buyers are African-American. About two-thirds of the buyers make 60–80% of the median income; a few make even less; and about 30% have incomes 80–115% of median (Smith, 1997).

The city is building trust by providing visible improvements in these neighborhoods. "The local governments really invest in this area. They keep the streets nice and have provided street trees, curbs and gutters, a hospital, a high school, and the parks department built a really nice community center. There are virtually no potholes or loose trash" (author interview with Jackie Walker, 1996).

The results of all this effort show not only in the provision of affordable housing but in many other areas. The Central Area now has an Arts Council, which sponsors cultural arts festivals, galleries and museums and also teams with the Langston Hughes Cultural Arts Center to present events such as a free summer concert series that includes hip hop, reggae, and Shakespeare. There is a Central Park Trail Steering Committee that works with the city and the CDCs to improve area parks and to develop "Seattle's first urban village trail" that connects schools, libraries, parks, and businesses and also ties into a citywide system of hike and bike trails. CADA (the Central Area Development Association) has been a primary catalyst for these projects and organizations; additionally it has developed mixed residential/commercial real estate projects, coordinated urban design and landscaping improvements in the area, administered a program that matches private funds invested in façade improvement for area businesses, hired youth to remove graffiti and trash, organized a senior housing improvement program, lobbied to obtain more than $200,000 worth of improvements to Jackson Street, recently established a web page (http:/www.aa.net/~cada), and is promoting web and community TV access for residents. Unified Community Economic Development Association (UCEDA), another Central Area CDC, has more than $10 million of renovation and development projects underway, including rent-to-own housing, rehab, assisted living for the elderly, commercial revitalization, and job creation programs.

Still, there is no doubt that the revitalization efforts which have accomplished so much in the Central and Southeast areas will be affected by the increased emphasis on mixing incomes and land uses in urban villages that is expressed in the new citywide comprehensive plan. In view of Seattle residents' activism and commitment to improving low income neighborhood quality of life, it seems likely that the urban village concept will be applied in ways that augment previous Central and Southeast neighborhood upgrading efforts. However, residents' suspicion of an effort which could change the fundamental character of the neighborhood is quite understandable. Whether the new approach will be successful or not remains to be seen.

Promoting Mixed Use and Income Downtown:
Pike Place and Pioneer Square

The new Urban Village planning approach is much more in harmony with the revitalization programs in the downtown area, which have been based on goals of mixing incomes and land uses since their inception. The Pike Place and Pioneer Square developments illustrate this point.

The Pike Place produce market had been a landmark in Seattle's downtown since the early 1900s; by the 1950s, however, its physical condition had deteriorated and most of its vendors had left. The market's decline was at the heart of deterioration of the surrounding neighborhood, which was home for many low income residents as well as transients. The market's downtown waterfront location inspired local officials and business leaders to plan to clear the site using urban renewal funds and redevelop it with a rather bland mix of offices, high rise apartments and hotels. But Seattlites had other plans: More than 50,000 of them signed a petition for a voter initiative to save the market, which passed easily in 1971. "It was an abrupt repudiation of the business community's goal of a thoroughly modern city," Frieden and Saga-lyn (1992) said, adding that the initiative's supporters "managed to change the debate over downtown from a narrow concern with economic development to one that considered issues of design, livability and historic value. . . . [They] wanted street activity and interest—a people city."

Once the market was saved, funds had to be found for its renovation. Mayor Wes Uhlman, whose urban philosophy was more in line with the voters than the city council and business community, did much of the fundraising himself. The largest source of funds was the federal government, which had already approved the 22-acre area (including seven acres devoted to the market itself) for urban renewal funding. From 1969 to 1970 Uhlman, with the help of Washington's U.S. Senator Warren Magnuson, increased federal funding for Seattle projects from $39 million to nearly $300 million. This was followed by HUD "urgent needs" funding, Community Development Block Grant funds, and Urban Development Action Grants. These funds provided leveraging for private lending. Historic tax credits and in-kind contributions were also used extensively, as were gifts from individuals. In the end, the city contributed about 34% of Pike Place's redevelopment cost along with $40 million in federal funding.

In keeping with the voters' wishes, Pike Place is much more than a middle class marketplace. It boasts a wide variety of retail establishments ranging from pawn shops to surplus stores, many of which cater to low income people. The clientele is also very diverse, and street people are actually encouraged to come to Pike Place as long as they do not annoy the customers. There are some walls on which graffiti are welcomed. As one retailer put it, "It's all part of the urban scene."

The diversity and attention to low income needs that is evident in the market itself is a reflection of the development in the surrounding 22-acre area. There are more than 400 market-rate-housing units in the area and about an equal number of low income units. But Pike Place is much more than a housing or retail project: It also includes a free medical clinic, a child and adult day care center, and a food cooperative. All of these entities have non-profit boards under the Preservation and Development Authority (PDA), and are operated by the PDA using its "surplus cash flow."

The voters' vision of a diverse, lively, human-scale mixed use area that welcomes the poor as well as the middle class has been a great success. In addition to reversing the trend of neighborhood decline that had adversely affected the area's residents for years, Pike Place has become a major tourist attraction which serves nearly 7 million customers per year.

The citywide vision that fostered this project is evident in several other neighborhoods, including Pioneer Square. This historic part of downtown had declined over the years to an extreme state of disrepair. Today, thanks to efforts to preserve and promote the area's historic resources along with significant investment in landscaping, urban design, transit, street repairs, and related items, the area offers a very diverse mix of restaurants, small shops, low income services and a variety of multifamily housing units, making it attractive to residents of all income levels as well as a magnet for tourists. Corporate investment and foundation support have also been evident. The most visible example is the Waterfall Garden pocket park, which was built in honor of United Parcel Service workers and was created by the Annie E. Casey Foundation on the site where Jim Casey began a messenger service that eventually became UPS. It seems likely that the area's designation as a major Urban Center, coupled with the efforts to direct low income housing and mixed use projects into downtown, will ensure that the area remains at least as dynamic and varied as it is today.

Promoting Mixed Use in a New Low Income Community: Sand Point

The proposed reuse of the Naval Station Puget Sound at Sand Point appears to be a good example of the city's commitment to creating mixed use communities, as well as commitment to providing housing for very low income people. Whether the project's potential is fulfilled, however, remains to be seen.

A former military base, most of the 151-acre site was acquired by the city free of charge (author's interview with city planner Mike Usen, 1996) using the public benefit discount provisions of three federal laws (PL 91–485,

PL 81–152, and the McKinney Act), which place restrictions on transferred property that limit its uses to recreation, education, and housing for the homeless, respectively (Seattle Planning Department, 1993a). The plan for the site calls for the northernmost 15 acres to be utilized as a recreation area, including a waterfront park, a sailing center and a pier; the 18 acres immediately to the south of this would house a variety of education and community service activities, including classes ranging from preschool to community college, city training centers, social services, and a film studio; the site's 17-acre centerpiece will be an arts, culture and community center; 49 acres in the south portion of the former base will be devoted to park, recreation, and open space uses; and a 21-acre adjacent parcel will be reused for low income housing and housing for the homeless.

Since this area is surrounded by a neighborhood composed mainly of wealthy retirees, the idea of reusing a portion of Sand Point for homeless housing was not accepted without a battle. "Originally the residential portion of the site was to be a mixed-income, mixed-use development, but the Coalition for the Homeless put a plan together, and the city ran with it. The fact that federal guidelines state that a high priority for acquiring base closure land goes to plans to house the homeless also helped," according to Fremont Public Association Director John Burbank (interview with the author, 1996). Phase 1 of Sand Point's low income housing redevelopment, which is confined to rehab and will take about 18 months to develop, will provide transitional housing for 1.5–2 years for homeless people in 52 single room occupancy (SRO) hotel rooms, and three group homes for recovering people. Phase 2 will be much more family-oriented, and will eventually provide housing for about 500 people.

The city plans to retain ownership but lease the site to either the Sand Point Community Housing Association (a 501c3 corporation) or its fiscal umbrella group/agent, the Fremont Public Association, which will redevelop it. The Seattle Conservation Corps, a city agency that trains homeless people in construction and is nearly self-supporting although it uses some city funds, will be active in project development. The project is funded with $5 million in HUD/HHS McKinney Act funds for operations and support, $3.5 million from the city's housing tax, and $2.5 million in state funds. Eventually the housing tax could provide the entire $12 million estimated city share of the capital costs for housing (author's interviews with Burbank and Usen, 1996).

CONCLUSIONS

Citywide policies and programs should actively support grassroots neighborhood revitalization efforts in low income areas. The role of community councils, neighborhood CDCs, and other grassroots organizations in Seattle's poor neighborhoods cannot be overemphasized. However, this case study also clearly illustrates how important citywide support can be. For example, local voters have repeatedly approved millions of dollars in city-wide funding for low income housing and related improvements; this strategy reflects the city's commitment to neighborhood improvement rather than displacement of low income residents. The city has made significant efforts to attract middle and upper income residents of all ethnic groups back to central city neighborhoods, and has encouraged a wide variety of housing types and land uses in the "urban village" tradition. It is now taking rather strict measures to encourage dispersal of low income housing and income mixing in higher income neighborhoods, although the success of this approach cannot yet be evaluated.

This focus apparently stems from an underlying attitude held by area residents, that the entire community should bear responsibility for helping to improve the quality of life in the poorest neighborhoods. Put another way, instead of viewing these neighborhoods merely as competitors for scarce resources, their improvement is seen by middle and upper class residents as beneficial, and thus in the public interest. Residents have chosen to tax themselves to provide financial support to these neighborhoods; they have supported high density mixed use zoning that includes low income housing, and regional growth management strategies that favor central cities at the expense of suburbs; and they have supported this approach "with their feet" by moving into areas that were previously in very poor condition and are still populated with significant numbers of poor and even homeless residents. The most recent evidence of this somewhat altruistic grassroots activism is the November 1997 passage of an initiative to extend downtown Seattle's one-mile monorail by 45 miles. The initiative, which was spearheaded by a disgruntled city bus driver, passed by a 54% margin despite complete lack of support from area newspapers and very little campaign activity.

Within low income neighborhoods, a full spectrum of government services should be provided. If the government is unwilling to invest heavily in ensuring that trash collection, transit, child care, medical services, alcohol/drug treatment, and so on are available, then beautification or physical rehab efforts will produce very limited revitalization success. Seattle has made major financial commitments to inner city neighborhoods, and these areas have been rejuvenated without displacing the poor population.

A microplanning approach that builds an atmosphere of teamwork and cooperation should be fostered. In less successful project areas, an adversarial relationship often exists between inner city residents and local officials (Bright, 1995). Seattle's empowerment of neighborhood-based organizations such as community councils and CDCs by providing staff, decision-making authority, and funding was an important factor in the success of its revitalization efforts. Another example is the use of surplus property. Although delinquent tax lands were not a factor in Seattle, in all three examples the making available of other government-owned property (acquired through highway clearance, urban renewal and military base closing) for reuse was a centerpiece of the revitalization effort. Community councils, CDCs, and other resident-led organizations generally took the lead in preparing detailed, lot-by-lot microplans for their neighborhoods, with technical assistance from the city, and even in many cases took the lead in allocating capital improvement funds, recommending zoning changes, and conducting other specific implementation activities.

In sum, although research throughout the country shows that low income residents must play the main role in designing neighborhood improvement programs (Ford Foundation, 1973; Glaser, Denhardt, & Grubbs, 1995; Taub, Taylor, & Dunham, 1984), in Seattle they are not expected to raise themselves up solely by their own bootstraps. As Gordon, Ulberg, and Locke (1996) said, "Currently, Seattle seems to have attained the mix of activists, organizations, relationships, and publicly and privately supported vehicles which together provide the necessary infrastructure for healthy communities." This wider support has been a key factor in the successful revitalization of the city's low income neighborhoods, and could be a valuable model for other communities.

NOTES

1. LISC is the Local Initiatives Support Corporation, a Washington DC-based corporate-funded organization which has a community development loan fund.

2. "Current Use" valuation involves having property appraised for its actual use rather than its zoning. The rationale behind this is that in inner city areas the zoning often is much more intensive than the use, thus producing overly high appraisals. This is just one of several ways in which standard appraisal practices can produce overvaluation, which leads to over-taxation, delinquency, abandonment and forfeiture. Appraising vacant and residential property based on comparable sales produces values that are too high if the immediate area has no listings or mortgage activity; appraising residential property based on replacement cost also produces overly high values in areas with homes more than 25 years old in declining neighborhoods; and averaging property values within neighborhoods results in over-appraisals of the less valuable properties (Bright, 1995).

3. Building code changes made include allowing an additional story in wood frame construction, which is less expensive than the previous concrete base requirement; allowing efficiency apartments that are smaller than the minimum Uniform Building Code requirements; allowing small homes to have only one exit; allowing larger mezzanines; allowing small lofts accessible only by ladders in individual dwellings; and allowing some lower cost materials to be used.

4. The Growth-related Fund has been in place since 1985 (Seattle Department of Housing and Human Services, 1996). With the advent of the urban village-based planning process, its focus is changing somewhat: "As part of the strategy to preserve existing low income housing and to mitigate the impacts of growth on low income housing, Seattle shall establish a growth-related housing fund for Urban Centers and

Urban Villages, that will capture a portion of the additional property tax revenue generated by growth and allocate this revenue to a fund for preserving existing housing in Urban Centers and Villages" (Seattle Planning Department, 1993b).

5. Transfer of development rights is a technique designed to encourage preservation of agricultural land, historic sites, and so on, by allowing property owners to sell the rights to develop these properties to a nearby landowner. Density bonuses are increases in project density that are awarded to developers in exchange for providing amenities such as plazas, childcare, or affordable housing. According to the Seattle plan, "Seattle shall investigate the potential for using Community Redevelopment Financing to subsidize low income housing in CRF districts" (Seattle Planning Department, 1993b).

6. A "deferred payment loan" is a fairly common device used in cities throughout the nation to make the cost of housing more affordable by requiring no monthly loan payments, and often by forgiving the entire loan repayment after a certain number of years. The Seattle deferred payment loans are not repaid until the property is sold, the loan term ends, or the use changes. If the property is sold the City may waive the repayment requirement if the new buyer can assure the city that the property will remain in use as low income housing. Loan terms are a minimum of 20 to 40 years, with extensions to 75 years encouraged. There are rather stiff penalties for paying off the loan in fewer than 15 years. After 25 years, the city forgives 5 percent of the total accumulated interest (which is computed at a 1 to 3 percent simple interest rate) each year.

7. A Census block group is an area defined by the Census Bureau that contains a cluster of blocks with an average of 467 housing units (Seattle Department of Housing and Human Services, 1996).

CHAPTER 3

Regional Governance, Finance, and Service Provision
A Tale of Six Cities

Minneapolis/St. Paul, Toronto/Ottawa/Montreal, and Portland have all placed heavy emphasis on regional growth management, service provision, and/or finance as ways to solve the problems of low-income urban neighborhoods, although there are variations among the cities studied. For example, in Portland the focus is on providing regional growth management and citywide financial support: Portland has made heavy infrastructure investments in the poorest areas while strictly controlling suburban growth. In Minneapolis/St. Paul, many innovative strategies have been employed, but perhaps the most heavily emphasized is regional finance. The Canadian cities have a strong tradition of regional governance, which supports not only regional growth management strategies that help preserve the economic value of inner city property, but also regional finance and service provision. Perhaps because of the regional approach taken to neighborhood revitalization, the story of these cities' efforts focuses much less on specific neighborhoods than is the case in any other city covered in this book. For example, Goetz, Lam, & Heitlinger (1996) point out that in Minneapolis policies have emphasized mixing incomes and the dispersal of public housing, so subsidized housing is scattered through much of the city.

Although none of these cities reached the level of population and job loss experienced by Cleveland or Pittsburgh, in recent decades they developed problems. This chapter will first examine the problems and solutions developed by each group of cities separately, then in comparison. Portland and the Canadian cities are included here for comparison of regional effort, and so will not be discussed in as much depth as will the Twin Cities.

REVIVAL AND REGIONAL FINANCE IN THE TWIN CITIES

Roots of Decline

By rights, St. Paul should have been the bigger of the Twin Cities: it was established several years earlier than Minneapolis (est. 1841 & 1852, respectively) and was on a navigable part of the Mississippi River, unlike its "big sister's" location ten miles upstream. But St. Paul lacked industry. Minneapolis attracted flour and lumber mills, while St. Paul remained a center for trade. This proved to be less unfortunate than it first appeared when Minneapolis's lumber supplies ran low and its flour processing moved south in the early part of the twentieth century. As Pillsbury, General Mills, and other food-related industries suffered and died, Minneapolis did too. Its peak population of 521,718 in 1950 had fallen to just 368,383 by 1990, a 29% decline (2.46 million people lived in the seven-county metropolitan area in 1990). See Table 2 for more complete trends. Nearly all of the 154,000 people who left, did so before 1980—the city lost less than 1% of its people between 1980 and 1990, and that was probably due to the growth of high-tech industries, services, financial institutions, and corporate headquarters in the area at that time which brought in some 13,300 new jobs. From 1980–1988, wholesale trade, manufacturing and construction all experienced job losses of between 16 and 19%. Yet the city maintained a median personal income level that was above the national average, accounted for 39% of total metropolitan region employment, and had an unemployment rate that was generally under 5% since the mid-1980s. Why? There was tremendous growth in service sector employment, which grew from 69,510 jobs in 1980 to 86,186 jobs in 1988. Double-digit growth in finance/insurance/real estate employment and in government

Table 2: Population Change in St. Paul/Minneapolis Area, 1950 through 1990

	City of St. Paul	Ramsey County	City of Minneapolis	Hennepin County	St. Paul/ Minneapolis MSA*	MSA Area Outside St. Paul/ Minneapolis
1950	311,349	355,332	521,718	676,579	985,101	152,034
1960	313,411	422,525	482,872	842,854	1,377,143	580,860
1970	309,980	476,255	434,400	960,080	1,704,423	960,043
1980	270,230	459,784	370,951	941,411	1,788,043	1,146,862
1990	272,235	485,765	368,383	1,032,431	2,464,124	1,823,506

Source: U.S. Bureau of the Census, 1950–1990
*Metropolitan Statistical Area

also helped, as did a rise of approximately 1,000 jobs in retail trade employment. Still, the 1990 population remained far below that of 1950. Not surprisingly, falling property values and housing abandonment were still common (Schwartz, 1995). Oddly, during the 1980s, the Euro-American population declined by 11%. Thus the 1980–1990 population stabilization was entirely due to increases in the African-American, Asian-American, and Native American populations, which represented 21% (13%, 5% and 3.3%, respectively) of the 1990 population but only around 13% of the 1980 population and just 6.3% of the 1970 figure (U.S. Bureau of the Census, 1970, 1980, and 1990).

During all these years, the main city focus has been on downtown. First came the Gateway project, which cleared and redeveloped about a third of the city's downtown using federal urban renewal funds. The well-known skyway system was begun in 1962; five years later ground was broken for the Nicollet Transit Mall, which was to become famous as an early downtown revitalization success story. In the 1970s the IDS Center, Minneapolis' tallest building, was constructed, along with more than two dozen others. The biggest boom for downtown was in the 1980s, which saw more than 70 downtown projects come to fruition (Schwartz, 1995).

Successful downtown redevelopment displaced the area's poorest residents. For example, between 1976 and 1985, 514 single room occupancy (SRO) rooms[1] in downtown St. Paul were displaced by redevelopment, and by 1985 the city estimated that the number of downtown rental units affordable to those with low incomes had declined from 410 in 1980 to 185 (Edmondson, 1986). In the late 1950s and early 1960s, 2,400 people—mainly single men—along with 450 businesses and 186 buildings, were displaced to make way for Minneapolis's Gateway downtown urban renewal project (Schwartz, 1995).

Meanwhile, CDBG and Section 8 housing funds were cut in the 1980s nationwide, and the federal Urban Development Action Grants (UDAG) program was eliminated. Fortunately, Minneapolis and St. Paul had several unique programs already in place that were able to make up for some of these losses.

Signs of Change

"In regional reform the Twin Cities area is the school of America. The successful political coalitions built between central cities and older suburbs there are a model for metropolitan areas across the country," former HUD secretary Henry Cisneros (1995) wrote. This regional approach is evident in several programs, as described below.

Regional Governance. Like Portland and the Canadian cities, the Twin Cities area has adopted "metropolitan-wide growth management, implemented by a distinguishable governmental authority," (Nelson & Milgroom, 1995) which in this case is a 30-year-old entity called the Metropolitan (Met)

Council (Cisneros, 1995). The Met Council, whose members are appointed from sixteen geographic districts by the governor, not only has power to control growth but also controls transportation planning, transit service, air and water quality planning, and sewer services. The agency also acts as the Twin Cities affordable housing and redevelopment authority.

Much of the regional cooperation found in the Twin Cities area required action from the Minnesota State Legislature. Thus, it is no surprise that in this region's revitalization, the "charismatic leader" who emerged as a champion of reform is not a local neighborhood resident but a state legislator, Myron Orfield. Orfield is largely responsible for passage of the many innovative pieces of state legislation that have made the area a model for the nation. One recent example is the Liveable Communities Act (LCA), passed in 1995 after years of debate. The battle for passage of this legislation was led by Orfield and is detailed in his most recent book (Goetz, 1998).

The LCA establishes a voluntary program for provision of affordable housing, using incentives such as funds for brownfield cleanup, development of transportation nodes, and attractive housing finance packages to entice communities into providing affordable housing. In return, each community must create a Housing Action Plan that includes specific, measurable affordable housing goals, which are usually the subject of much negotiation before being approved by the Met Council (Goetz, 1998).

Tax Base Sharing. The Twin Cities area boasts "the nation's most far-reaching regional revenue sharing mechanism," (Cisneros, 1995) covering the 7-county, 188-municipality area and known as the Fiscal Disparities Plan (FDP). Commonly known as tax base sharing, this plan was authorized by the state legislature in 1971 and has been in operation since 1975. The legislation that created the plan requires that 40% of all increases in taxes from commercial and industrial property in a seven-county area that includes Minneapolis and St. Paul must be pooled and redistributed to the municipalities. Redistribution is based on both population and need, which is determined by the ratio of each city's per capita property valuation to that of the region. For example, in 1991 the FDP fund contained $290.5 million, which is 30.8% of the region's assessed property valuation and is up from 15 percent in 1980 (Schwartz, 1995). Fund distributions that year produced net losses of tax revenue for 31 communities and net gains for 157 (Waste, 1998). "It has been wildly successful in whittling down fiscal disparities," according to state legislator Myron Orfield, a primary supporter of the plan (Olson, 1985). This success is reflected in the narrowing of the gap between total (including residential) per capita appraised property values in rich and poor communities from 17:1 in 1971 to just 4:1 in the 1990s (Rusk, 1993). The FDP may also be partly responsible for the fact that the City of Minneapolis has become a net contributor of revenues to surrounding aging suburbs, instead of its original role as the program's largest recipient (Waste, 1998).

It seems that the FDP has succeeded in retaining businesses within the central city: As one analyst said, "Cities in the five counties neighboring the central cities get to tax the [central cities'] high commercial activity, which they undoubtedly contribute to, without having to persuade urban businesses to relocate" (Adams & VanDrasek, 1998). However, evidence also shows that counties outside the reach of the FDP are successfully luring businesses from the FDP region. "Much of the metro area's economic activity is occurring beyond the reach of the (FDP), and many communities are not benefitting from it" (Adams and VanDrasek, 1998).

A different sort of tax base sharing was authorized by the 1993 State Legislature, which approved a half-cent sales tax for the City of St. Paul to finance expansion of the city's Civic Center along with a neighborhood revitalization program in the city's Cultural Corridor. Neighborhood and business organizations can receive loans, grants, and seed money for capital projects. In 1995, a total of $3.7 million was available. Imposition of special sales taxes to finance large public projects is hardly new; what makes this one somewhat unique is its inclusion of neighborhood revitalization as part of the package (author's interview with Soderholm, 1996).

Tax Increment Financing (TIF) and the Neighborhood Revitalization Program (NRP). Tax increment financing (TIF) is a financing technique for funding capital improvements in declining but marketable areas. First, boundaries of a TIF district are drawn. Within this area, the taxable value of each property is then "frozen" on paper. Any tax revenues that are generated by increases in the value of district property which occur from that moment until the end of the life of the district (usually about 15 years) are then pledged to repay revenue bonds to finance improvements in the district. The bonds are then sold, with the expectation being that property values will rise as a result of the improvements' completion—thus providing the "incremental" tax revenues needed to repay them.

Minneapolis began using TIF in the early 1970s to do what many other cities have done, namely, fund downtown commercial and office development. The method was wildly successful. Property tax revenues committed to TIF districts grew from $437,000 in 1974 to $56 million in 1984. It was not uncommon to find mayors of municipalities in the region devoting half their time to real estate projects. The list of financial success stories began with the nine-block Loring Park area, the city's first TIF district, in which a $37 million investment in acquisition, relocation, and construction of housing (including some for low-income residents), a hotel, a merchandise mart, two campuses, an orchestra hall, and an extension of the Nicollet Transit Mall raised property tax revenues from less than $400,000 annually when the project began in 1972 to more than $5 million in 1990. From 1980 to 1991 thirty new projects were built downtown with the help of TIF financing. These included more than 750,000 square feet of office space added each year; City

Center, a mixed use development featuring an office tower and a mall that yields nearly $10 million per year in TIF revenue (which is 17% of the city's total TIF revenues); nearly 3,700 housing units; a Hilton Hotel which features the Minneapolis Community Development Agency (MCDA)[2] as part owner; and two theaters that were renovated by the MCDA (Schwartz, 1995).

But during this time, criticism was mounting: Opponents claimed that budgets were not well scrutinized, voters were shut out of the process, marginal projects were being funded (Frieden & Sagalyn, 1992), and all the city's funding and attention was being directed at downtown (author's interview with Hagen, 1996). This led to development of the unique TIF program that the city has today: Revenues generated by large downtown developments are used to fund revitalization in residential neighborhoods. The TIF funding is possible because in 1990 the state legislature took a very unusual action. It approved continuation of the downtown TIF districts after the bonds are retired, with the provision that the revenues that were paying off downtown bonds be made available for use in low income neighborhoods (author's interview with Pettiford, 1996). This allowed the MCDA, which runs all but one of the city's 39 TIF districts (including all the downtown districts, which constitute about half of the city's TIF districts and include the most financially successful ones), to consolidate most of them into a single TIF project area and to refinance remaining TIF revenue bonds at lower interest rates over a longer time period (Schwartz, 1995).

The proceeds from this innovative approach go into the city's Neighborhood Revitalization Program (NRP) program, which was approved by the State Legislature in 1990. The NRP involves the City, the school board, park board, library board, county, and various community organizations. Under NRP, residents develop an action plan with city assistance, then are given funds to implement it. The residents have some control over these funds, although the approval of a number of agencies is needed. Housing is emphasized, and typically an NRP plan allocates more than half its funds to housing stock improvements. The program covers much more than housing (author's interview with Billig, 1996) with its main purposes being to build neighborhood capacity, redesign public services, increase government collaboration, and create a sense of community. The MCDA acts as program coordinator, and manages the housing and economic development components of the program (which also encompasses safety, health, recreation, economic development, social service, environment, and transportation issues). NRP funds under these two program components have been used for everything from construction of a women's shelter to microenterprise startup funds to construction of a school playground (Minneapolis Community Development Agency, 1996).

All of the city's 81 designated neighborhoods are participating in the NRP program, which receives $20 million each year from a $400 million, 20-

year allocation (Fainstein, 1994). This constitutes about 30% of the $84 million per year that is expected to be spent annually for the next 20 years on neighborhood revitalization. The vast majority of the remaining 70% of the revitalization budget is generated by MCDA activities, supplemented by federal CDBG and HOME funding (typically, the city has allocated 100% of its CDBG funds to neighborhood revitalization). In recent years the downtown tax base has been eroding and federal funds have also been cut; how the city will continue its ambitious inner city neighborhood revitalization program in the wake of declining TIF and CDBG funds remains to be seen.

In St. Paul, the city's Housing Division of the Planning and Economic Development Department (PED) has established a program to preserve, rehabilitate, and construct new multifamily housing using pooled funds from tax increment financing as well as from the Minnesota Housing Finance Agency (MHFA, a state agency), tax-exempt revenue bonds, the Minneapolis–St. Paul HRA Low-Income Housing Development Fund, and the McKnight Foundation's Family Housing Fund, which is described in more detail in the next section. Several buildings have been rehabbed into loft housing for artists, housing for the elderly, and housing for disabled residents.

Another innovative use of TIF was passed by the Minnesota Legislature in 1995. The law allows the Twin Cities and two nearby communities to establish Housing Replacement TIF Districts in which TIF funds will be used to acquire and remove substandard housing. In Minneapolis, up to 100 parcels can be designated to be included in the district (only vacant and substandard houses and vacant lots can be included in the district). TIF funds can cover up to 75 percent of the project costs, with the city putting up the remaining funds. The goal is to prepare these TOADS to be "sold for market rate housing," which in Minneapolis translates into single family housing sold at $118,124 or less (for comparison, the mean house price in Minneapolis was $78,749 in 1996—see Minneapolis Community Development Agency, 1998). Parcels remain in the TIF for 15 years, and the revenue generated by development of one parcel can be used to improve another. This program is certainly an innovative approach to the problem of reusing TOADS. Its success should be monitored over time; if successful, it could be a useful model for other cities.

Joint Housing Assistance Programs. Besides the unique regional governance and financial arrangements described above, the Twin Cities' long history of cooperation has led to a large number of joint programs designed to assist low income neighborhood residents throughout the region. A few of these are highlighted in this section.

The Minneapolis/St. Paul First Time Homebuyers Bond Program provided approximately $10 million in Phase 10 (which covers a two-year period that began in November 1994) for use in below-market mortgage lending to buyers with incomes below $51,000 in the Twin Cities. In St. Paul the average loan amount is $58,330, and the average family income of buyers was $29,000. The program, which began in 1981, is funded through the sale of tax-exempt housing revenue bonds.

Over time it became clear that new construction was occurring, but housing rehab was not taking place as fast as had been hoped. The reason was also clear: "Regrettably, most of the lending community is not accustomed to lending with an emphasis on home repair or improvement" (Minneapolis Community Development Agency, 1998). For this reason, in 1987 MCDA itself became an approved lender. "This meant that . . . all of the loan underwriting standards were under the control of the MCDA rather than FHA, VA or other investors" (Minneapolis Community Development Agency, 1998).

The PHA (Public Housing Agency) Home Program is a partnership that provides financial counseling and training to would-be first-time homebuyers now living in public housing. The St. Paul Housing Division and MCDA act as mortgage bankers for these buyers, also occasionally using Special Assistance Monies, which are provided in conjunction with the MHFA and can be used for closing costs, down payments, and loans for equity or rehab.

Joint programs in which the McKnight Foundation (see the next section) is involved include Take Credit! which provides a federal income tax credit equal to 20% of the annual mortgage interest paid on buyers' homes. In lieu of the below-market mortgages described above, lenders issue the buyers "mortgage credit certificates." The Minneapolis-St. Paul Housing Finance Authority offers low-interest 30-year fixed financing for low and moderate income homebuyers (moderate includes some families making up to $90,000 in annual income) (author's interview with Pettiford, 1996). The Home Ownership Center provides home ownership counseling and education through community-based organizations in both cities.

The McKnight Foundation: A Catalyst for Regional Revitalization. The Twin Cities area is blessed with corporate headquarters that have played an active role in revitalization for many years. Minneapolis's first major downtown and neighborhood redevelopment projects were initiated by businesses, and the city boasts one of the nation's largest corporate philanthropy programs: Many corporations routinely donate five% of their pretax earnings to charity (Schwartz, 1995).

The McKnight Foundation, a private philanthropy founded in 1953 by William McKnight (an early leader of the 3M company), stands out as an important contributor to neighborhood revitalization throughout the Twin Cities. "McKnight is involved in every multifamily deal MCDA does," Pettiford (in interview with author, 1996) said, adding that the foundation has also been invaluable in "filling gaps" in many government-sponsored revitalization programs. The foundation gives hundreds of grants each year for child abuse prevention, child care, emergency assistance, employment services, teen pregnancy education, assistance to battered women, at-risk children, literacy, legal aid, mediation, parenting, computers, outreach and social services, neighborhood groups, CDCs, minority outreach, transitional housing, Boy Scouts, and many other youth development organizations, housing, economic development, education, health, crop research, neuroscience, the environment, public affairs, international aid, and the arts (McKnight, 1995).

Support for low income housing throughout the region. The McKnight Foundation's interest in regional revitalization programs coupled with the Twin Cities' long record of political and economic cooperation is reflected in an array of joint programs aimed at providing or rehabbing low income housing. One of the most innovative of McKnight's programs is the Family Housing Fund of Minneapolis and St. Paul, one of the first organizations of its kind in the nation. Founded in 1980 as a public-private partnership with the Twin Cities, the fund is a private nonprofit corporation supported with private funds; initially, capitalized with $10 million. From 1980–1995 McKnight contributed more than $32 million to the fund, and has committed $16 million from 1995–2000. The money has leveraged $266.7 million from the city of St. Paul and $345.9 million from the city of Minneapolis since 1980. Some other examples of Family Housing Fund programs are given in the section on urban homesteading, below.

McKnight also contributes about $500,000 each year to the Century Homes program to recycle TOADS, which is described in detail in the section on the vacant lot sales-recycling program, below.

Support for Lowertown. Another program in which McKnight has been instrumental is the revitalization of Lowertown, an 18-block neighborhood near downtown St. Paul. Once the site of Mississippi steamboat docks for the fur trade, Lowertown became a commercial area of warehouses and wholesale houses during the expansion of the railroads around the turn of the century. Thereafter the district declined as commercial establishments were abandoned (Olson, 1985). By the 1970s Lowertown had declined into a shabby district of abandoned warehouses, rail yards and parking lots; although, it still had the residual charm of turn-of-the-century buildings, narrow alleys and tree-lined streets (Peirce, 1985). In 1978, then-mayor George Latimer approached the McKnight Foundation and persuaded it to put up $10 million to stimulate new Lowertown development (Peirce, 1985). Approximately $8.5 million of this was used as a revolving fund to finance projects and the remainder was devoted to administrative costs of the Lowertown Redevelopment Corporation, or LRC (Olson, 1985). LRC is a private, nonprofit corporation that coordinates design and financing, and orchestrates the interests of city government and the private sector. It also administers the program-related McKnight investments, makes other loans and loan guarantees at below market rates for selected projects (such as the Galtier Plaza, described later in this section), and works with the city government to secure federal grants for redevelopment. For example, the LRC received a $4.8

million federal Urban Development Action Grant (Olson, 1985) and subsidizes housing costs so that low-income people can afford to live in Lowertown (Peirce, 1985).

In 1984, St. Paul condemned a YMCA, eliminating 145 SRO rooms. This proved to be a catalyst and brought the ongoing problem of loss of affordable downtown housing to a head. One effort to rectify this problem was to create a 56-unit, SRO apartment complex on four floors of Lowertown's five-story American Beauty building (the street level was left open for commercial development), which was completed in 1986. The city struck a deal with Asset Development Services, Inc., the building's former owner and a local developer, in which the city and the federal government absorbed much of the cost—the company contributed just $700,000, in exchange for a limited return. This project was funded in part by a $4.8 million federal Urban Development Action Grant (HUD denied another grant application because the proposed shared kitchens and baths did not meet federal regulations), and the city granted the project $4.4 million in TIF funds (Edmondson, 1986). Another housing project within Lowertown is Market House, a warehouse converted to loft-style condominiums. Specialty retail space is located on the first and second floors of the six-story structure. Residents of the building as well as others living in new housing nearby are expected to support the retail area (Olson, 1985).

One of the largest projects in Lowertown was Galtier Plaza, a 1 million square foot mixed use development. Galtier Plaza encompasses one square block and includes a 113,000 square foot, three level mall and two high rise towers. The towers contain 150 luxury condominium units and 350 rental apartments. A 6-story YMCA and 60,000 square feet of office space are incorporated above and around the mid-block mall area. Galtier Plaza is a joint venture between Boisclair Corporation and Omni Venture Ltd. (Olson, 1985). The LRA also contributed $2 million to the development.

In Lowertown and surrounding areas more than 70 new projects were built in the 1980s, and at least 15 more have been finished since then; about 80 rehabilitation efforts have also been completed. The riverfront is gaining attention, with plans for revitalization well underway. Today the area boasts a variety of lovely renovated historic buildings as well as high-rise condo towers and apartments, artists' studios, theaters, shops, offices, boat landings, a growing list of computer-related companies, which LRC Director Weiming Lu is trying to link to form a "cybervillage," and a rich diversity of people. "The result of LRC's unique partnership with the City and the private sector has been the successful planning and execution of a development strategy . . . which has succeeded beyond anyone's expectations" (Lowertown Redevelopment Corporation, 1998). This is a modest assessment of a redevelopment which was called "a model for urban villages" by columnist Neal Peirce (1997).

Supportive City Programs. Regional cooperation has been the primary method used in the Twin Cities for low income neighborhood revitalization. Programs like the Fiscal Disparities Plan (FDP, otherwise known as tax base sharing), tax increment financing (TIF) transfers between downtown and surrounding neighborhoods, regional cooperative efforts with the McKnight Foundation, and regional governance have been described in previous sections. But regional cooperation alone has not revitalized the Twin Cities' low income neighborhoods. An important local activity that was necessary to achieve successful revitalization was the reuse of TOADS. In the Twin Cities, TOADS come from many sources. Cities could acquire property owned by the FHA, VA, railroads, and the RTC, as well as toxic sites. The biggest source of land was acquisition due to nonpayment of property taxes.

Nicollet Island, a quarter-mile-long island in the Mississippi River between Northeast Minneapolis and downtown Minneapolis, provides an early example of revitalization using government-owned property. The city's wealthy elite built mansions on the island in the 1870s but within 25 years they were converted into apartments, and eventually became ill-kept rooming houses. In 1966, local historian Lucille Kane described the area as "obscured by a shabby cover of houses, stores, secondhand shops, and missions." Eventually, many were foreclosed for nonpayment of property taxes. The city's Park and Recreation Board acquired much of the island's acreage along with 22 homes and 5 undeveloped lots that were later made available as locations for relocating historic homes. Today most of the island is a park, owned by the Minneapolis Park and Recreation Board. There are five quadruplexes and one duplex all under 99-year land lease from the Park Board to the Minneapolis Housing and Redevelopment Authority, which constitute a co-op of 22 units; 17 of these are rented to low and moderate income people (60% of median SMSA income).

The remaining homes on the island's northern tip are historic treasures, a remnant of pioneer days. The island provides a unique living experience, offering a small-town rural forested environment next to downtown. The residents of the 1960s, composed mostly of hippies and retirees, successfully defeated several proposals to "renovate" the island by building high-rise apartments (Paine, 1995). Perhaps the apparent city neglect of the area, which is easily spotted by the casual observer is the result of this neighborhood/city antagonism: The condition of the island's residential streets and small neighborhood parks is deplorable, and devalues the evident efforts of the homeowners to maintain their properties.

In Minnesota, as in many other states, the task of foreclosing on tax-delinquent properties and then auctioning them falls to the counties. Both the cities of Minneapolis and St. Paul receive lists of these properties and have "first right of refusal," before they go to auction. They can select some from the list and can hold them for a year, after which they must either be sold or put to use (author's interview with Hagen, 1996). Meanwhile, under Chapter 249 of the Minneapolis code, vacant housing must be boarded up and after 60 days, demolition can be authorized (author's interview with Pettiford, 1996). In 1993, the city spent about $4 million to acquire and demolish vacant houses and another $6 million in rehab, with funding coming from the federal HOPE3 program. As of January 1994, the city of Minneapolis had an inventory of 405 vacant houses; the city of St. Paul had 550 (St. Paul Division of Housing, 1995).

In the past, when property taxes were not paid the city assessor would "wipe out" the liens, then offer the property for sale at "fair market value" which was determined by an appraiser—but then, after the property was sold, the purchaser would receive a bill for the liens.[3] This method made purchase of tax-foreclosed property unpopular, so the policy was changed (author's interview with Pettiford, 1996). Both cities have since developed programs designed to recycle their extensive inventories of city-owned property but those in Minneapolis will be the focus here. There are now three main programs for recycling city-owned property, as described below.

Urban Homesteading. Urban Homesteading was pioneered in 1973 in Wilmington, Delaware. By 1975 the federal government had taken notice of the activity. In an effort to encourage reuse of its foreclosed homes, HUD began urban homesteading programs in 23 cities, providing money for acquiring vacant properties in need of rehab. In order to qualify for the $1 sales price, homesteaders must agree to bring the homes into compliance with city codes within 18 months, and to occupy the homes for 3–5 years. Urban homesteading programs soon sprouted in cities and towns throughout the nation. In 1990 the federal program was replaced with the HOPE3 program, but Minneapolis chose to retain the previous name. At that time the program was substantially changed: Among other things, the sale of property for $1 was replaced with a requirement of sale for an amount equal to the after-rehab fair market value.

In Minneapolis, urban homesteading recycles the TOADS that are in the best condition, because these buyers must keep rehab costs down (author's interview with Pettiford, 1996). MCDA works with neighborhood CDCs and housing corporations (author's interview with Hagen, 1996). The developers, which include nationwide (Neighborhood Housing Services), regional (Greater Minneapolis Metropolitan Housing Corporation, or GMMHC), and local organizations, either build new houses or rehab the ones that are there.[4] Federal home improvement loans (3% interest for 20 years with a cap of $27,000) were supplemented with local financing: The below-market-interest-rate MCDA mortgages described earlier are given based on the property's value after rehab, so the buyer has immediate access to funds for completing the rehab work. Closing costs are included in the mortgages. MCDA also provides a $2,000 subsidy for some mortgages, and low income buyers with a dependent child may also receive loans for closing costs and/or "equity participation" loans for up to 10% of the purchase price through the Minneapolis–St. Paul Family Housing Fund described earlier. These loans have no interest or monthly payment, and are due only when the home is sold, paid off, or the buyer moves. Buyers are selected via a lottery that is held several times a year. They must have incomes between $18,000 and $43,500, and must make a $750 payment when their mortgage application is approved.

For very low income buyers the MCDA works with Habitat for Humanity, selling them homes for a low price which are then rehabbed and sold using Habitat's sweat equity/zero interest loan program. The city of St. Paul has a similar program. Placement of homes is important here too, with the goal being mixed income neighborhoods: "We don't want the Habitat homes to become islands," Pettiford (in interview with author, 1996) said.

HOW and RIF. Under the Home Ownership Works (HOW) program, MCDA contracts with nonprofit developers to do plans and specs, then develop property. The HOW program is for moderate income buyers, who purchase the homes after rehab at subsidized interest rates. They also attend counseling sessions to correct credit problems and learn money management. HOW is funded through the federal HOPE3 program as well as local government money.

The MCDA Rehabilitation Fund (RIF) gives grants to developers to do the plans, specs, and rehab work on major renovation. The grant amount covers the difference between the total development cost and the post-rehab appraised value, providing "gap financing" for the nonprofit group to cover rehab costs before the units are sold; there is a maximum of $45,000 for single family and $75,000 for duplexes. "MCDA loses about $25,000 per house here," Pettiford said, referring to the typical grant amount. This program, which is funded locally, gets the "second cut" homes, after urban homesteading (author's interview with Pettiford, 1996).

Vacant lot sales/recycling program. Finally, MCDA makes its vacant lots available for purchase and construction. Under this program, "We'll sell to anyone—for example, 60 townhouses near the river are high-dollar, one buyer owns 25 banks! We're very committed to mixed income. We need an economic mix in order to have the buying power to attract retail, and a racial mix in order to retain neighborhood elementary schools so busing is not necessary," Pettiford (in an interview with the author, 1996) said. MCDA makes subsidized loans available to low-income buyers for closing cost or down payment assistance on these properties; it also has a closing assistance program in which buyers "work off" these costs by doing something the nonprofit agency says is needed—for example, coaching soccer (author's interview with Pettiford, 1996).

MCDA's Century Homes program, which was begun in 1994 and operates all over town, aims to provide new homes on MCDA-owned lots. The program's goal is construction of 100 new homes each year for five years. It is capitalized with $500,000 from the McKnight Foundation, $350,000 from General Mills, and $850,000 (mainly CDBG funds) from MCDA (Minneapolis Community Development Agency, 1998). The City of Minneapolis also contributes $2–3 million worth of acquisition and demolition work (author's interview with Pettiford, 1996). Nonprofit developer GMMHC, which manages the program, has built 800 single-family units under this program so far, and they also advise on multifamily development.

Some buyers are moderate income but about 80% are low income (author's interview with Hagen, 1996). Century Homes has no restrictions on income—"We're there for everybody," Pettiford said. A typical sales price is $89,000 for a 1,600 square foot 3-bedroom, 2-bath home with a basement, security system, and so on. The low income buyer could receive a $10,000 "equity participation" loan plus a $15,000 "affordability loan," both of which are "deferred payment"—that is, they become grants after five years of occupancy by the purchaser. A typical new home under this program costs more than $100,000 to construct; matching grants from MCDA and other public and private entities bridge the gap.

Results

Evidence of Success. Evidence of the success of some programs is considerable. The Family Housing Fund has financed more than 14,000 apartments and single family homes for low-income families with children since 1980. Not surprisingly, it has become a model for programs throughout the country (McKnight, 1995). In 1994, under Take Credit! lenders issued the buyers "mortgage credit certificates" worth $1.2 million in St. Paul alone, and a total of $352,054 was awarded to 56 homeowners under the SAM program. Of the 474 PHA participants from 1991–1994, 97 have already become homeowners. The St. Paul/Minneapolis First Time Homebuyers Bond Program has approved nearly 7,000 mortgages since its inception in 1981, and 42 families received $2.4 million in loans during a three-year period in the early 1990s alone (St. Paul Division of Housing, 1995). In 1995, 15 homes were rehabbed under the housing rehab matching fund program, with an average ending value of $89,000 (author's interview with Pettiford, 1996). In 1995 alone, nearly 40 homes have been rehabbed under HOW and Urban Homesteading, with a construction value of more than $2.2 million (Minneapolis Community Development Agency, 1995).

Completion of projects like the American Beauty SRO housing conversion and the Galtier Plaza mixed use development attest to the success of cooperative efforts in Lowertown. As of February 1985, $200 million of redevelopment was completed or underway in the neighborhood (Olson, 1985). Peirce (1997) stated that McKnight's initial $10 million investment has attracted $428 million from other sources, resulting in 4,300 jobs and 1500 housing units, one-fourth of which are for low and moderate income people.

Other neighborhoods have also experienced some degree of success. The Near North and Willard-Homewood areas of Minneapolis were viable, but declined as people moved in that were displaced by renewal elsewhere. Revitalization (which began in the 1970s) involved building 130 new homes in Lynn Park (a part of Near North) with prices starting in the upper $50s. The existing poor residents were paid an amount equal to the cost of a new home (not merely the value of their present home) to relocate, so they also benefited by obtaining better housing (author's interview with Pettiford, 1996).

There are many neighborhoods in which the City of St. Paul has utilized tax-delinquent property as a catalyst for revitalization. In Lyton Park Place the city assembled six blocks, then built 22 single family homes and an industrial park (author's interview with Soderholm, 1996). In Wabashon Terrace at East 3rd and Mariah, the city also assembled tax-delinquent property in order to provide housing. There are "many other things going on there besides housing," Soderholm added.

Remaining Problems. State law regarding recycling TOADS appears to be in need of reform to streamline the process and reduce costs. For example, filing suit to quiet title before offering any delinquent tax property for sale is costly: The city of St. Paul paid $12,000 to quiet title on six lots. They city is trying to reduce this cost. Total cost to the city of recycling tax-delinquent property runs $3,800–6000, which is covered by CDBG grant money and general city funds in order to keep buyer costs low.

The NRP program has not accomplished as much as its supporters hoped, apparently because the program involved numerous independent government agencies, the city generally does not have a tradition of longstanding strong neighborhood organizations, and the residents were not truly in charge of the program for their neighborhoods. As Fainstein and Hirst (1993) said, "The participating jurisdictions with minor exceptions, failed to modify their normal practices to accommodate the neighborhood plans and, therefore, had reallocated hardly any of their own funds to conform with neighborhood desires. . . . The NRP office's ability to improve the program was limited by its lack of leverage over the participating jurisdictions," adding that most city staff are not familiar with the city's neighborhoods and neighborhood activists had to obtain approval from several agencies for their proposals. Changes are being implemented, but whether public officials and staff can "adapt to a different, and possibly diminished role"—enough to let the residents put the program to work, remains to be seen.

The Minneapolis/St. Paul area suffers from significant affordability gaps between wages and both rent and purchasing power, according to data collected for the McKnight Foundation by consultant Warren Hanson (1996). In St. Paul, the more affluent population is moving east and the St. Paul neighborhoods are becoming majority minority as a result. A state Affordable Housing law that required replacement of affordable homes that were removed was repealed in 1996 (author's interview with Soderholm, 1996). Thus, it is reasonable to expect that the affordability gap will remain large, or possibly even enlarge, in the near future.

REGIONALISM IN PORTLAND

Roots of Decline

The idea of Portland's decline is somewhat of an oxymoron, since the city has experienced very few of the population losses and related problems that have been endured by nearly every other large U.S. city mentioned in this book. Since 1960, the city itself has added some 65,000 residents to its 1960 population of 372,676; the city population declined only in the 1970s, when 16,000 people left for the suburbs. The metropolitan area has grown by roughly 2 million people every decade since 1960 (see Table 3). Even the city's share of families in poverty fell in the 1980s (Nelson & Milgroom, 1995). Yet the data also show that Portland has not been immune from the employment shifts that were at least in part responsible for the massive population losses experienced in other cities. From 1967–1987 the city's manufacturing employment fell from 41,000 to 32,700 jobs, while the surrounding suburbs added nearly 27,000 manufacturing jobs. Portland residents had the same opportunities to participate in FHA and VA loan programs for suburban homes, and to tap into DOT funds for highway construction to suburbia. What stopped people from fleeing the city here? The answer appears to lie in "regional development management that directs development opportunity toward the center rather than facilitating its continued outward expansion" (Nelson & Milgroom, 1995).

Signs of Change

Regional Growth Management. Like San Francisco and Seattle, Portland is characterized by a compact, livable, mixed use urban form which has been described as "A Mecca for urban design, architecture, and planning enthusiasts" (Nelson & Milgroom, 1995). But the form taken by Seattle, San Francisco, Manhattan, and other dense urban areas is at least in part dictated by geographic constraints. In Portland, this structure is the result of a conscious decision to direct growth. "Portland has experienced the nation's highest level of regional development management," according to Nelson & Milgroom (1995), referring to the area's combination of limits on sprawl, aggressive redevelopment, transit, regional infrastructure planning and management, and high density requirements for new development. The program

Table 3: Population Change in Portland Area, 1950 through 1990

	City of Portland	Multnomah County	Portland/ Vancouver CMSA*	CMSA Area Outside Portland
1950	373,682	471,539	704,829	331,147
1960	372,676	522,813	821,897	449,221
1970	382,619	556,667	1,009,129	626,510
1980	366,423	562,640	1,242,594	876,171
1990	437,398	583,887	1,477,895	1,040,497

Source: U.S. Bureau of the Census, 1950–1990
*Consolidated Metropolitan Statistical Area

started in the 1970s, when the state of Oregon adopted a wide-ranging state land use planning program designed to protect farms and forests in danger of succumbing to the pressures of sprawl. This Growth Management Act established urban growth boundaries that ensured that new development would occur within pre-established city and suburban areas.

The provisions of this Act are carried out by an elected regional government, the Metropolitan Services District (MSD). The MSD, which was created by the State Legislature in 1970, is run by a 12-member nonpartisan commission elected from districts that cover three counties and 24 municipalities, essentially all of the Portland urbanized area in Oregon. The MSD is a large and powerful governmental body, with taxation authority, 1,200 employees and an annual budget of more than $200 million. Originally formed to oversee regional solid waste facilities, the MSD is now in charge of planning and construction of a convention center, air and water quality programs, parks, the zoo, and "has the primary planning responsibility for the Portland regional area" (Waste, 1997). The MSD's Portland 2040 "Future Vision" and "Regional Framework Plan" establish urban growth boundaries, promote balanced regional housing distribution, coordinate transportation investment, and "are widely regarded as among the preeminent participatory and comprehensive metro-wide planning documents in the United States" (Waste, 1997). Local plans must be concurrent with regional ones, thus it is not surprising that Portland's city plan declares it to be in accordance with the adopted plans of the MSD (Portland Bureau of Planning, 1991), nor that regional planning directly affects comprehensive city planning and even neighborhood plans (Nelson & Milgroom, 1995).

Regional Transit. A prime example of how regionalism supports the central city, including its lowest income neighborhoods, is the area's transit system Tri-Met. The entire downtown area (inside I-405 to Hoyt on the north to the river on the east) is a "ride free" transit zone, and there is a 16-block transit mall within this area (between 5th and 6th Streets/Main St. and Union Station). These downtown services are supported by revenues from the system's more lucrative routes. The system, which was voted America's Best Transit System, serves over 600 square miles in three counties with 86 bus routes and a 15.1-mile light rail line, MAX (Metropolitan Area Express), that runs from downtown east to Gresham.

Completed in 1986, the 29-stop MAX line cost $214 million and was mainly financed by federal funds that had been reserved for construction of a highway through southeast Portland. The city lobbied state and federal agencies to cancel the freeway and make the funds available for light rail instead, a concept endorsed by the state legislature in accordance with regional plans to reduce traffic congestion, foster more dense urban areas, and contain growth within its predetermined boundary. Ridership is growing steadily, and evidence shows that Max has stimulated downtown development as well as encouraged more than $800 million worth of development along the line itself (Nelson & Milgroom, 1995). Experts believe that this success is largely due to "regionally coordinated land use and transit planning aided by regional urban containment strategies" (Nelson & Milgroom, 1995). Not surprisingly, funds have been secured to build another line heading west from downtown, and Tri-Met is considering construction of a 20-mile north-south line from Vancouver, Washington to Oregon City.

Local Support for Neighborhood Revitalization. Regional growth management and transit provision alone would not have been enough to improve the city's low-income neighborhoods. Political support from Portland's elected officials has also been a key element in successful neighborhood maintenance and revitalization. One example of this support is the city's Office of Neighborhood Associations—established by former mayor (1973–81) and governor (1987–91), Neil Goldschmidt—which coordinates and provides support for community organizations (Perry, 1987). The office is divided into components that focus on the northeast, north, east, southeast, and southwest parts of town, with staff assigned to each area. Another is the $24 million fund created in 1995 to leverage private funds for the provision of affordable housing, using general city revenues.

Affordable housing is an especially serious problem for the city's poor neighborhoods. In the first five years of the 1990s, housing prices had increased 50% citywide and had risen over 150% in some lower income neighborhoods. Thus, providing housing that low income people can afford—one might say, fighting rampant gentrification—is a challenge. For example, the area in northeast Portland that is bounded by Lombard, 15th Street, and the waterfront used to be the worst part of town but now is being gentrified rapidly by children of the baby boomers. In the early 1990s almost 1,000 properties in this area were subject to seizure for nonpayment of delinquent property taxes, but since the housing stock was sound, when demand rose the area attracted new people (author's interview with Runkel, 1995). Although demand seems to have kept the delinquent tax problem in check, it has also decreased affordability.

When poor residents do achieve homeownership, city support has been needed to allow them to retain their homes. The Dominion Capital story, which one interviewee described as a case of "a slumlord victimizing poor homeowners with bogus land sales contracts," is an example. Apparently, the company went bankrupt, throwing 350 properties into federal bankruptcy court and causing the residents to lose their equity and titles. There was pressure for the city to buy the homes and return them to their owners, but there was not enough local money to do this. So Councilman Erik Sten sponsored a plan that provided an $11 million loan guarantee from U.S. Bank to Portland Community Reinvestment Inc. (a CDC) to purchase all 350 homes and return them to their owners. The money was repaid via Model Cities mortgage repayment funds (author's interview with Runkel, 1995).

Another example of city involvement in revitalization efforts is the Belmont Dairy, a mixed-use project at S.E. 30th and Belmont, which transforms a dilapidated dairy into ground floor retail shops with about 80 housing units above. "Councilman Sten worked hard for two years to encourage the banking industry to believe that mixed-use projects such as this are good investments, and are the type of development that we need to finance to meet city and metropolitan planning goals," activist Marshall Runkel (in author's interview, 1995) explained. City council members also support programs such as HOST (Home Ownership One Street at a Time) and Community Reinvestment Initiatives, organize community banks, and they were instrumental in supporting development and implementation of the Shelter Reconfiguration Plan.

Results

The results of these efforts are far too extensive to include here; a single example must suffice. Perhaps nowhere is the broad-based citywide political support (coupled with the effects of regional growth management and transit) more evident than in the efforts of a city-county-nonprofit-business-church-activist coalition to improve the quality of life for Portland's homeless. Rising prices and resultant losses of SRO housing have contributed to marked increases in the number of homeless people in U.S. cities (Baum & Burnes, 1993) including Portland, where one of the elected officials' major concerns was the preservation of SRO hotels. The city has been able to secure both public and private funds for rehabilitation and operation. A group in the Burnside community, Central City Concerned (CCC), has renovated and manages at least 454 units for rent to low income singles, over 300 of them SRO housing. One of CCC's and Portland's biggest achievements was the securing of the SRO Section 8 Demonstration Program. Under this program, low income

tenants pay about 30% of their income for housing, while rents are fully subsidized for tenants with no income. Social services are also provided through
a joint effort of the city, Multnomah County, area churches, nonprofit groups
such as CCC, the Portland Chamber of Commerce, and social service agencies. In 1987 these groups created a "city assistance program" modeled after
employee assistance programs to provide services to those homeless people
who were alcoholic, addicted, and/or mentally ill. Under this program (Perry,
1987), specific plans are made for getting appropriate detoxification and
other services to people found on the street, and responsibility for them is
assigned to participating agencies. For example, CCC operates the CHIERS
wagon (CCC Hooper Inebriate Emergency Response Service) wagon, which
"deploys deputized persons to respond to 'person-down' calls and transports
individuals to a sobering station," (Baum and Burnes, 1993). Another option is the Everett Hotel, which houses patients just completing a treatment
program. The city assistance program also encompasses treatment, outreach,
employment opportunities, public education, coordinated planning and
fundraising, and supervised substance-free housing.

A site visit to the area containing most of these SROs was revealing. Chi-
natown occupies several blocks adjacent to this area—its ornate gates delin-
eate the neighborhood boundary and its residents stroll freely through the
adjacent SRO area, which is rapidly becoming characterized by mixed use
and mixed income. The impetus for much of this redevelopment undoubtedly
comes from the east, where the Skidmore/Old Town district (a 20-block area
that forms the area's eastern border and continues south across Burnside) has
undergone a remarkable renaissance. Once the center of Portland, the area
declined to become the city's "Skid Row." Now, it is filled with restaurants,
nightclubs, art galleries, and small shops. The southeast corner of the SRO
area is marked with a large fountain (the Skidmore Fountain) and pocket park
(Ankeny Park), an impressive government investment in public amenities for
a low income neighborhood to receive. The fountain, which was installed in
1888 to provide drinking water for "horses, men and dogs" as requested in
Stephen Skidmore's will, marks the city's historic heart. On weekends, the
pocket park and nearby area are filled with artists and craftspersons selling
their wares. Directly to the east, the north end of Governor Tom McCall Park,
which was installed after demolishing a freeway that cut off the city from the
Willamette River, now invites residents to the riverbank. Burnside Street, a
major arterial, borders the area on the south. To the west lie the North Park
Blocks, six blocks of linear park which preserve one of the largest groves of
elm trees in the country. The blocks were created in the 1850s as part of a 25-
block urban greenway. To the north the neighborhood's edge is marked by the
Greyhound Bus station, several large public buildings, and the railroad tracks.

Unlike similar districts in many other cities, both the area and the numerous SROs themselves are clean and well maintained. Extensive government

investments have also been made on infrastructure, police, buses, trees, litter control, and streetscaping. There are also many small businesses, ranging from coffee shops and art galleries to warehouses, giving the appearance that revitalization of business is taking place. Interspersed with the SROs and businesses one finds numerous loft apartments and an occasional gallery. In sum, the visual clues people use to judge both neighborhood quality and personal safety are all present here. On first glance, one could easily mistake this area for a gentrified, upscale central city neighborhood. Clearly, the upgraded appearance and apparent gentrification taking place have succeeded in accommodating, rather than driving away, the existing homeless and SRO population. There are still many "street people" here, and conversations revealed that they still perceive the area as theirs. Further, observed behavior makes it clear that although an attractive physical environment improves the quality of life of these residents, it does not solve all their problems. This conclusion is reinforced by the lingering presence of a few boarded-up buildings decorated with graffiti; by window signs letting passersby know that the area is a "Drug-Free Downtown Zone, dealers and buyers are not welcome"; and by the formation of a Neighborhood Business Watch (similar to the neighborhood crime watch groups found in residential areas) to help deter business-related crime.

In conclusion, Portland's neighborhood revitalization can be credited to coalitions between residents and community groups working closely with the city, in a regulatory environment established by the state that favors city life over suburban living. The resulting programs address every aspect of quality of life as listed in Figure 1 in Chapter 1, even for the city's homeless residents. Thus, at least in this case, the combination appears to have been successful.

TORONTO, OTTAWA, AND MONTREAL

Regional control is common in Canada, thanks to a system of government that is quite different from that of the United States. Each of Canada's ten provinces has its own variations in governmental structure, with each province able to determine the specific form. This variation extends to the local level (localities are creations of the provincial government), where one even finds wide variations in the nomenclature used for municipal and other local governmental bodies. For example, "regional municipalities" in Ontario, "district municipalities" in British Columbia, and "parishes, townships, united townships or municipalities without designation" in Quebec (Cullingworth, 1993). All refer to municipal governments. In urban areas the provinces are often also divided into regions, which encompass several municipalities. For example, in the province of Ontario, the Ottawa region includes three municipalities, the Toronto region covers seven, and British Columbia has established 28 "regional districts," the best known being the Greater Vancouver Regional District.

Provincial Power

The province is the ultimate authority, setting policies to which regional and municipal policies must conform—for example, most provinces require that municipal plans and zoning ordinances be consistent. This governmental structure reflects Canadians' longstanding dislike of local government and opposition to the property taxes they engender, a position which is understandable when one remembers that in Canada the preferred model is that in which services are financed and provided directly by the provinces or regions (Cullingworth, 1993). Canadian planning and zoning law also gives much broader discretion to the provinces and regions than do their U.S. equivalents. For example, like the State Enabling Acts that authorize planning and zoning in the United States, in Canada, each province has its own Planning Act. Unlike the U.S. enabling acts, however, there is a great deal of variation among provinces regarding the provisions of these acts. The Canadian equivalent of the Fifth Amendment to the U.S. Constitution, which protects private property from being taken without compensation, substitutes "security" for "property." Thus, "The taking issue and the property rights argument simply do not operate in Canada" (Lapping, 1987). Further, the Canadian constitution (the British North America Act) says little about democracy or popular sovereignty; reserves all powers not given to the lower levels of government to itself (a reversal of the U.S. Tenth Amendment declaration that all powers not expressly given to the national government are reserved for the states); and even contains a provision that allows a national or even a provincial legislature to escape Constitutional restrictions by stating that the law in question shall operate notwithstanding these restrictions. The court system is seen as an arm of the state rather than an independent branch of government, and rarely deals with land use planning cases. Finally, Canadians hold a much more cooperative, trusting view of their national and state governments—both elected officials and bureaucrats—than do U.S. citizens. Canadians value "peace, order, and good government" over "life, liberty, and the pursuit of happiness" (Friedenberg, 1980). Given these differences, it is not surprising to find that the Canadian national and provincial governments wield much more power in planning than do the national and state governments in the United States. As Goldberg and Mercer (1986) said, "The relatively greater role played by bureaucrats in Canada would be anathema to most Americans, as would be the broad discretionary powers wielded by senior officials."

One result of these differences is that Canadian provinces have not only zoning such as is found in the United States, but also utilize a system of discretionary controls and approvals that gives wide leeway in project approvals to administrative officials. As Cullingworth (1993) describes it, "The system . . . is one in which the owner's right to develop is controlled not by a zoning bylaw but by a planning authority's discretion." There are wide variations among the provinces, and even the regions and municipalities within provinces, regarding how much discretionary control is exercised. In most parts of the country the power is utilized much as the power to review and approve planned unit developments is used in the U.S., but some areas, such as Vancouver, go further. Here, the city has been given the power to create zoning districts in which there are no uniform regulations; developers simply submit plans for council approval. The regional policies and regulations have overriding authority over those prepared by regional municipalities, but not over the provincial ones.

Ottawa: An Enforceable Plan. The Ottawa region illustrates the extent of regional authority. Here the mayor and city council are elected by the region, which provides all public facilities (water, sewer, transit, and so on), has a budget of $1 billion Canadian and includes 640,000 people. The region creates the regional municipalities where local zoning must conform to the official regional plan. The regional staff (not elected officials) approve all local subdivisions, and also control water and sewer access. The region even has the authority to prevent development of wetlands and agricultural lands without compensating the owners, because the Ontario Planning Act is one of the strongest provincial acts—giving much more power to regulate and even take land than is the case in the United States.

The Official Plan for the Ottawa-Carleton region "is a legal document that sets the future development patterns within the region over the next 25 years" (City of Ottawa, 1996). It calls for no increase in urban boundaries (that is, all development will be infill) and gives priority to proposals that support walking, cycling, and transit rather than auto transportation. The main selling point for this plan was its lower public cost. The regional planning staff evaluated many alternative regional growth patterns, costing them out in detail, and discovered that rural development was the most expensive, so they chose to "grow in, not out," emphasizing redevelopment. Most jobs are already downtown, and the modal split is very high—50–70% of city travelers ride the bus. Many other advantages also helped this plan alternative win approval: It was seen as helping support downtown, provide more housing choice (as opposed to suburban growth which is usually 3–4 bedroom, 2 bath, single family homes), and so on. The impetus for the planning effort described above was the failure of Ottawa's greenbelt to control sprawl (although common in Europe, Ottawa's is the only greenbelt in North America designed to control sprawl). Developers were leapfrogging over the greenbelt, and pressuring the region to provide services. Whether the new approach produces better results remains to be seen.

Remaining Problems

Despite the heavy regional controls, sprawl is a problem in all three Canadian cities for several reasons. First, innovative Canadian planning and zoning are recent additions to the urban scene. As Carver (1960) said, "In both the U.S. and Britain the foundations of present planning ideas and methods were laid down during the period between the two wars. In Canada this did not happen. . . . So in 1946 we almost literally started from scratch with no plans or planners and we immediately hit a period of tremendous city growth" (author's interview with Sweet, 1996). Second, shortly after World War II the Canadian government created the Central Mortgage and Housing Corporation (CMHC), which provided financing and related services to suburban housing developers in a somewhat analogous manner to that of the Federal Housing Administration and Veterans Administration loan programs in the United States. Before creation of the CMHC there was a serious housing shortage: Suburban development boomed after its creation.

But the impact on Canadian central cities was less devastating than in the United States because Canada did not have nearly as comprehensive a highway program or urban renewal program as did the United States. There is only one national road in Canada, and the provinces have invested heavily in creating high quality transit systems more than in urban highway building. Urban renewal did occur briefly in the 1960s in Canada, but national funding was much less than U.S. levels. In spite of this, the program was very controversial and was soon replaced with a Neighborhood Improvement Plan that stressed central city neighborhood preservation and citizen input in the planning process (Cullingworth, 1993). Much renewal in Canada was spearheaded by the private sector as contrasted with the conspicuous absence of the private sector in U.S. urban renewal efforts, which is widely cited as a reason for the Canadian program's adverse effects on central cities.

There are variations in the degree to which growth has been controlled. For example, Montreal (in the province of Quebec) is not faring as well as Ottawa financially because the city has not stopped sprawl. They recently closed 11 schools in the city and spent $69 million on new schools for the suburbs, a concrete example of the costs of sprawl (author's interview with Sweet, 1996).

Toronto: A Troubled Model. Toronto, too, is surrounded by plenty of sprawling suburbs. Yet Toronto in particular may offer lessons in what can and cannot be accomplished with regional control to improve the quality of life in central cities even though development has exploded around it.

Metropolitan Toronto, established by the province of Ontario in 1953 to govern a 240-square-mile area, is one of the oldest metropolitan governments in America. Originally, amalgamation of the city of Toronto with its surrounding municipalities was proposed, but this met with stiff opposition, so a two-tiered system was developed, with a metropolitan government serving the entire region and the municipalities remaining intact. The impetus for the formation of Metro Toronto was the inability of the existing local governments to cope with providing services for the explosion of postwar urban growth in the region. "In the 1950s and 60s, Metro sprouted suburbs that required massive construction of water and sewer infrastructure. Dreams—and nightmares—of piping schemes to satisfy the need contributed to a public vision of technology tinged with terror" ("METRO VOTES," 1995). In its first ten years, 75% of Metro's construction spending went for roads, sewers, and water mains. Metro Toronto became a model for the establishment of other regional governments, but these did not always retain a similar structure. For example, in 1959 the province of Quebec established the Montreal Metropolitan Corporation based on Toronto's model, but it suffered from internal political problems that led to its restructuring in 1969 as an indirectly elected regional government known as the Montreal Urban Community (Cullingworth, 1993). Recently, Metro Toronto became the central city of a new provincially-created regional body, the Greater Toronto Area, which covers more than ten times the area of Metro Toronto. Thus, the province has assumed responsibility for regional planning and service provision in the Toronto area (author interview with Frances Frisken, 1992).

Even regional governance has not produced a noticeably higher quality of life in Toronto's low income neighborhoods, which have plenty of problems typical of declining urban neighborhoods throughout the United States and Canada. Although downtown is a very lively place, even at midnight, the area is thick with the homeless, the mentally ill, and the addicted. They mingle freely with tourists, businesspeople, and teenagers who congregate around the night clubs and music shops on Yonge Street. Of all the cities visited, only in New York did the author see a comparable number of destitute people attempting to survive on the streets literally in the middle of urban activity; and like New York, the passersby simply navigate around them as if they were objects. A walk through nearby blocks at 6 A.M. can be an unsettling experience, as only the homeless are about at that hour. Especially in view of the city's cold weather and the Portland experience, one wonders why more has not been done to help these people. Despite this problem, Toronto's downtown and surrounding neighborhoods are full of activity, residents and small businesses. It seems that the city's efforts have engendered a remarkable amount of business activity and attracted residents of all incomes and ethnic groups, but the poorer surrounding neighborhoods still suffer from property abandonment (although not nearly as severe as that found in many U.S. cities), poor litter control, and building code violations.

The Parkdale neighborhood is an example of these problems. "Located on the western fringe of downtown Toronto, Parkdale is a community of mixed incomes, education levels, and building types including fine examples of Victorian architecture. In recent years this once very desirable neighborhood has been plagued with problems such as drugs, street prostitution, safety, the deterioration of buildings and the impact of de-institutionalized patients from a nearby regional mental health center" (ACSP-AESOP Tours, 1996). Planning efforts to reduce these problems began in the fall of 1992 when development of a South Parkdale Neighborhood Improvement Plan was recommended in response to an investigation into unrelated persons living as "family units" in subsidized housing in the area. By early spring 1993, area residents had established the structure of a Community Coordinating Committee to guide the area's community input—prioritizing issues identified by residents, informing residents, communicating with the City Council, and holding public meetings. The committee consists of nine residents with at least three years' tenure in the neighborhood (four tenants, four homeowners, and one homeless or formerly homeless person), three business representatives who have been in business in the neighborhood for at least three years, and three service providers (Ward 2/3 Community Project, 1995). This group acts as a Steering Committee, forming subcommittees of area residents and businesspeople to develop recommendations on specific issues. It is as yet too soon to tell whether Parkdale's planning response will be successful.

In sum, like residents of Minneapolis and Portland, residents of the eastern Canadian cities seem to have a sense of protecting the public good that is not often found in the United States. In Canada, these feelings are exacerbated by the residents' desire to compete with the cities in their southern neighbor. As one resident expressed it, "An asset we possess is the pride which people in the Toronto area and across Ontario clearly have in the high quality of social and community life relative to North America. For a majority of Canadians the difference between our country and the other one [the United States] is in the quality of public goods and public environments, whether it's health care education or basic community services. It points to the presence of positive civic values in our society and the importance of civic cohesion" (author interview with Jean Novick, 1995).

CONCLUSIONS

Mechanisms that produce regional business and government participation in supplying financial resources for inner city revitalization should be fostered. Mechanisms such as the Twin Cities TIF program (which redistributes taxes paid by downtown businesses to the neighborhoods), the Minnesota tax base sharing approach (which forces local government to redistribute business taxes to tax-base-poor areas), regional service provision (such as the Tri-Met in Portland), and/or strict growth management measures which should raise the value of inner city property are all helpful, since they force new development to occur within the existing city boundaries and/or water/sewer service areas (such as those in Portland and in Canada, especially Ottawa). Without these programs, localities can make a case (albeit an ethically weak one) for neglect of infrastructure and services in poor areas based on a shortage of funds coupled with political pressure to respond to the needs of more politically powerful (and more tax-generating) neighborhoods.

To force localities to cooperate, states may have to take action such as Oregon's, mandating concurrency between regional and local plans and encouraging the formation of regional levels of government with elected officials and power over spending. The federal government can also do much to encourage regional cooperation and even governance, using grant incentives and mandates. This may be necessary not only to make central city neighborhood revitalization viable but also for the financial benefit of all. As Nelson and Milgroom (1995)—perhaps referring to the ideas of David Rusk (1993) and others—said, "A growing literature demonstrates that unmanaged regional development results in inefficient dispersion of development away from the central cities," raising the cost of transportation, utilities, energy, solid waste disposal, and land. "In the absence of regional or state-level coordination of development patterns that reverse the effect of sprawl-inducing policies on regional urban form, central cities are at a distinct disadvantage in attracting new investment. . . . The bottom line is that more compact patterns of urban development, anchored by relatively high density central cities, result in greater economic development" (Nelson & Milgroom, 1995).

Citywide decisions should support, not undermine, inner city neighborhood revitalization efforts. If the government is unwilling to invest heavily in ensuring that trash collection, transit, child care, medical services, alcohol/drug treatment, and so on are available, then beautification or physical rehab efforts will produce very limited revitalization success. This is evident in Minneapolis's commitment to fiscal redistribution to the city's neighborhoods through the TIF-funded NRP program, and in Portland's decision to invest heavily in a full spectrum of infrastructure and services for the city's poor neighborhoods. Portland in particular has made major infrastructure investments in its inner city neighborhoods immediately adjacent to downtown. This strategy reflects the city's commitment to neighborhood improvement rather than displacement of existing low income residents. This level of support is based on an attitude of teamwork and cooperation, rather than the adversarial relationships that too often exist between inner city neighborhoods and local officials in less successful project areas. All cities studied here have made significant efforts to attract middle and upper income residents of all ethnic groups back to central city neighborhoods, have encouraged a wide variety of housing types and land uses in the "urban village" tradition, and have assigned staff to specific neighborhoods. This focus apparently stems from an underlying attitude held by area residents that the entire community should bear responsibility for helping to improve the quality of life in the poorest neighborhoods. Put another way, instead of viewing these neighborhoods merely as competitors for scarce resources, their improvement is seen by middle and upper class residents as beneficial, and thus in the public interest. Perhaps one reason for this attitude can be traced back to the way in which programs designed to help poor areas are structured: These cities' decisions to take a regional approach has meant that most aid programs are universal instead of targeted. That is, all parts of town are eligible to apply for funds under Minnesota's tax base sharing and NRP programs; all Portland residents benefit from investing in Tri-Met. By designing regional programs, officials have at least reinforced the idea of a unified urban area. These programs give the illusion, or hope, that neighborhoods of all income levels should cooperate. This may be a powerful argument in favor of universal rather than targeted aid programs.

As is the case in Seattle, these cities' residents have chosen to tax themselves to provide financial support to these neighborhoods. They have supported high density mixed use zoning that includes low income housing, and regional growth management schemes that favor central cities at the expense of suburbs. Also, they have supported this approach "with their feet" by moving into areas that were previously in very poor condition and are still populated with significant numbers of poor and even homeless residents. In short, although research throughout the country shows that low income residents must play the main role in designing neighborhood improvement programs (Medoff & Sklar, 1994; Rooney, 1995; Kotler, 1978), in these cities they are not expected to raise themselves up solely by their own bootstraps. This wider support has been able to sustain some successful revitalization efforts even when major roadblocks to success exist in other key areas, for example, problems with state law regarding delinquent tax properties.

Residents should lead revitalization efforts to the greatest possible extent. The city of Minneapolis typically allocates 100% of its CDBG grant funds to neighborhood revitalization. The residents complete action plans for their neighborhoods, then get CDBG and other funds through the NRP program to implement the plans. In other words, they are in control of project funding.

Foundation support is very helpful. The importance of the McKnight Foundation's efforts in the Twin Cities cannot be overstated. It gives testimony to the importance of working with whatever large corporations are in a given community to direct some of their resources toward the least wealthy neighborhoods.

Other factors must be addressed. Although the revitalization efforts found in these cities were impressive, they were far from complete. For example, in Minneapolis there still are considerable infrastructure needs to be addressed, while in Portland the infrastructure is impressive but the need for social services remains greater than their availability. Toronto appears to lack both, although it also may have a larger problem to deal with than do the U.S. cities. Still, the level of success that was achieved rests at least in part on the programs' efforts to address a wide spectrum of quality of life factors. For instance, in Minneapolis the NRP program addresses safety, education, transportation, and environmental and services needs as well as improving shelter.

One of the most important factors is support from the state and federal governments. None of the cities could have accomplished what they have without support from higher levels of government. In this regard, Alex Schwartz's conclusion regarding the need for outside funds is applicable to all these cities, and is worth emphasizing.

> If Minneapolis, with its prosperous economy, homogeneous population, and relatively harmonious relationship with the state government, cannot rely on its own resources to sustain downtown and neighborhood development, it is not reasonable to expect the same of any other major city. Without federal and state assistance, Minneapolis and other cities are unable to foster downtown and especially community development. This is particularly true of low- and moderate-income neighborhoods, which are by themselves unable to generate tax revenues necessary to support development projects. CDBGs and project-based housing subsidies such as the Section 8 New Construction program (and federal tax breaks) are critical to the funding of neighborhood development.

In conclusion, Minneapolis/St. Paul, Toronto/Ottawa/Montreal, and Portland are similar in many ways. Most notably, they have all made significant efforts to attract middle and upper income residents of diverse ethnic groups back to the central city neighborhoods, have encouraged a wide variety of housing types and land uses, and have placed heavy emphasis on regional growth management, service provision, and finance. There are also interesting variations among the cities studied. For example, in Portland the focus is on providing regional growth management and citywide financial support. Portland has made heavy infrastructure investments in the poorest areas while strictly controlling suburban growth. In Minneapolis/St. Paul many innovative strategies have been employed, but perhaps the most heavily emphasized is regional finance. The Canadian cities have a strong tradition of regional governance, which supports not only regional growth management strategies that help preserve the economic value of inner city property, but also regional finance and service provision. All these strategies reflect the cities' commitments to neighborhood improvement rather than displacement or dispersal of existing low income residents.

Perhaps the most obvious result of the emphasis on regional efforts is dispersal of subsidized housing. Although every city still has neighborhoods that are clearly poor, subsidized housing is widely scattered throughout many parts of these cities. Income mixing seems to have been achieved to a greater extent than is usually the case; this fact is reflected in the focus of this chapter on programs rather than on specific neighborhoods. Beyond that, it appears that fiscal regionalism in the Twin Cities has not worked as well as has growth management coupled with regional service provision in Portland and the cities in Canada. For example, it appeared that investments in infrastructure and maintenance were lagging in some of the Twin Cities' low income areas. Still, in view of the magnitude of the Twin Cities' problems compared to the Canadian cities and Portland, its efforts can be deemed a qualified success. The relatively new NRP program's effects may not yet be evident, so there is further reason to hope for future improvement. Portland and the Canadian cities have achieved impressive neighborhood improvement, but the level of regional control in Canada would not be acceptable to U.S. residents and Canada's form of government is quite different, and Portland certainly did not experience anywhere near the magnitude of problems with safety, shelter, services and other "quality of life" determinants (as outlined in Figure 1, Chapter 1) that most other northern U.S. cities did; these factors limit wider applicability of their approaches, particularly in the case of the Canadian cities. Still, the regional financial mechanisms used and the important role played by the McKnight Foundation in the Twin Cities, along with the regional growth management and infrastructure investments in Portland, are all features worth consideration by other cities.

NOTES

1. SROs are single room occupancy hotels, which provide housing for the nation's elderly, homeless, and mentally ill who have been adversely affected by a shortage of affordable housing. For the most part they offer single furnished rooms that may have a private bath, a shared adjoining bath, or a public bath down the hall. They often have a sink, they may have a refrigerator and/or stove, and they may have a front desk or lobby. SROs tend to cluster in central cities (Saffrin & Goldberg, 1985).

2. The MCDA has been operating without a general property tax levy for nearly 20 years although in 1995 it generated nearly $184 million in revenue. It is "the housing and economic development arm of the City," and, although it was created by the Legislature as a separate legal and financial entity, it is run by a Board that consists of the City Council. In addition to the NRP activities described later in this chapter, it administers more than 100 housing and business development programs, including some that acquire blighted residential properties, demolish deteriorated structures, build new housing, issue hundreds of mortgage loans, issue rehab loans and housing revenue bonds, give rehab grants to nonprofit developers, issue housing revenue bonds and low-income housing tax credits, acquire land, decontaminate deserted factories and contract with private developers to recycle them to new uses, disperse public housing, sell properties, encourage riverfront and downtown development, and offer a wide variety of services to business and industry.

3. This practice is still the norm in some other cities. For example, in Ft. Worth, unsuspecting buyers of delinquent tax properties can receive bills amounting to more

than the delinquent taxes which they originally paid after purchasing the properties at a tax sale, and can lose their ownership rights in these properties if the additional bills are not paid.

4. Goetz, Lam, and Heitlinger (1996) examined the comparative effects of subsidized multifamily housing provided by CDCs, public agencies, and the private sector on nearby property values, crime, and neighborhood stability indicators (residency, race, income, and rent measures) in Minneapolis. Interestingly, they found that CDC-provided housing actually had a positive effect on surrounding property values, perhaps because the CDCs are community-based organizations and thus take the welfare of nearby residents more seriously. Further, the incidence of crime dropped after CDCs purchased the properties, and there was much less transience. There was a much higher incidence of minority and low income residents in the subsidized housing and convincing evidence of a large unmet need for more affordable housing in many Minneapolis census tracts. The authors conclude that "multifamily housing rehabilitation is an effective strategy that can be profitably continued in the central cities of this metropolitan area. . . . dispersal of subsidized housing is not necessary for the sake of inner city neighborhoods," but should be undertaken to broaden resident neighborhood choices, access to employment, and educational opportunities.

CHAPTER 4

Boston
An Empowered, Supported Neighborhood

ROOTS OF DECLINE

Founded by John Winthrop in 1630, the Puritans' "city upon a hill" and its surroundings are the sites of many urban "firsts." Boston Common, the first public park in the nation, was established in 1634. This was swiftly followed by creation of the nation's first free public school (1635), establishment of Harvard (1636) in nearby Cambridge, and enactment of the first tidelands legislation (1698). Nearby Lowell, the first planned industrial community in the country, was established in 1821. In 1826 another nearby community, Quincy, was the site of the nation's first railroad. The country's oldest regional park system was born with the 1893 creation of the Metropolitan Park Commission, and the city unveiled the nation's first subway system in 1897. The string of "firsts" in public works continues today. After the state invested $4 billion to clean up Boston Harbor, in 1997 the National Park Service dedicated the Harbor Islands National Park and began developing a plan for its 31 islands. And most notably, America's largest construction project—the Central Artery/Third Harbor Tunnel construction, popularly known as the "Big Dig"—has been underway since 1991.

The city also has a long tradition of neighborhood activism dating back to the town meetings held in the 1700s, which has continued in recent years and led to more "firsts" for the city. "Almost 25 years ago, in a classic grassroots crusade, a disparate group of Bostonians succeeded in stopping a proposed inner belt segment of Interstate 95. They secured the nation's first transfer of highway funds, leading to the creation of the Southwest Corridor, which covers an Amtrak rail line. The effort stitched together the South End and Back Bay, black and white, old and young, in a superb display of incremental and overall planning" (Kay, 1998).

This tradition of leadership extended to the planning profession. In 1909, Harvard offered the country's first course in city planning. This was followed by the establishment of a City Planning Board in 1914 and enactment of zoning enabling legislation in 1920, well before the Commerce Department published its famous Standard City Planning and Zoning Enabling Acts for use by the states as models. Boston passed a local zoning ordinance in 1924, a mere five years later the nation's first planning school opened at Harvard, capping two decades of innovative planning activity (Thomas, Foster, Bowyer, Chester, & Southworth, 1998). Even today "the hub, the city's traditional nickname, boasts more architects and planners per capita than most American cities" (Kay, 1998).

The city of Boston is, at a mere 48 square miles, one of the smallest in the nation. By contrast, the CMSA is 1,100 square miles. Still, the city is the largest in New England and serves as a transportation hub for it. With 72 colleges and universities in the area serving 260,000 students, the city has been called "one of the largest college towns in the nation." It is no surprise that the city ranks third out of the 20 largest cities in the nation in terms of% of the population holding a college degree. It is also a national center for the health care industry, with 27 hospitals in the city alone (Hodges, 1998a).

Boston annexed Roxbury in 1867 and Dorchester in 1870. This and other annexations helped make Boston a city of neighborhoods, including Roxbury, North Dorchester, South Dorchester, and 13 other large ones, which are in turn divided into 69 smaller neighborhoods. Not surprisingly, neighborhood pride is still very important in Boston (Hodges, 1998a). The city's relatively young median age (30.4 as opposed to 33.5 for the nation) and an influx of a variety of immigrant groups over the past 20 years have helped to keep central city neighborhoods viable as their existing populations age.

Despite these strengths, like many Snowbelt cities, Boston has experienced severe population losses since 1950. The city's population fell by 13% from 1950 (801,444) to 1960 (697,197) and continued downward to 641,071 in 1970, a loss that was parallelled in the surrounding county (the city accounts for 87% of Suffolk County's population) but was the opposite of regional trends. From 1950–1960, the SMSA experienced a 7.4% increase in its population (2,410,572–2,589,301) and continued growing to 2,887,191 in 1970, with growth outside the city of Boston rising at a 17.6% rate from 1950–1960 (1,609,128–1,892,104) and climbing to 2,246,120 by 1970. But from 1970–1980 the economy suffered so badly that, amazingly, even suburban populations declined. The SMSA as a whole lost nearly 150,000 residents (the addition of Framingham to the SMSA in 1980 makes adjustments to raw figures necessary), with about 50,000 people leaving the area outside the city of Boston. Since 1980 the postwar suburban expansion trends have reappeared. The SMSA population grew from 2,805,911 to 2,870,669, with the portion outside Boston rising from 2,242,917 to 2,296,386. But, in what appears to be a major demographic change, for the first time in 40 years the

Table 4: Population Change in Boston Area, 1950 through 1990

	City of Boston	Suffolk County	Boston SMSA*	SMSA Area Outside Boston
1950	801,444	896,615	2,410,572	1,609,128
1960	697,197	791,329	2,589,301	1,892,104
1970	641,071	735,190	2,887,191	2,246,120
1980	562,994	650,142	2,805,911	2,242,917
1990	574,283	663,906	2,870,669	2,296,386

Source: U.S. Bureau of the Census, 1950–1990
Note: Framingham added to SMSA in 1980.
*Metropolitan Statistical Area.

central city is also experiencing significant population growth. During this decade, its population rose from an all-time low of 562,994 to 574,283 as Table 4 shows. Strangely, the number of housing units grew in the city and the SMSA as a whole even during the 1970–1980 recession. 1990 population density was 11,865.4 people per square mile in the city (467.4 in the surrounding SMSA).

Boston's racial diversity has increased dramatically since 1960. The city's racial makeup in 1990 was 63% White (360,875), 26% African American (148,829), 5% Asian (30,388), and 7% (34,191) "other race." Further analysis shows the "other" category to be mainly (28,655) persons of Hispanic origin; thus there is some overlap between the Hispanic origin category and the white (22,141), the African American (10,058), and the Asian racial categories, as well as the "other" category. Comparisons with 1960 are not possible regarding Hispanic origin, since this category was not then defined the same; however, it is interesting to note that the "other" category, which accounted for nearly half the city's Hispanic population in 1990 (28,655), was just 2,057 for the entire SMSA in 1960. Thus it seems reasonable to assume that the Hispanic population in Boston has grown exponentially since 1960. In 1990 the vast majority of Asians were Chinese (16,701), with a significant number coming from Vietnam (4,754). In 1960 the majority of Asians were also Chinese, but Vietnamese were not separated out, and overall the numbers of Asians were minor: just 7,254 out of a total SMSA population of 2,589,301. Thus, the number of Asians in the city of Boston alone in 1990 was more than four times that of the SMSA in 1960. The story is very similar with respect to African-Americans. The city's black population in 1990 (360,875) was more than four times the SMSA black population in 1960 (77,781).

In 1990 Boston had 251,000 housing units of which just 39,124, or 15.6%, were single family. The 32% owner occupancy figure indicates that many multifamily units are owner occupied; most of these are condominiums and row houses. With an average household size of 2.37, it is safe to assume that the city is home to more single adults and fewer nuclear families than are the surrounding suburbs. In the past decade, rents have soared. "Asking rents for one-bedroom apartments ranged from $550 to $800 in the neighborhoods in 1995 and from $995 to $1,300 per month in the downtown and Back Bay-Beacon Hill neighborhoods." Likewise, house prices are high: "Median house prices in Boston's lower-cost neighborhoods in June of 1997 ranged from $85,500 to $145,000 while medians ranged from $180,000 to $320,000 in the pricier neighborhoods. Condominiums have a wider range of prices . . ." (Hodges, 1998a) High price not withstanding, property sales are up by 10% in recent years (Kay, 1998).

With a city labor force of about 295,000, "Boston's employment in 1997 reached 641,000 full and part-time jobs up from a recession low of 587,000 in 1992." Unemployment was at a nine-year low of 3.7% in January 1998 after falling from a recession peak of 8.4% in 1991. Four years earlier, however, it was at an all-time low of 3.2%. The 1991 recession was not the worst, though; the all-time high unemployment was 12.8% in 1975. "Boston is one of the few cities in the nation—along with San Francisco and Washington, D.C.—to have more jobs than residents. This is due to a large commuting population—65% of the total workers" (Hodges, 1998a). This is not a new development. Even in the early 1980s, Boston residents held only 30% of the jobs in the city (Powell, Walsh, & Healy, 1986). Likewise, "In contrast to more decentralized metropolitan areas, the city and its adjacent suburbs account for 40% of the new jobs . . ." (Kay, 1998)

In addition to having a high percentage of commuting workers, only 40% of city residents drive to work alone: The remaining workers use transit (32%), walk (14%), carpool (11%), or use other means (3%). About 632,000 of the MBTA service area's 1.7 million residents ride the bus or subway on weekdays, with another 98,000 using commuter rail (Hodges, 1998a). "To this day, a legacy of excellent public transit enables Bostonians to enjoy a car-lite lifestyle. Residents of the metropolitan area travel half the 15,000 vehicle miles of those who live in more spread-out areas . . . a million passengers in 78 communities depend on [transit]" (Kay, 1998).

The city's ten largest private sector employers, which provide jobs for one out of every five city workers, include five hospitals, one university, one bank, one investment firm, and two insurance companies. This situation reflects a shift which has occurred in the city since 1960 from blue-collar occupations to white-collar and service work. "As of 1990, 67% of city residents were white-collar workers, 17% were service workers, and 16% were in blue-collar positions." This shift is also reflected in vacancy rates, which are low for office space (3.7% in September 1997, the lowest rate among all 47 of the largest U.S. office markets) but high (18% in 1997) for manufacturing and industrial space. Two of the city's three industrial parks are located in Roxbury (Crosstown) and Dorchester (Alsen-Mapes); thus, these areas are especially affected by the shift away from manufacturing (Hodges, 1998a).

The city's poor have not benefitted from Boston's economic recovery as much as most residents. One out of ten residents lives in the city's 15,000 public housing units, a rate comparable to that of New York. Reduced welfare benefits, HUD's withdrawal from housing provision and the recent loss of rent control statewide have worsened conditions: As architecture and planning critic Jane Kay said, "Stays at emergency shelters were at an all-time high this winter [1998]. At Christmas, hunger strikers sat in to protest the death of a homeless man on Boston Common" (Kay, 1998). Although the city ranks fifth nationwide for its level of household income, it ranks 16th in income disparity between rich and poor. "Boston had a median household income of $29,180 in 1989, well below the median for the metropolitan area as a whole of $40,491. Boston had a poverty rate of 18.7% which did show an improvement from the 20.2% rate posted in 1979" (Hodges, 1998a).

A Tradition of Neighborhood Revitalization

"The most significant accomplishments in Boston's revitalization have resulted from deliberative public policy decisions by Boston's elected officials, such as deciding to extend transit and commuter rail instead of building inner belt and southeast expressways; limiting downtown parking for clean air reasons; and developing large mixed use complexes such as Quincy Market[1] and Copley Place,[2] the establishment of administrative structures (such as the Boston Redevelopment Authority, described later in this section), and most importantly, the influence of strong neighborhood and special interest groups . . . to foster planning" (Koff, 1998). Neighborhood, interest group, professional, and business groups have lobbied for "building preservation, pedestrian improvements, quality design, assisted housing, code enforcement, economic development, employment, health care, and public safety" (Koff, 1998), concerns which have led to the development of "sub-area" plans for the city's lower income neighborhoods such as those developed for Blue Hill Avenue, Washington Street, and Erie-Ellington,[3] as well as planning for more upscale communities such as the Back Bay and Beacon Hill.[4] In the low income Dudley Street neighborhood, similar plans have been developed by the residents themselves. But neighborhood activism did not arise spontaneously; rather, it was triggered by a history of government-led redevelopment disasters.

The West End multiethnic neighborhood, which abuts Beacon Hill, was bulldozed from 1959 to the mid-1960s and replaced with an urban renewal project. The project included Government Center (site of a paved wasteland of open space which is now the subject of major redesign efforts), "the much-lamented Boston City Hall," (Keane, 1998), and Charles River Park, a market-rate high-rise apartment complex in a suburban-style setting, "totally out of context with historic Beacon Hill across the street," which converted to condos and sold out in the 1990s. "The urban renewal process was so devastating to the former residents and the City of Boston, it eventually changed the way clearance and redevelopment practices were conducted as part of the Federal Urban Renewal Program."

The neighborhood's former residents never lost their view of the West End as home, as can be seen in the case of West End Place, a cooperative apartment complex at the corner of Merrimac and Staniford Streets. The complex "was built in 1997 on the last parcel of the West End Urban Renewal Area. However, its realization has not provided closure to a very controversial urban renewal project and process. The 1.6-acre parcel lay undeveloped and vacant for 30 years. Now, the attractive red brick and granite, mixed income development offers 183 units, including 77 market-rate units priced between approximately $160,000 and $350,000 for 700 to 1,500 single family units, respectively. The impressive building was built by a private developer and the Archdiocese of Boston. . . . The original developer of Charles River Park, who controlled the site, wanted to develop it more densely and at market rate. The former West Enders wanted affordable housing so they could return to their old neighborhood. The City intervened on the side of the original residents. Over 2,000 applications for the subsidized units were received, and were assigned by a lottery. Many West Enders who didn't get in are unhappy and are pursuing their case in court" (Hodges, 1998a).

The legacy of the West End experience can be seen in the presence of many active local community-based organizations (CBOs) in the low income neighborhoods, reflecting residents' mistrust of government and the resulting desire to organize and control the process. Community groups were galvanized into action by the West End experience, the assassination of Dr. Martin Luther King in April 1968, and especially by the continuing threats to their own neighborhoods which the federal government, the city, and the Boston Redevelopment Authority (BRA)[5] posed. For example, just a few weeks after King's assassination, community organizer and future state representative Mel King led a weekend sit-in by Community Assembly for a United South End (CAU.S.E). The location for the sit-in was on a site in the South End[6] (the neighborhood immediately to the north of the Dudley Street area), across from what is now Copley Place, which had been acquired and razed by the BRA, displacing 100 families. "After 23 were arrested, community support grew and a spontaneous 'Tent City' emerged. After 20 more years of battles with city government, a mixed-income development was finally built on the site, with two-thirds of its units affordable to low and moderate income tenants. It is called Tent City" (Medoff and Sklar, 1994). The event also sparked "linkage,"[7] a 1980 mechanism which "allocated a percentage of costs of major development projects to a fund to provide affordable housing in neighborhoods" (Hodges, 1998a). Tent City and Harbor Point, formerly the Columbia Point public housing complex that has been rehabbed into a mixed income complex, have won praise for the Boston Housing Authority and the Massachusetts Housing Finance Agency (Kay, 1998).

The origins of many of the current financial assistance programs which have helped revitalize Dudley and other low income neighborhoods can be traced to the efforts of a CBO in the Fenway area, which lies just west of Back Bay. No one in the Fenway lives more than five minutes from the gardens, playing fields, and ponds of the Back Bay Fens, part of Boston's "Emerald Necklace"—the most complex of the urban park systems laid out in the 19th century by Frederick Law Olmstead. More than 40 arts groups call the Fenway home, and the close-in location makes carless living a real possibility. Yet as the urban population declined, the area began to experience problems. The Fenway Community Development Corporation (CDC), one of the city's oldest and most active CBOs, was formed to combat these problems. Through its Fenway Condo Coalition, it is an advocacy group for neighborhood stabilization. The Fenway CDC owns and operates over 300 rental and coop housing units including West Fenway Apartments (107 units for families, elderly, and disabled residents that opened in 1989 and were the first housing built in the West Fens since the Depression) and 71 Westland (a 20-apartment building that was one of the first projects in the state to bring together public and private funding to house a mix of market-rate and subsidized tenants). But the group's major interest is in promoting ownership. Discovering that no low-downpayment mortgages were available for people wishing to buy in Fenway condo complexes with relatively low owner-occupancy rates (25%), the Coalition worked with the City and with Fannie Mae to establish the "Condominium Stabilization and Resident Homeownership Project, [which] aims to make condominium ownership accessible to more residents, with a broad range of incomes" (Davis, 1996). The project spawned some of the city's major financial assistance programs (Boston-MORTGAGE, BostonHOME Certificate Initiative, HouseBoston-PRO, Boston HomeWorks)[8] which have since been extended by Fannie Mae to other Boston neighborhood CDCs, including Allston-Brighton and Dorchester Bay. The programs have been instrumental in overcoming the devastating effects of redlining, providing mortgage and rehabilitation money, which has been crucial in turning around neighborhoods such as Dudley Street.

The community-based effort that renewed the Dudley Street neighborhood has its roots in this long tradition of neighborhood activism in Boston. "Name a project, a neighborhood, or a cause and you'll find a grassroots group—or three. . . . 'In terms of citizen input, there's only one city that can compare with Boston. That's San Francisco,'" Harvard professor Alexander Krieger said (Kay, 1998). Dudley's success is also partly due to the web of financial and political support forged by other groups from the 1960s on. But Dudley's residents have built upon these citywide strengths in many unique ways, and the results have been remarkable.

Decay Hits Dudley Street

In 1965, Dr. Martin Luther King, Jr. gave a speech in Boston Common in which he said, "Boston must become a leader among cities. The vision of a New Boston must extend into the heart of Roxbury and into the mind of every child. Boston must conduct the creative experiments in the abolition of ghettoes which will point the way to other communities" (Holding Ground Productions, 1997). His words have proven to be prophetic, as the story of the revitalization of Dudley Street will show.

The Dudley Street neighborhood is a 1.5 square mile area within two miles of downtown Boston that straddles the historic communities of Roxbury and Dorchester. Before World War II the neighborhood was mainly inhabited by Irish and Italian working class immigrants. But most of the area's factories were gone by the 1940s and young couples began moving out after World War II, leaving their elderly relatives behind. These people became "a caring core of long-time residents with deep historical roots to the community" (author interview with Patrick McGuigan, 1996). The ethnic composition also changed dramatically over the years. One of the growing number of African-American residents was Malcolm Little, who later became famous as Malcolm X. He fell in love with the west Dudley area at age 15 while visiting his half-sister Ella in the summer of 1940. "The house was on Waumbeck Street (near Humboldt Avenue) in the Sugar Hill section of Roxbury, the Harlem of Boston," he wrote. "Ella was busily involved in dozens of things. She belonged to I don't know how many different clubs; she was a leading light of so-called 'black society.'" The following summer, immediately after finishing the eighth grade in Mason, Michigan, he moved in with Ella (Malcolm X, 1966) and stayed until New York beckoned later that year. Malcolm X describes his awe, arriving from a small Michigan town, at life in the neighborhood.

> I didn't know the world contained so many Negroes as I saw thronging downtown Roxbury at night, especially on Saturdays. Neon lights, nightclubs, poolhalls, bars, the cars they drove! Restaurants made the streets smell—rich, greasy, down-home black cooking! Jukeboxes blared Erskine Hawkins, Duke Ellington, Cootie Williams, dozens of others. . . . The biggest bands, like these, played at the Roseland State Ballroom, on Boston's Massachusetts Avenue—one night for Negroes, the next night for whites. . . . This was the snooty-black neighborhood. . . . Their quiet homes sat back in their mowed yards. . . . they called themselves the "Four Hundred," and looked down their noses at the Negroes of the black ghetto, or so-called "town" section . . . which was no further away than you could throw

a rock. . . . Any black family that had been around Boston long enough to own the home they lived in was considered among the Hill elite. It didn't make any difference that they had to rent out rooms to make ends meet. Then the native-born New Englanders among them looked down upon recently migrated Southern home-owners who lived next door, like Ella. And a big percentage of the Hill dwellers were in Ella's category—Southern strivers and scramblers, and West Indian Negroes, whom both the New Englanders and the Southerners called "Black Jews." Usually it was the Southerners and the West Indians who not only managed to own the places where they lived, but also at least one other house which they rented as income property. . . . In those days on the Hill, any who could claim "professional" status—teachers, preachers, practical nurses—also considered themselves superior. . . . I'd guess that eight out of ten of the Hill Negroes of Roxbury . . . actually worked as menials and servants." (Malcolm X, 1966)

Beginning in 1960, the minority population rose dramatically in the Dudley Street area. Urban riots in 1968 and court-ordered busing in the mid-1970s fueled the exodus of European-Americans from the area. However, the political influence and bank support which the Irish-Americans and Italian-Americans had enjoyed was not extended to other minorities. By the 1970s disinvestment and abandonment were rampant, and in the late 1970s and early 1980s wholesale razing took place. Arson became a serious problem; more than 20% of the neighborhood had been denuded of buildings by arsonists in the 1960s. As resident Clayton Turnbull said, "When I came here I was 10 years old in 1966 and what I saw was a lot of fires and I think that's what I remember. It was the smell of fire every night—two, three fires every night. On my street, two homes out of six were gone by the year 1970" (Holding Ground Productions, 1997). The neighborhood suffered dramatic population losses and soon became one of the most impoverished areas in New England. "By the 1980s, decades of disinvestment had created the most economically disenfranchised neighborhood in the state, with over 40% of the residents living below the poverty line" (Holding Ground Productions, 1997), and by 1990 Dudley had an unemployment rate of 16%, twice that of the city as a whole (Medoff & Sklar, 1994). Not surprisingly the Dudley Street neighborhood soon had the highest concentration of delinquent tax land in the city. A recent newspaper article described the area as follows: "These are tough streets. Streets where children get caught in gang crossfires. . . . streets where weedy, vacant lots long ago replaced the double decker homes that once stood in proud rows" (McFarling, 1994).

Rather than look to city hall for help, residents from the area launched their own revitalization initiative "out of fear and anger to resist the redevelopment and gentrification that had already pushed low-income people out of the South End and the West End" (Dudley Street Neighborhood Initiative, January 1996). As State Representative Byron Rushing said, "Most of the people in the Dudley Street Neighborhood Initiative [DSNI] neighborhood, and certainly the activists in the community, had the experience of urban renewal in other parts of the city: planners came in from outside and decided what was best for people" (Gallagher, 1997). Many Dudley Street area residents came to the area after being pushed out of other neighborhoods by planned gentrification, and Dudley residents did not want to repeat the displacement experience. For example, Boston's South End used to be a low income area but is now completely gentrified, complete with businesses like Neiman Marcus. The poor were pushed out to Roxbury, Dorchester and Mattapan, including the Dudley Street area. The original residents still return for church, and have to double park due to the gentrification's elimination of adequate parking (author's interview with Yelder, 1996).

Signs of Change

The community's rebirth began, ironically, as a reaction by residents to this "urban renewal"–type neighborhood revitalization when it was proposed for the Dudley Street area by outsiders (Gallagher, 1997). In 1984, the local social service agency La Alianza Hispana asked the Mabel Louise Riley Foundation, a small Boston-based trust, for $30,000 to buy carpeting for its offices. But when Riley board members visited the area they were so shocked at the neighborhood's condition that they soon decided to try to renew not only the carpeting but the entire neighborhood. Attorney and Riley trustee Robert Holmes then sponsored a meeting with several social service, religious, and community development groups in which a top-down organization—a 23-member board with only three seats for residents—was proposed to develop a renewal plan for the area. Residents attending the meeting refused to accept it. "We thought we would present our ideas and the residents would welcome it. We made a mistake," Holmes said. Resident and single mother of three Che Madyun (a charismatic person who was to become DSNI's President in 1986) expressed the frustration of the residents: "I asked how many of the people up there [running the meeting] lived in the neighborhood. Not one. And then I asked, How can you say the residents are going to be represented? You always have people from downtown or somewhere else telling you what you need in your neighborhood. This is important: planning never happens without people who are going to have to live with the results day to day being involved, from the beginning" (Walljasper, 1997; New Day Films, 1997).

Two weeks later, Roxbury Community College sponsored a community meeting with many area stakeholders including members of La Alianza Hispana, the Roxbury Multi Service Center, St. Patrick's Catholic Church, the Orchard Park Tenants Association and the Mt. Pleasant Neighborhood Association. The approximately 200 attendees "approved a different governing structure, which they would dominate . . ." (Andrews, 1997). They formed the Dudley Neighborhood Coalition, which soon metamorphosed into the 1,300-member Dudley Street Neighborhood Initiative. The governing structure of the DSNI is indeed radically different from that originally proposed, and reflects the residents' determination to take control and to reflect the neighborhood's diversity. DSNI is now governed by a board of 29 members, 27 of which are elected every two years in a communitywide open election and the other two are community residents appointed by the Board. The 27 elected board members include 3 African-American residents, 3 Cape Verdeans, 3 Latinos, 3 European-Americans, two youths, and representatives of seven nonprofit agencies, two CDCs, two religious institutions and two small businesses (Gallagher, 1997). To its credit, the Riley Foundation put up $70,000 in startup funds despite its loss of direct control—a supportive action rarely seen in philanthropic circles. "We allowed the neighborhood process to happen on its own. Some people thought we were crazy. They thought we were throwing away our grant money," Holmes said (Walljasper, 1997).

Peter Medoff, a community organizer who also had good connections at City Hall, was hired in 1986 as the group's first executive director; Che Madyun was elected DSNI board president. Their leadership ensured that neighborhood organization for political activism in order to put the condition of the area back in the hands of its residents would be the first priority, rather than developing affordable housing or providing social services. In order to accomplish this goal Medoff and the Board launched some campaigns to achieve small successes right away, such as restoring rail service to a nearby commuter station and improving the safety of a major intersection. "By setting achievable goals, DSNI kept the level of participation high even though the bigger things like getting the dumps out of Dudley Street and providing affordable housing were slow in coming" (Walljasper, 1997).

But DSNI faced formidable challenges to more comprehensive revitalization. The ethnic diversity which has since been turned into one of the neighborhood's strengths was a barrier at first, as residents were fragmented and the immigrants' limited command of English required communication in several languages (a situation which is still reflected in the publication of DSNI materials in English, Spanish, and Cape Verdean). Beyond that, the list of problems faced by the neighborhood seemed insurmountable. A resident survey conducted by Roxbury Community College had revealed extensive concerns about arson, poor street lighting, rodents, inconsistent trash collection, abandoned cars, uninhabitable housing, and especially illegal dumping on the neighborhood's vacant lots, which constituted one out of every five parcels. "Red-lining, disinvestment, and arson fire combined to physically, financially, and spiritually devastate this community, a devastation symbolized by 1,300 vacant lots filled only with rubble and trash dumped by outsiders" (Dudley Street Neighborhood Initiative, January 1996). "There were unscrupulous contractors from throughout the greater Boston area who would come and dump their garbage (even including rotten meat) on these lots. You would go to sleep one night and the next morning you would find a car that was completely stripped, several refrigerators, a washing machine sitting in front of your house," said La Alianza Hispana Director Nelson Merced (Holding Ground Productions, 1997). "You had to hold your nose when you drove down the road—it was terrible," adds Che Madyun (Walljasper, 1997). Not surprisingly, the group's first major project was the "Don't Dump On Us" cleanup campaign, a grassroots effort complete with leaflets, buttons, and political pressure. When Mayor Raymond Flynn's verbal pledges of support were not backed by action to clean up the numerous city-owned trash-filled lots, residents enlisted the help of a neighborhood radio station, picketed City Hall, and even threatened to transfer some of Dudley's trash to the building's steps. As Che Madyun said, "There's nothing that says because you don't have a lot of money, you have to live in filth" (New Day Films, 1997). Eventually the Mayor, who had campaigned in 1983 as a populist representative of the city's neighborhoods but had little support from minorities, saw DSNI's campaign as a potential road to increased minority support and took action to get some of the city-owned lots cleaned up and to close two of the illegal dumping and trash transfer operations which were widespread throughout the neighborhood, even padlocking the gates of one operation with Che Madyun while TV cameras rolled (Walljasper, 1997).

After the DSNI achieved success in the cleanup campaign, "people were galvanized in seeing that they could change things," Ros Everdell said (Walljasper, 1997). New street lights and signs were installed to improve safety, especially for the area's children, and a commuter rail stop was restored at Upham's Corner. "We fought to get the commuter rail to stop here. There were only two buses, and they were packed. The government's response was to hire truant officers to take away children's bus passes instead of adding more buses or a train stop," DSNI staffer Trish Settles explained (in interview with the author, 1996). Then, members turned their attention to creating the housing, parks, community centers, and businesses that would eventually fill the vacant lots. The city's Public Facilities Department (now the Department of Neighborhood Development, or DND) offered to do "joint planning and decisionmaking." But DSNI members viewed the City as something of a neighborhood juggernaut, conspiring with the Boston Redevelopment Authority to plan the destruction of neighborhoods whose residents found out only when they read the local newspapers. This attitude is not surprising when one recalls the destruction/gentrification of neighborhoods such as the West End. So they rejected the offer, countering with a proposal to create the plan themselves with the department's participation. The department agreed, and also called a moratorium on the disposition of city-owned vacant land until the plan was completed. DSNI then used $123,000 (including $100,000 from the Riley Foundation and $20,000 from the Boston-based Hyam's Trust) to hire a minority-owned consultant, DAC International of Washington, to work with the community. DAC's Technical Director David Nesbitt was an African-American who spoke Spanish and Portuguese, and had previously worked as a director with the Rouse Company, developers of many innovative residential and commercial areas including Fanueil Hall. More than 150 residents helped shape the plan in eight months of trilingual meetings. In 1987, nine months after the planning effort began and three years after DSNI's first meeting, a renewal plan had been completed. The "DSNI Revitalization Plan: A Comprehensive Community Controlled Strategy" "envisions a diverse, economically viable neighborly urban village" (Andrews, 1997). It covered the 507-acre Dudley Street core area and called for $135 million to be invested over the next five years in creating Dudley Village, an "urban village" with playgrounds, bike paths, apple orchards, community gardens, outdoor cafes, fountains, art programs, concerts to be held in a new central park (Town Commons), a business district, and much rehabilitated housing. Former DSNI Executive Director Gus Newport explains why the urban village approach was selected by area residents. "What you have here are a lot of people who grew up in the rural South and the Cape Verde Islands and the Caribbean. They want to work with the land. They want open spaces for kids to play in. They don't want to live in tall buildings. They want to know their neighbors. They understood all by themselves that they wanted to get back to the village" (Walljasper, 1997). In a victory for resident control, the city adopted the document as its redevelopment plan for the Dudley Street area.

Residents and planners quickly realized that the key to the neighborhood's future and the plan's implementation was its vacant land. More than a third of the neighborhood's land was vacant, creating a checkerboard pattern of abandonment that was a major source of neighborhood blight. But this did not mean that the land was available. The largest problem the group was having was that most of the vacant land they wanted to build upon was not easily acquired, for two reasons. First, more than one third of the 1,300 vacant parcels in the 507-acre core area were already owned by governments (the city, the BRA, the state, and HUD), mainly the city which had taken them for nonpayment of property taxes. Second, their acquisition from the city was prohibitively expensive due to the amounts of back taxes, interest, and penalties that had to be repaid (the remaining two-thirds of the vacant lots were privately owned, and about half were tax-delinquent) (Medoff and Sklar, 1994). After much negotiation, the city's Department of Neighborhood Development (DND)—the entity that takes ownership of delinquent property tax parcels and also does neighborhood planning—agreed to waive all back taxes, liens and judgments, then donate all its vacant tax-delinquent parcels within the Triangle. This area, a 64-acre area extending from the Hampden-Dudley intersection on the north, down Blue Hill and Dudley Streets on the east and west to a southern border defined by Howard Avenue and Brookford, Hartford, Robin Hood, Folsom, and Harlow Streets, is home to about 2,000 residents and has the greatest concentration of empty lots in the Dudley area (Andrews, 1997). Under the terms of the agreement, DSNI and the city's DND formed a joint land disposition committee to funnel properties to Dudley Neighbors Incorporated (DNI), an "urban development corporation" formed in August 1988 which acts as the landowner and lessor, acquiring and retaining ownership of the land in an independent nonprofit community land trust. DNI is run by an 11-member Board of Directors: six appointed by the DSNI Board, and one each appointed by the Roxbury Neighborhood Council, the 7th District Boston City Councillor, the Mayor's Office, the State Representative for the 2nd Suffolk District and the same for the 5th Suffolk District. These last two are nonvoting. All homeowners are voting members of the community land trust, which makes their role somewhat equivalent to that of stockholders in a corporation. DSNI serves as the "watchdog" group, in charge of planning and monitoring. About 15 acres of vacant city-owned land worth over $2 million (author's interview with Yelder, 1996) have been transferred to DNI ownership.

One hundred and eighty-one properties on 15 acres in the Triangle were abandoned but still in the hands of private owners; many of these were speculating and so did not want to sell, and 101 were tax-delinquent (Medoff and Sklar, 1994). DSNI mounted a massive lobbying campaign which paid off in November 1988 when, creating another "first in the nation" for Boston, the Boston Redevelopment Authority and the City acted under Chapter 121A of state law—a little-known chapter which gave eminent domain power to redevelopment authorities and to "urban development corporations authorized by the BRA" to develop low and moderate income housing (Medoff and Sklar, 1994)—to authorize DNI to use the power of eminent domain "to acquire any vacant parcel in a section of neighborhood containing over 15 acres of privately held vacant land in the center of the neighborhood," (Houston Planning Department, July 24, 1994) specifically within the Triangle. This grant of power was followed by four years of court challenges, but eventually it proved invaluable in the neighborhood's revitalization.

Meanwhile, DSNI hired a consultant (Comunitas) to complete a Triangle buildout plan, the development of which involved more than 100 residents. A microplanning approach was followed here: "Residents looked at the area block by block to determine the preferred use for each site. They wanted lower density housing, tot lots, community centers, day care, off-street parking, and open space, including a town common" (Andrews, 1997).

Unlike typical uses of eminent domain, however, DNI does not take any property that the owners have chosen to develop (DNI, 1994). DNI only handles vacant land, giving ground leases to developers and homeowners for 99 years. A $500 annual "ground lease fee" is charged to each home, mainly to cover the real estate taxes (which are charged to DNI since it retains ownership of the land) but also for DNI operating costs. Deed restrictions are added that ensure resale to low and moderate income buyers. Further, the price at which units are sold must be approved by DNI: "The price at which a resident may resell his/her unit will be restricted by a 're-sale formula,' which will allow for a certain amount of growth in value and for a recovery by the residents of any additional investments s/he made in improving the property. The price must be approved before the sale can take place—but in its review, DNI must respond within 45 days of being notified of a resident's intention to sell. If a resident wants to sell but has no buyer, DNI may purchase the unit at the allowed value, and then must re-sell it to a low- or moderate-income buyer. The current re-sale formula allows 0.5% annual increase in each of the first ten years and 5% thereafter" (DNI, 1994). This arrangement allows DNI to control the properties' use, maintaining the area's residential character, as well as to help ensure they remain low income by setting caps on sales prices and keeping the lease amounts minimal. "In the extreme case of wilful and non-resolvable violation of the rules, DNI has the power to cancel the ground lease and force the offending residents to leave his/her premises" (DNI, 1994).

It is a noteworthy but somewhat ironic accomplishment that this community has taken the tactics—eminent domain, land trusts, and restrictive covenants—which have been used for years to evict the poor, keep vacant lands unused and segregate affluent neighborhoods, and employed them to accomplish opposite goals. Land trusts are most commonly used as an open space preservation tool; in wealthy Marin County California, for example, a land trust employed "preemptive buying" of strategically located parcels to render nearby private land useless for large-scale development (Hart, 1991). Restrictive covenants have been used extensively to provide extra protection for wealthier neighborhoods, and in many cities before the 1970s covenants commonly included clauses that prevented minorities from purchasing homes in the area. Eminent domain, one author explained, "is the legal tool that has been used to devastate many urban neighborhoods, where people are forced to sell their homes and businesses to make way for freeways, convention centers and other megaprojects" (Walljasper, 1997).

The next hurdle was obtaining financing. According to DNI's Executive Director Paul Yelder, bank financing for construction on the 15 acres of donated city-owned lots was arranged but the banks backed out when the real estate crash hit in the late 1980s; even though the city put up its CDBG funds as collateral, the bank still would not give a letter of credit to DNI. Finally, the DND had to loan the startup funds itself. Financing for purchase of the private properties acquired through eminent domain was even more difficult. Most of the tax-delinquent land was classified as residential and was worth $2.75/square foot, but commercial parcels are worth up to $8.00/square foot with the average value being $4.30/square foot. Thus, the 4 acres of commercial land was worth about $750,000 and the 11 acres of residential land were worth slightly over $2 million. Consumers United Insurance Company gave a $1 million credit commitment, but more was needed. After four years of effort, in 1992 the Ford Foundation made a $2 million program investment loan (a Project-Related Initiative) to DSNI for nine years at 1% interest for land acquisition in the Triangle. This results in an annual interest payment of $20,000/year, but DNI's interest earned from keeping funds not yet needed for acquisition in the bank produces enough to make the payment and also cover some operating costs. The four-year battle to obtain Ford funds meant that DSNI had to ask for an extension of its eminent domain authority, which had originally been granted for just three years. The request was granted, and the authority was extended for a second three-year period that expired in 1994. Meanwhile, all 15 acres of initially authorized private land have been acquired.

Results

Housing: The First Challenge. Next the developer for Phase 1 of housing construction backed out, forcing DSNI to take the job (DNI could not take on this role because the Ford Foundation did not want DNI to have any debts). DSNI broke ground for the first of 38 duplex houses in 1993, completing the effort in 1994. The same year, this development (dubbed Winthrop Estates) was selected as one of six national affordable housing developments to receive a Maxwell Housing Excellence Award from the Fannie Mae Foundation (DSNI, 1996c).

Ironically, permanent financing for homebuyers was available, largely due to pressure brought to bear through the Community Reinvestment Act on a bank which was seeking a merger coupled with the DSNI housing director's move to a job at the bank. Former Berkeley, California, mayor Gus Newport, who was hired as DSNI's executive director after Peter Medoff left in 1988 and served until 1992, was also instrumental in obtaining both lender and city support. The city has developed several financial assistance programs for homebuyers, described in this section. The fact that DNI retains ownership of the land was not a financial barrier, since banks commonly finance large commercial buildings on ground-leased land, and recently, the technique has been used in other affordable housing developments as well. "The land trust usually agrees that a bank may foreclose on a housing unit if the owner repeatedly fails to keep his or her payments current, and in that case, the bank is exempt from the ground lease. In return, however, the bank must agree ahead of time to:

1. give the residents a longer-than-usual time to cure any defaults,
2. give DNI an additional period of time to solve the situation, and
3. make best efforts to convey the unit to another low- or moderate-income household" (DNI, 1994).

The Winthrop Estates units are single family two-story 1300-square-foot townhouses built in a traditional New England style, with three or four bedrooms, one and a half bathrooms, clapboard-style siding, bay windows, front porches, back yards, and off-street parking. With its traditional house designs, sidewalks, compact lots, and narrow streets, Winthrop Estates looks more like an urban neotraditional town development than a transplanted suburbia. The homes are priced at around $90,000, but with city subsidies (based on the buyer's income and including closing costs, interest rates and equity), they were affordable to families making as little as $18,000 annually (Andrews, 1997) as monthly payments ranged from $495 to $800. A portion of the 5% down payment and the closing costs are also covered, using a $50,000 private contribution to DSNI (Mimram, 1995).

After the first phase, DSNI began emphasizing limited income mixing and was able to share the role of developer. Phase 2, which was begun in the spring of 1994 and completed in 1996, consists of 36 units built by a DSNI-selected private developer (Nuestra Comunidad CDC) and DSNI that are available to people making up to $42,000 (considered low income) or $77,000 (moderate income). But housing for very low income people is still a major focus. During the same time, 41 co-op units have been built by the same CDC and DSNI in the Stafford Heights development adjacent to Winthrop Estates that are available for purchase by families with incomes less than $19,000, which is 60% of the median family income. They are priced so a family earning as little as $15,000 can afford them, depending on family size. Another 46 units of housing were completed in 1992 and 1994 by Dorchester Bay EDC and Project Hope (DSNI, 1996b).

Paul Yelder, former DNI executive director, explained that in 1996 DNI started its third phase of development, which included construction of 50–60 additional new units. The new phase, dubbed Woodward Park Homes, is developed by New Boston Housing Enterprises and JTS Consulting—DSNI does not have to act as developer—and consists of single-family and duplex owner-occupied homes. Applications for the homes are given via the City of Boston Home Center (DSNI, 1996c). Typical new single family homes in the Woodward Park development sell for $95,000–99,000 and feature 3 bedrooms, 1.5 baths, wall to wall carpet, laundry hookups, a two-car driveway, fenced backyard, and landscaping.

As of January 1996 more than 225 new affordable homes have been built, more than 300 housing units have been rehabbed, and more than 300 of the 1,300 vacant lots have been returned to productive use as homesites, play areas, gardens and community facilities (DSNI, 1996a). A typical example involved the DND using Community Development Block Grant funds "to restore two 19th-century homes taken in tax forfeitures and boarded up for years" (Anand, 1995) on Woodville Park Way, which were then sold to low-income residents.

The DND subsidizes the construction cost of the units, since construction costs run about $140,000 per unit. "It's very costly to build here," DSNI employee Trish Settles (in interview with the author, 1998) said, adding that an "equity subsidy" is available from the state, but this neighborhood is in competition for it with communities around the state, and since construction costs are much lower in western Massachusetts, Dudley Street often loses out.

Much of the cost is due to environmental remediation (site cleanup). Brownfields are a big problem in Boston, where the incidence of hazardous waste sites in the city's neighborhoods is twice the national average (Neighborhoods Against Urban Pollution [NAUP], no date). The Environmental Protection Agency (EPA) has designated the Dudley Street neighborhood as a brownfields cleanup area, and the Brownfields collaborative (a coalition of local groups including DSNI) has selected six sites to receive loans, grants, free legal and technical assistance, and so on under the EPA program (DSNI, 1996c).

Homebuyer classes are offered free to low-income people by DSNI, the DND, and prvate nonprofit agencies such as NOAH, Neighborhood of Affordable Housing.[9] Upon completion of these, graduates are certified to participate in special mortgage programs offered by Fannie Mae (mentioned earlier, see note 8) and the Massachusetts Housing Finance Agency (MHFA).[10] After moving in, homebuyers can still turn to DSNI for counseling on home-ownership-related matters if needed (Mimram, 1995).

The Dudley Street area residents' efforts in housing have begun to be noticed. In 1995, HUD personnel visited the area, later incorporating some of DSNI's housing provision techniques into a 1996 $50 million HUD initiative to fund new construction of low income housing nationwide (New Day Films, Fall 1996). Two years later, DSNI's development of Winthrop Estates won the Current Topic award from the American Planning Association (Andrews, 1997).

Other Major Accomplishments. The community changes have extended well beyond housing. DSNI's comprehensive, wholistic approach to revitalization is reflected in its slogan, "Building Houses and People Too," and in its wide range of programs, goals, and activities. In the fall of 1991 DSNI started Dudley Pride (People and Resources Investing in Dudley's Environment), a block-by-block organizing effort designed to raise residents' self respect, community pride, spiritual and emotional well-being (Medoff & Sklar, 1994). Since then, much has changed. A committee concerned with the safety of children going to and from school and a network of family day care providers have been established; the W.A.I.T.T. House offers adult education for high school dropouts; the city's renovation of the Vine Street municipal building (Cape Verdean Community House) into a $5.3 million community center has been completed after five years of planning (author's interview with Settles, 1998); and a multicultural festival is held each year.

At the same time community gardens are being created, some raised for wheelchair-bound residents; the Food Project, a learning/service organization for youth, works with DSNI to allocate the garden space to residents, hires people to grow food, and sponsors a Farmers Market for the sale of this locally-grow produce in the Town Common several afternoons a week every summer. Several times a year, DSNI sponsors neighborhood cleanup days: Tools are available for free use, and residents are urged to cooperatively "adopt a lot" to clean on their streets; a cookout is held by DSNI afterwards. DSNI, the City's Environmental Strike Team, local block associations, Alternatives for Communities and Environment (ACE), and other groups also collaborate to forge "consent agreements" with landowners in which the owners agree to "eliminate illegal trash transfer and dumpster storage operations, piles of refuse, and underbrush" (DSNI, 1996a).

The old Dudley Mill Works building has been converted into DSNI's offices plus Youth Build Boston's training headquarters, a charter school, and commercial space. Originally a turnaround building for horse-drawn cable cars, the multistory Mills building later served as a munitions plant and a cabinet factory, both of which contributed their share of toxic substances to the site. Eventually, it was taken by the FDIC as a distressed property and sold to DSNI for $1. DSNI obtained a $1.1 million EDA rehab loan in 1994; the addition of $400,000 from the City for YouthBuild-Boston to renovate the building meant that by 1997 the work was done (author's interview with Settles, 1998).

Another project of special interest is the focused effort to revitalize the historic Shirley-Eustis house. It was visually connected with the recently renovated historic Dudley Mills building on Dudley Street that serves as DSNI headquarters (by removing four homes that separated the house from the Mills building). Built in the mid-1700s by Massachusetts Bay Colony Governor William Shirley, the house resembles a part of Shirley's home in England; in 1820 it was purchased by State Governor William Eustis, and it is now being restored to its condition at that time by the Shirley-Eustis House Association. The Association had purchased the building in 1911 but was unable to begin restoration until the 1970s.

The Town Common at Dudley Street, Blue Hill Avenue, and Hampden Street opened in the summer of 1996 and serves as "the gateway to Dudley Village" (DSNI, 1996a). The Common consists of two pocket parks linked by "interpretive art tiles of cultural and historic symbols of the community inset into bollards for seating; an abbreviated version of the DSNI Declaration of Community Rights expressing the DSNI fundamental objectives . . . and proudly declaring the independence of the neighborhood residents; paving bricks engraved with cultural symbols inspired by neighborhood youth artists with images . . . and names of significance to the neighborhood selected by the community." Special lighting had been placed along the connecting block of Dudley Street and in the parks themselves. The parks also contain a garden trellis, large gateway structures, a dozen bronze plaques depicting the neighborhood's history from 1630–1996, a fence with musical notation from a local jazz pianist/composer, areas for "ongoing art murals," mosaic bench sculptures, shading, and a stage complete with nighttime lighting. "North Park is a green haven and passive park with an emphasis on the cultural/historical interest of the community. South Park is an active urban festival park emphasizing the cultural/contemporary arts of music and dance . . ." ("Dudley Town Common," brochure, undated). The Common resulted from a partnership of the State Department of Environmental Management (which contributed $700,000), the City DND, and the Office of Cultural Affairs and the Parks and Recreation Department (which together contributed $500,000), and DSNI. Area residents played a key role in its design, suggesting art elements, selecting artists and locations, and reviewing the artists' proposed forms and materials.

Perhaps nowhere is Dudley's resident-based, comprehensive approach to revitalization more noteworthy than in its attention to the needs of the area's children. "The DSNI provides local youth with a central role in neighborhood revitalization. Children and teens make up more than one-third of the population of the Dudley Street neighborhood (10,000 of the neighborhood's 24,000 residents are under age 20, and half of these live in families with incomes below the poverty line). They were encouraged to become involved in identifying critical problems and devising solutions to them from the earliest days of organizing. Children are welcome in the DSNI offices and serve on its board. Evidence of their involvement is pinned to the walls in the form of drawings and poems, and is found in their frequent presence just "hanging out" in the DSNI offices. To date, community organizers, architects, and designers have engaged local youth in projects ranging from neighborhood clean-ups and park reclamation to mural painting" (Breitbart, 1995). Painting the now-famous Unity Mural on the side of Davey's Market was the first project of the neighborhood's Nubian Roots Youth Committee. Another outstanding effort was the initiation of summer day camp and evening youth programs, such as recreational sports leagues, in Mary Hannon Park as part of an extensive push to rid the park of drug dealers. In 1991 the park was a "stop and shop" drug market, so DSNI made an agreement for the police to be there every day; residents also provided activities all day at the Bird Street Youth/Community Center, which helps sponsor the sports leagues. Most of the drug customers were white men in their 30s from the suburbs. Although successful, neighborhood antidrug dealing efforts must continue to prevent reoccurrence, as happened in 1993 when residents had to fight the dealers for the park again (New Day Films, 1997).

Mary Hannon Park is not the only place where serious drug dealing has been successfully combatted. Woodville Park, a 200-yard-long unpaved street in the Triangle, had become "the hottest drug zone in the city" by the early 1990s, a street with "hooded, knife-carrying young adults standing guard at the corner . . ." Deputy Police Superintendent Bobbie Johnson said, "A year and a half ago, my officers were wary of coming down this street. We were going to do a stakeout here but they advised against it. They said it was too dangerous. People lived in terror" (Anand, 1995). Residents called the police for years without results. As resident and DSNI Board member JacQuie Cairo-Williams said, "My question was always, 'Why can't you stop the drug dealing?' You know who's dealing the drugs. You know who's taking the drugs" (Anand, 1995). Then, in 1993 Tom Gannon, head of the newly formed Ten Most Wanted Drug Houses Task Force, brought a crew of building and housing inspectors to the street, ready to combine code enforcement with police surveillance in order to close the drug houses. The crew has since managed to foreclose and tear down several notorious dealing spots, including one next door to Cairo-Williams which was the center of neighborhood drug deals (Anand, 1995).

"In March 1991 DSNI established Dudley's Young Architects and Planners, a focus group to involve youth in community vision development and provide them with basic architectural skills. The following month the youth presented drawings for a community center that would include a gym, weight room, indoor track, swimming pool, and day care center. Architects are also teaching the youth basic surveying and related skills by helping them build models for two community centers (as the neighborhood's plan suggests) and the surrounding open space. In a foreword to a report on the group, former DSNI President Che Madyun explains how this project "integrates DSNI's commitment to community control" by providing an important "outlet for the transformative power of youth. . . . [this project] is based on the dreams and creativity of youngsters too often written off by others as worthless" (Medoff and Sklar, 1994). The success of involving local youth directly in physical revitalization efforts and in collaborations with design professionals has convinced local organizers and those studying the DSNI as a possible model for urban renewal elsewhere, of the importance of youth to the whole community development enterprise" (Breitbart, 1995).

> Connected to the DSNI is Youth Works/Art Works, a project which seeks to involve young people in photography, poetry writing, and urban art and design as part of a larger scheme to revitalize a long thoroughfare that runs

through the Boston neighborhoods of Roxbury, Dorchester and Mattapan. The project provides low-income, at-risk teenagers with summer jobs, pairing them with professional community artists who run a variety of workshops. The objective, according to director Pamela Worden, is "not only to give kids a chance to learn new skills and to earn pay, but also to try to get the kids to look at their communities through the eyes of an artist, to see [them] . . . in a slightly different way and to understand that they have a relationship to their community that can be a productive one." (*Boston Sunday Globe,* 17 April 1994) (Breitbart, 1995)

The Dudley Area Today. The 1.5 square mile Dudley area is now home to about 24,000 people. The neighborhood is estimated to be 37–40% African-American, 29–30% Latino (mainly from Puerto Rico and the Dominican Republic), 24–25% Cape Verdean, and 6–7% European-American (mainly Irish and Italian residents who have lived in the area since the 1950s) (Jackson, 1997; Walljasper, 1997). Half of these live in the 507-acre core that has been the focus of redevelopment efforts (Andrews, 1997). The neighborhood's population is now growing, for the first time in many years. DSNI itself has grown to a membership of 8,000; 2,400 of these come from the focus area, pay $1 dues and are able to vote for DSNI Board members (350 voted in a recent election) (author's interview with Settles, 1998). DSNI's staff of 18 is also composed mainly of neighborhood residents. The staff works with local CDCs and forms partnerships with agencies at all levels of government.

The area's land use is now extremely mixed, with heavy industry and warehouse operations within a stone's throw of elementary schools, churches, a wide variety of small neighborhood businesses, a large grocery store, parks, and homes. Massachusetts Avenue, which forms one of the neighborhood's borders and has attracted a conglomeration of medical-related services, boasts a high concentration of large businesses and industry, as do several other neighborhood streets. Within walking distance of most of these areas are small retail businesses, churches (there are two dozen in the neighborhood), ballfields, tot lots, five parks, three elementary schools, a middle school, a library, a police station, a fire station, two bus lines, two CDCs, a homeless shelter, a citywide Latino service agency, and a variety of homes (Hindley, 1992). These homes are mainly older, detached two- to three-story wood frame and brick houses containing several families, interspersed with a smattering of new, smaller wood frame single-family homes (referred to by some residents as "doll houses") along with many newly built duplexes and a smattering of still vacant parcels, on which elderly men congregate in folding lawn chairs. The DSNI headquarters and the nearby Davey's Market also serve as gathering spots; here the multicultural character of the neighborhood is clear, as people converse in Cape Verdean, Spanish, and Caribbean-accented English. Children walk home from school without fear, watched over by elderly women tending their gardens and talking to their neighbors over the low picket fences that separate back yards while preserving neighbor interaction and visibility. As resident Iman Soloman put it, "There was a time when I wouldn't walk on Dudley Street after 5 P.M. New homebuyers are now bringing healthy activity into the neighborhood" (Mimram, 1995). A typical mixed-use revitalized, formerly vacant area is found at an intersection along Cottage Avenue. Here newly built "doll houses" occupy one corner; raised-bed wheelchair-accessible community gardens cover another; a cross street separates these from a small new apartment complex for the elderly, with the fourth corner still vacant.

Remaining Problems. Despite the overall improvements, problems remain. The neighborhood's $8,631 per capita income is still just half that of the city of Boston, unemployment is twice as high, drug dealers are still evident, half the families have absent fathers (Spaid, 1994), and more than 40% of families still have incomes below the poverty line (DSNI, June 1996).

Banking, lending, and corporate (other than via foundations) activity in the community appears to still be largely absent. "We will need the banking community to be a partner with us to realize this vision," Watson (1995) said; indeed, the most glaring "missing player" in the case study is the private for-profit lender and developer. This is no doubt due to the perceived difficulty of making a profit in inner city redevelopment; it appears to be a very high-risk venture. In Boston, DSNI had to take over the role of developer when the private one backed out. Even today, participation of private developers is confined to nonprofits. As for lender involvement, without the CRA, an "insider" at the bank and the city's willingness to pledge its CDBG funds as collateral, bank financing would have been a dream. Still today, extensive city involvement is necessary to get banks to consider lending in the area. Clearly, greater enticements are needed to lure the private development industry back to areas such as Dudley Street.

The lack of strong regional planning and growth management hurts not only Dudley Street, but many other central city neighborhoods. There is "an alphabet soup of uncoordinated (regional) agencies . . . along Route 128 (the highway loop around the city) and beyond, growth is uncontrolled, old towns spoiled, wetlands and forests threatened. . . . the Metropolitan Area Planning Council has only an advisory role for its 1422 square miles of which Boston proper occupies a scant 46. The agency has no real power to alter development plans" (Kay, 1998). Asked if there was any effective regional cooperation for economic development, one planner replied, "There's competition. Boston has to fight for its share" (Thomas interview, 1998).

City support is still lacking in some important areas. There are still many trash-covered vacant lots in need of reuse. Half the lots in many residential areas fall into this category, and a recent summation showed more than four million square feet of vacant property (Hindley, 1992). DNI does not take ownership of city-owned lots[11] until it is ready to use the land, and its eminent domain power is limited to the 15 acres of vacant land within the Triangle. Thus, many lots remain abandoned and blighted. Illegal dumping is still a big problem. As DSNI employee Trish Settles said (in interview with the author, 1998), "We need more eyes on the street, and more support from the city," adding that it took two months to get the city to provide trucks for a recent cleanup effort. "The city still doesn't enforce codes well, particularly in the areas with heavy industry like Norfolk and Hampden," a staffer added (author's interview with Sepulveda, 1998). A local businessperson agreed: "The City's Office of Inspectional Services still doesn't do much enforcement. We have to push them all the time" (author's interview with Lloyd, 1998). Despite the progress made in neighborhood cleanup, residents reported that garbage is only picked up once a week in Dudley whereas wealthier parts of the city have pickup two times a week. City studies have found asthma and bronchitis rates twice that of the city as a whole, and an average of two houses per street "house children poisoned by lead." Loose zoning has allowed toxic-using or toxic-producing businesses to locate near homes. There are 54 hazardous waste sites (brownfields), as well as a dozen unpermitted waste-related industries still operating. "It's a place that's been poisoned," said Russell Lopez, executive director of Boston's Environmental Diversity Forum; "You either vacate the area or you stay and pitch in," added Dorchester native Louise Hamilton, now a senior toxicologist with the city Health Department (McFarling, 1994).

Settles explained how the neighborhood is pitching in. "Our residents are very active, very giving, always ready to help. We are developing a leadership curriculum on how to deal with the city bureaucracy. We want to give our residents the confidence to go back and really feel like they can make a change," she said (in an interview with the author, 1998). Other difficulties are handled in a more informal way. For example, recently DSNI staffers advised some young residents on how to lobby their school for a permanent math teacher and better instruction while the kids were dropping by DSNI headquarters (Walljasper, 1997).

From the city's point of view, forming workable partnerships among all the major stakeholders is viewed as both essential and difficult. "It's tough to obtain the trust of community groups; there is a lot of suspicion," one staffer said (in author's interview with Thomas, 1996). Community groups, developers, and funders all have different goals. Putting the financing packages together that make $110,000–120,000 condos affordable to low income buyers is also quite a challenge.

Despite these problems, optimism regarding success in the long run remains high. As DSNI Board member Clayton Turnbull said, "[The neighborhood] didn't take two years to get this way . . . it took 20 to 30 years, and it may take 20 to 30 years to correct" (Spaid, 1994).

Future Prospects. What lies in store for the neighborhood's future? Construction of 76 new units along with some commercial development was recently completed with 44 more to be completed soon; the DSNI's long-term goal of 350 new homes will then have been achieved. This is 40% lower than the originally proposed goal of 550 units, because residents wanted more open space, yard space, and garden space (author interview with McGuigan, 1996). "Overall, the 250–300 units of new housing planned for the Triangle . . . must be affordable to individuals in these income categories: 40% low-income, 30% moderate income, and 30% market rate" (DNI, 1994). Expected land acquisition costs should approximate $2 million. Developers are assessed a "land acquisition fee" of $7,000 per unit as an initial lease fee, to cover this cost. The vacant land within the neighborhood remains the focus of DSNI's efforts; eventually, the group hopes to put all the remaining 1,000 vacant lots in the 507-acre core area into productive use.

DSNI was born in part as a reaction to threats of gentrification, and preventing gentrification is still a real concern for the future. For example, in 1990 the neighborhood was offered a Nehemiah grant from HUD, but since federal regulations prevented the $20,000–30,000 per-unit HUD subsidies from being assigned (that is, transferred to the next buyer) they were due upon the sale of the home, thus assuring that the unit would be affordable for a low income person for only one ownership cycle. Through the deed restrictions and sales price approval policies described earlier, DSNI hopes to prevent extensive gentrification; however, income mixing is now a goal of DSNI and some home sales are being opened up to higher income buyers.

The 1987 plan was updated in 1996, with planning extending to the year 2010. One product of the update was a widened vision of what the neighborhood could become. As former DSNI executive director Greg Watson said, "We want this to be a place where, ten years from now, people will come into Logan Airport and say, I want to go up to 'The Village.' We want it to be to Boston as Greenwich Village is to New York. We want it to be a place that, if you didn't come here, you did not get the complete Boston. Right now, people just know us for getting the land. Ten years from now, we want people to know Dudley Street for what it *did* with the land" (Jackson, 1997). Others have compared the vision to the Adams-Morgan area in Washington, D.C., and to closer areas that were toured by residents, including Boston's Newbury Street, Brookline Village, and Somerville's Union Square. The development of such a vision is itself a sign of the success of the neighborhood's past efforts at revitalization: whereas the overriding original goal was gaining resident control over the immediate problems of abandonment, dumping, and so on, residents can now take a more proactive, longterm view.

DSNI's objectives still include reusing all the remaining vacant land, rehabilitating the remaining distressed structures, creating affordable housing, and neighborhood cleanup. The city and the state Department of Environmental

Protection's Environmental Strike Force are cleaning up more empty lots and citing polluters more frequently. But "cleanup" has been expanded to encompass "a massive effort to create a map showing the many environmental hazards," using sources ranging from residents' memories to federal databases (McFarling, 1994), and an aggressive campaign for environmental remediation.

One aspect of this campaign is toxics removal. For example, an abandoned incinerator near Atkinson and Massachusetts Avenues was being used as shelter by homeless people despite the presence of high levels of asbestos, dioxin, and oil in the soil. Funds were obtained from the EPA for a pilot project, and the site was decontaminated and a methadone clinic built. DSNI has also "organized a successful petition for the Public Involvement Process to be implemented with 17 of the 54 hazardous waste sites . . . identified the first cases of illegal dumping and storage of hazardous materials for action by the Massachusetts Environmental Justice Network organized by the Boston Bar Association . . . focused Americorps teams to engage youth in environmental education and action, including lead poisoning . . . created a collaborative with Boston Urban Gardeners to train youth in landscaping and apply these skills to creating interim improvements on vacant lots . . . (and) organized a soil-lead testing and compost distribution campaign to encourage safe urban gardening" (DSNI, 1996b).

Another aspect is the reduction of exposure to lead. Current lead levels in soil range from 80–8,000 parts per million (ppm); 400 ppm is the level at which cleanup is supposed to be done, but this is often prohibitively expensive so DSNI is proposing to cover the contaminated lots with about a foot of compost and use them for community gardens, with the help of the EPA and CityYear (Settles's interview with the author, 1998). This level of attention to cleanup is new. The area's City Councilman Gareth Saunders explained, "We didn't really have the luxury to think about the environmental issues that might 'do us in' in the long run" (McFarling, 1994).

Besides cleanup, the focus of the original rehab and infill goals has shifted from housing to business. The encouragement of gardens will support neighborhood business development, such as farmers' markets, which is the primary objective of Phase 4 (the current phase). "The same resident-driven process that found the solution to affordable housing in the Dudley community also has spawned a strategy for the economic rejuvenation of the neighborhood. It is . . . multicultural, community entrepreneurship. In addition to meeting the needs of local residents, this model . . . holds the key to attracting visitor dollars as well," said Watson (1995). One example of this new focus is the group's plan to redevelop the abandoned Swifty brownfield site as a location for the incubation of auto-related businesses. Another is DSNI's selection of a site for construction of a greenhouse, in hopes that this along with the community gardens and Dudley Market will create an economic base of produce and flower production for the neighborhood (Homsy, 1998). Some food-related businesses have already benefitted. For example Glen Lloyd (in an interview with the author, 1998), owner of the CityFresh Kitchen on Dudley Street, said his business now generates half a million dollars a year, has recently expanded from 2 to 16 employees, and now does a wide range of catering as well as providing food for the Meals on Wheels program. There are several large food-related industries in the area already. Newmarket, for example, is a major employer in the wholesale and retail food business. DSNI staff hope someday to see a "bioshelter" the size of a city block (up to 3 acres), "where residents could grow produce, and perhaps even fish, for neighborhood restaurants and [the] farmers market . . . [complete with] a fresh-food café" (Jackson, 1997). The entire neighborhood is part of an Enhanced Economic (Empowerment) Zone, and thus area CDCs are eligible for many job development programs and incentives.

Neighborhood organizers hope that successfully enticing food-related and other neighborhood businesses (including an ice cream parlor) will allow them to achieve other objectives, such as the establishment of a neighborhood bank or credit union, and eventually achieve the larger Dudley Village vision. As Watson said, "If we can get things like a hardware store, a pharmacy, and grocery stores that are buying the locally made produce, people can keep ther money in the neighborhood and begin to create a web of interdependency. That would give a bank the confidence to establish itself here. Then could come clubs, bookstores, art galleries, . . . a theater and an outdoor café. We might even get a bicycle path, too" (Jackson, 1997). DSNI has put teeth into the rhetoric regarding keeping residents' money in the neighborhood with "The Buck$ Stop Here!" campaign. More than 200 neighborhood businesses are participating in this program by issuing "Frequent Buyer" tickets to customers, which can then be redeemed for raffle tickets.

The overriding principles of DSNI's business selection efforts are community control, and hiring of local residents. This means that—in sharp contrast to the economic development efforts of many low and moderate income areas—industries, large grocery or department stores, anchor stores and strip malls are not welcome. DSNI Organizing Director Ros Everdell said, "The community has already said no to a check-cashing store. It has said no to an auto spray-painting shop. It has said no to an asphalt plant" (Jackson, 1997). Settles (in an interview with the author, 1998) added that the group has fought with the city several times to keep other unwanted uses (for example, a proposed jail) out. Crime control and zoning are important factors in encouraging neighborhood business development. DSNI is now attempting to map crime patterns, and to prosecute the many area businesses that were conducting illegal activities. The City is now rezoning Dorchester and did Roxbury 2 years ago, incorporating the proposed land uses in DSNI's plans into the zoning scheme (author's interview with Settles, 1998).

Perhaps most important, political power is being restored, and the area now has responsive elected officials (a city councilperson, state senator, and state representative) who attend neighborhood functions and keep up with DSNI activities. "They're very aware. They now come to us before something is proposed," said DSNI Director Frank Sepulveda (in an interview with the author, 1998). Mayoral support also seems likely to continue. Mayor Thomas Menino, who in 1997 was unopposed for reelection and has a degree in planning, said, "My planning heroes are the people in the neighborhoods and in the community development corporations. . . . the neighborhood people understand what (revitalization) is all about" (Lewis, 1998).

But beyond these changes in the community's power within traditional larger levels of government, there may be a more profound (and in some ways more exciting) change in political empowerment occurring within the neighborhood itself. At DSNI's 12th annual town meeting held in the last week of June 1997, it seemed as if DSNI had actually become a neighborhood governing body in the purest tradition of grassroots small-town democracy which stretches back to the New England town meetings held to govern communities in Revolutionary War times. Forty-one candidates competed to be elected to 27 seats on the DSNI board, speeches were given, neighborhood issues discussed, and votes cast to elect what was clearly perceived to be a slate of elected representatives of the people. One could not help but wonder whether neighborhoods of all ethnicities and incomes would not benefit from adopting such a governance structure.

Support from Others. Although they deserve much credit, the rebirth of the Dudley neighborhood has not been due to resident efforts alone. A wide varfiety of support has been given by public agencies.

Unlike some other city departments, the DND is supporting DSNI's revitalization efforts with several important business-related planning efforts. Both the Dudley Square area in the northwest corner of the DSNI neighborhood and the Upham's Corner area on its eastern edge have been designated to receive help from the Main Street Program.[12] Another Main Street area, Washington Street, runs just west of the DSNI area and "is beginning to revive. Housing for homeless elderly has opened, built from a former bread factory" (Hodges, 1998a). Blue Hill Avenue intersects Dudley Street and, like Dudley, has become the focus of intensive planning efforts, particularly in the one-mile segment that runs through the DSNI neighborhood. Implementation efforts have been significant, too. As Mayor Thomas Menino said, "Ever since the riots of the 60s . . . there have been plans up the ying-yang for the neighborhoods along Blue Hill Avenue. I said no more plans. We have to do something. We invested over $50 million, and today there are new businesses and new jobs in those neighborhoods" (Lewis, 1998).

The Boston Housing Authority is also supportive, completely rebuilding the Orchard Park public housing project in the northeast Dudley area (childhood home of soul singer Bobby Brown).[13] Originally built in 1942, the project had 770 units in a setting without landscaping or street furniture that was designed to be isolated from the surrounding neighborhood. Maintenance budgets declined and poverty increased, until by the 1980s "Orchard Park was plagued by high rates of gang violence and drug dealing. The vacancy rate was 42%, over 80% of the units did not meet HUD's housing Quality Standards, and rent collection hovered around 70%" (Massachusetts Department of Housing and Community Development [MDHCD], 1998a). Plans began in 1991 with a $20 million commitment of HUD modernization funds which was followed by the granting of Low-income Housing Tax Credits from the Massachusetts DHCD.[14] In 1996, the Orchard Park Tenants Association (OPTA) and the BHA obtained a $50 million commitment of HUD HOPE6 funds (author's interview with Sepulveda, 1998) for housing renovations and the creation of playgrounds, and selected a joint venture of Madison Park CDC and Trinity Financial to develop and manage the project (MDCHD, 1998a). A new community center opened there in the fall of 1995 (DSNI, 1996b) and about 200 units of public housing on Dearborn Street have been demolished. When completed, the three-phase redevelopment will cut the project's density by more than 50%. The three phases are described below.

> Phase I is the reconfiguration and complete renovation of nine buildings which will contain a total of 126 units [originally there were 183]. Common hallways, which used to serve as the entrances for 12 units each, were eliminated. Now 80% of the units have private entries and the highest number of units on a common hall is three. HOPE VI provided 23% of the funding, BHA public housing modernization 48%, and tax credit equity accounted for 29%. Phase II consists of the new construction of 90 units on the western portion of the site (Dearborn Street), replacing 246 demolished units. There will be 62 townhouse units along the periphery of the site and 28 units in 14 duplexes located on new streets cut through the site's interior. HOPE VI provided 36% of the funding, BHA . . . modernization 41%, and tax credit equity 36%. Phase III consists of the new construction of 90 townhouse units on the eastern portion of the site . . . HOPE VI would provide 53% of the financing and tax credit equity would provide 47%. (MDHCD, 1998a)
>
> Although HOPE VI projects are typically more expensive than other types of housing rehabilitation activities, they also provide some of the most sweeping physical improvements. . . . violent crime rates have declined by 40% over the past few years and rent collections have increased from 70% to 98%. (DHCD, 1998a)

Conclusions

A comprehensive, wholistic approach to addressing problems was taken, with a wide variety of difficulties tackled. This wholistic approach can be seen from the subjects covered in the 1987 DSNI comprehensive plan as described by the American Planning Association (APA): "The meaning of 'comprehensive' is broad and deep. It includes 13 strategies that go far beyond physical development and financing, from anti-displacement measures to volunteerism to ethnic pride and diversity, child care, employment and training advocacy, an earning and learning project, and locally based business development and training" (Andrews, 1997). In short, the DSNI attempts to improve all four major contributors to quality of life: safety, services, shelter, and social support. A comparison of the revitalization effort with the detailed items listed in Figure 1 (in Chapter 1) shows that projects and programs were developed to deal with every one of them. Special attention has been made to reducing drug dealing, exposure to environmental toxins, providing adequate garbage service, access to adequate business and social services, providing sufficient affordable housing, access to homeownership, neighborhood maintenance, development of a network of people, urban design that encourages interaction, and access to political power. This is truly an impressive list of accomplishments.

In housing, new construction and rehab, single family and multifamily units were emphasized; thus a "critical mass" of diverse space was created which was large enough to improve the housing market in the surrounding neighborhood (Andrews, 1997). DSNI also strove to encourage and even celebrate its ethnic diversity; now, income diversity and more diverse business development are also being sought. As former DSNI executive director Gus Newport said, "A lot of these urban programs do only housing. I think planners take it for granted that poor people don't need culture, vital businesses or beauty. If you had these things in inner cities, you'd have a lot less crime . . . [residents] want more than houses. Beauty—no matter how small it is, just a few flowers—is what matters most" (Walljasper, 1997). Thus, one can conclude that in order to achieve successful revitalization of a neighborhood such as this, all major strands—both the substantive problems and the people and institutions that influence them—of the web that determine the quality of life in low income neighborhoods must be addressed. Changing just a few of the substantive problems affecting the neighborhood is not likely to produce lasting improvement.

The DSNI experience also shows that **successful revitalization is based on "microplanning"**—that is, obtaining a thorough, detailed knowledge of the neighborhood itself, as well as the web of people, institutions, and substantive issues that affect it, then developing highly detailed programs or plans based on this information—as was done in the Triangle. "[Residents] believed that a specific sequence of events, caused by economic, social, and political systems and policy decisions, had led to the decline in their neighborhood and that rebuilding it would require addressing those forces directly"

(Gallagher, 1997). Detailed microplanning allowed those forces to be discovered and their specific consequences identified and addressed.

Help and support was also enlisted from a wide variety of agencies at all levels of government, private foundations, and service providers outside the neighborhood. Cleveland State professor Norman Krumholz described DSNI's uniqueness in this regard among the thousands of CDCs operating nationwide as follows: "Some are ahead of Dudley Street in terms of affordable housing production, but none that I know of has the power of eminent domain, and very few could have gained the support of city agencies, foundations, and lenders" (Spaid, 1994). Clearly, the residents' ability to successfully partner with government agencies (especially the city's DND and the BRA) was critical to the successful revitalization of this neighborhood. For example, the city DND still provides major annual financial support to DSNI, and local governments streamlined procedures to allow recycling of tax-delinquent properties with relative ease. As APA member Todd Bressi said, "That's what making places is all about, making a commitment and staying with it over a long period of time. . . . The best places result from a long period of incremental steps, incremental action" (Andrews, 1997).

But partnership with the city has not been easy. The support of ex-Mayor Flynn was an important factor in getting city help in later stages of the project, but it was very difficult to obtain; it took time and effort from both residents and the mayor to establish an atmosphere of teamwork and cooperation, rather than the adversarial relationship which exists between residents and local officials in less successful project areas and which had existed in the Dudley neighborhood, too. In a similar vein, Yelder said that the biggest roadblock the neighborhood faced was having to fit into the city government's political (4 year terms for a mayor, for example) and budget cycles and dealing with the "loss of memory" that a new local administration brings. Also, not all city departments have been helpful. For example, although Mayor Thomas Menino and the DND have teamed with DSNI to improve the area, the message seems not to have reached the city's Public Works Department, which took years to provide even a minimum of streetscaping, sidewalks, or paved streets in redeveloped areas. Some of the trouble was caused by lack of coordination: "The public works department would pave, then the DND would tear it up to put in a house," one DND staff member explained (author's interview with Thomas, 1998), adding that the two departments are now working with each other. But even today many basic services such as quality education and trash pickup that are routinely provided in wealthier neighborhoods had to be demanded by Dudley residents, a situation whose unfairness is compounded by the fact that these people have less money and so must devote more of their time and energy to the basic jobs of keeping a roof over their head and food on the table. These problems lend support to the idea that, despite the increased political power the neighborhood now enjoys,

Dudley residents still have less political power to back up their needs for public services than do residents of wealthier neighborhoods.

Many others in addition to government also played important roles. Chief among these is the role of private foundations, several of which have helped bring the Dudley plan to reality. Certainly the Ford Foundation's $2 million loan was critical. But some of Ford's restrictions are difficult, so the Riley Foundation's flexible startup funds were also crucial: "We were fortunate to have a funder [the Riley Foundation] that gave us time. Without initial flexibility in the funding source we wouldn't have time to go through an adequate community involvement process, especially given the city budget" (author's interview with Yelder, 1996). Riley's initial investment of $70,000 had grown to more than $1.4 million given directly to DSNI and another $1.5 million given to other neighborhood social service agencies by 1997; it also arranged for the pro bono legal work, and is still supporting DSNI today. The Charles Stuart Mott Foundation and the Boston Foundation, which has a history of community support dating back to its funding of settlement houses, also contributed funds for implementation. "As Boston's *community foundation,* the Boston Foundation works in partnership with our donors, creating the 'community capital' to provide flexible resources . . . at the heart of all we do . . . is a deep conviction that our community's greatest strength—and greatest hope—lies in its diversity" (Hindley, 1992). Major funding for the video "Holding Ground," which documents Dudley's rebirth, was provided by Ford, Riley, and the Annie E. Casey Foundation, with many local foundations and individuals also contributing (Holding Ground Productions, 1997). Research for a chronicle of the neighborhood's redevelopment, *Streets of Hope,* was underwritten by the Riley Foundation, which had been interested in an evaluation of the project since 1989; the Ford Foundation and the MacArthur Foundation also donated. The book, which was written by former DSNI director Peter Medoff and writer Holly Sklar, was unveiled on April 12, 1994; a few days later, Medoff died of AIDS-related illness at the age of 37. The street on which DSNI's first new homes are located was soon renamed Peter Medoff Way in his honor (Morgenroth, 1994).

Personal and corporate ties were also important. "We never could have done any of this without tremendous support from the legal community," Yelder said. Three large law firms, including Rackemann, Sawyer & Brewster; Goulston & Storrs; and Powers & Hall (Hindley, 1992) donated $1 million worth of assistance (Spaid, 1994) including all the title work on the properties, the eminent domain application, all ground leases, and Ford Foundation contracts. Powers & Hall became involved due to personal contacts with Yelder and the Riley Foundation. Riley Trustee and Powers & Hall attorney Bob Holmes served as DSNI's free general counsel for years. Another attorney used to be the city's corporation counsel (author's interview with Yelder, 1996). Area architects contributed free expertise to the two youth-designed community centers, and the Bank of Boston also donated many hours of pro bono service work. Finally, other neighborhood associations and churches played a role, giving meeting space and being involved with DSNI from its inception. DSNI still holds an open meeting annually at St. Patrick's Church, with childcare, translation, and dinner provided.

Being able to put surplus properties back into productive use is an activity of primary importance if successful revitalization is to be achieved. Yet the instances in which other cities and residents have cooperated to successfully accomplish this mission (as they did on Dudley Street) are rare: A large amount of land in many low income inner city residential neighborhoods remains vacant, abandoned, and government-owned. Greenberg and Popper (1994) explain the devastating effects of this on neighborhoods: "Abandoned properties produce no legal revenues. They lower nearby property values, create public costs, and are expensive to police. They often frighten residents and business owners into leaving the vicinity, producing more abandonment. . . . they also mean a substantial loss to the municipality in foregone taxes." But the Dudley Street case shows that ownership of this land by the government can also present an invaluable opportunity to improve these neighborhoods. Perhaps nowhere is the importance of outside support for resident-based efforts illustrated more clearly than in outside agencies' work with DSNI to recycle this derelict property. Foundations provided funds for reusing the property, and private legal and architectural firms donated services that were essential in order to proceed with reuse. The city and the BRA gave eminent domain power to the residents' group in order to facilitate the assemblage of privately held abandoned land and waived all back taxes, penalties, interest, and fees on city-owned land, which it then donated to the residents' land trust. Such activities are not only unusual, but prohibited by a variety of laws in many other parts of the country. In order to take advantage of the opportunity this land presents, discriminatory state and local laws and policies that prevent their reuse in many parts of the country must be changed.

Of all the factors that contributed to DSNI's success, the most important factor is resident control. "The last 15 years have seen a tremendous flowering of community-based capacity to solve problems. [DSNI has] pushed it a little farther than most everybody else has been able to push it," said Stephen Perkins, associate director of Chicago's Center for Neighborhood Technology Services. Former DSNI executive director Peter Medoff said, "Our best accomplishment had to do with organizing the community. People that had been abandoned found that together, they could have power" (Morgenroth, 1994). This cooperation has led to the creation of a "village" atmosphere, including social infrastructure and support networks which are of primary importance to many residents. For example, although DSNI's efforts benefit everyone in the neighborhood, undoubtedly the assistance this "village" provides to women and children cannot be overstated. Adult males are present in only about 50% of the neighborhoood's households, and not surprisingly these are generally the ones with relatively higher incomes. A typical family in one of the low income homes (such as those in Winthrop Estates) consists of either a single mother and her children or of a grandmother, her grandchild (and often, but not always, the child's mother too), and sometimes a younger child or two of her own. The revitalization of Dudley Street has succeeded in large part because of its focus on creating a "village"—a neighborhood where people know and watch out for each other, providing family-style ties and values despite the relative paucity of nuclear families and proving the truth of the African proverb, "It takes a village to raise a child."

"What has been proven here is that when neighborhood people are given the chance, they will fill the leadership void. This was an area that had hit rock bottom. It was a monument to the failure of urban development. But the people themselves have changed all that," former DSNI Executive Director Gus Newport said (Hindley, 1992). But as Medoff pointed out, resident-led redevelopment does not occur overnight. "Deep, grounded, real community building takes time. When you're talking about community building, the quick fix mentality simply doesn't work. You have to have patience, and you have to have faith in the people who live in the neighborhood. Every neighborhood has people who want things to be better and are willing to work for it." Yelder (1996) adds, "My advice to others would be, most of all, to insist on a real community-led process—that is, plan to include residents in all aspects of revitalization; fund projects proposed and supported by the community rather than imposed on it; and provide more flexible funds with longer time frames, particularly in the startup years. The key to Dudley's success is commitment to resident control, as can be seen from the makeup of the Board. It takes longer, but it's worth it. You get a real transformation of people, a building of leadership within the community. [DSNI President 1985–1995] Che Madyun, for example, has become a national spokesperson for community development. [Our housing production] may not seem too impressive by CDC standards, but the community changes are equally, or more, important." Rev. Paul Bothwell, a resident and area pastor, explained, "This community has suffered a lot. It's taken a lot of wounds over a lot of years. It's been pulled apart, it's been exploited, but no more—because we decided to work together. We decided that together we would find a way to make this place different" (Holding Ground Productions, 1997).

Is a program like DSNI's worth the time, money, and effort invested? Although successful in providing housing and many other improvements, the relatively small number of homes built, the high level of subsidy needed per housing unit, the still-present extensive environmental contamination, and the remaining problems beg the question. Undoubtedly, a cost-benefit analysis or fiscal impact study would conclude that construction of a new community for Dudley residents in an unpolluted, unplatted suburban location would be far less costly.

If cost is the only measure of interest to the community, then DSNI's efforts should not be replicated or even applauded. But economic efficiency was never the main goal of the revitalization effort; rather, DSNI's mission is "to empower Dudley residents to organize, plan for, create and control a vibrant, diverse and high quality neighborhood in collaboration with community partners [that is, neighborhood organizations]" (DSNI, 1996c). Clearly, after more than a decade of hard work and the investment of hundreds of millions of dollars, that goal is being achieved.

The question of whether DSNI's approach should be emulated depends on each community's goals. However, communities that answer this question on economic terms alone will fail to consider what many perceive to be the most important benefits produced by inner city revitalization. A DND staff member touched on some of these benefits when he said, "Absolutely, revitalizing the Dudley neighborhood was worth it. I've seen big pockets of the neighborhood filled in. It also stopped the spread of toxics from the industrial areas. People are getting jobs out of the process. There are people who work at DSNI who wouldn't have ever thought of this line of work—it opened their minds to new possibilities" (author's interview with Thomas, 1998). A Dudley resident put it more bluntly: "People's only crime here was they were poor, powerless, and had no advocate. That's changed now" (New Day Films, 1997).

NOTES

1. The city of Boston was incorporated in Fanueil Hall in 1822, and not surprisingly the city was instrumental in its redevelopment. The Hall faces Quincy Market, which is the central one of three long rectangular buildings (North Market, Quincy Market, and South Market) stretching back toward the bay. Famous for its revitalization by developer James Rouse, the area is now one of the top three retail centers in eastern Massachusetts (Hodges, 1998a).

There are many other noteworthy examples of the city's interest and willingness to become a major partner in commercial redevelopment projects. One is the Prudential Center, which "is built on air rights over the Boston and Albany Railroad yard, which has since been removed, and the Mass Pike extension. The 52-story tower was the first large new office building in Boston in over three decades and was built in response to real estate tax abatements." Opened in 1965, "The Pru" was greatly expanded in the 1990s, when 500,000 square feet of shopping space was added. It sold in 1998 for about $700 million; part of the sale involved approval to add 1.6 million more square feet of space, including sidewalks, alleyways, open space, and connections with the Sheraton and the Convention Center. It is already linked by pedestrian bridge to many nearby areas, including Copley Place (Hodges, 1998a).

2. Copley Place is built on air rights above a Mass Pike interchange on 9.5 acres, $530 million, and opened in 1985; "The project's land use planning concept exhibits a successful use of valuable air rights, filling an enormous gap between the Back Bay

and the South End and now connecting the two neighborhoods. The architectural design was controversial, however, largely due to its scale" (Hodges, 1998a)—that is, it and Prudential "could be anywhere. The interior environments are anonymous; they don't read 'Boston'" (Hodges, 1998a).

3. The Erie-Ellington neighborhood, a ten-street area in east Dorchester bordered by Blue Hill Avenue on the west and Columbia Avenue and Washington street on the north, immediately south of the Dudley Street neighborhood, has also been the subject of intensive planning and revitalization efforts. More than 50 tax-delinquent lots were offered by the city for redevelopment; Neighborhood Housing Services (NHS) submitted a proposal to develop condominiums on 30 lots, but financial and other problems caused NHS to close down the effort after developing just 12 units. The Cogman Square CDC has since taken over the properties, and the city has worked with them to develop a neighborhood plan that Department of Neighborhood Development (DND) staff hope will eventually lead to the redevelopment of all the neighborhood's vacant property (author's interview with Thomas, 1996).

4. Boston's tradition of neighborhood activism is not confined to low income areas; in fact, some of the most active neighborhoods (for example, Beacon Hill and the Back Bay) are also its wealthiest. The Back Bay (which begins just west of Boston Common and runs to the West along the Charles River, with the Fenway area in the Back Bay's western part) "is a model of urban planning, sort of a 19th century Levittown in brick and brownstone. Once a dank swamp whose fetid airs reputedly made more than one Brahmin swoon, the area was filled in over a period of 23 years with dirt brought by train from Needham, an outlying suburb that was once much hillier than it is now. Well before public-private partnerships were a political science infatuation, the Back Bay used private development, limited by strict rules regarding lot size, building height and style, to create an entirely new residential community. . . . The Back Bay today remains a successful blend of commercial and residential uses, a community whose vitality seems to grow with each passing year. [It] abuts another one of Boston's successful neighborhoods, Beacon Hill" (Keane, 1998).

Beacon Hill "is decidedly not a model of urban planning. It grew like Topsy, and its urban environment reflects that. Architectural styles vary widely and the streets are spaghetti-like, laid out, some say, by the meandering paths of cattle. . . . Residents think of their neighborhood as an 'urban village,' filled with small, quirky spaces. The Back Bay is grander and more stately. Each has its own distinctive character, so much so that there are residents of Beacon Hill who could never imagine living in Back Bay, and vice versa. . . . The differing reactions of the Back Bay and Beacon Hill neighborhoods (to recent planning efforts) is instructive. The Beacon Hill meetings have been rancorous. The overwhelming sentiment is that the neighborhood has no need of city planning, particularly of the kind proffered by the BRA. The fear of Beacon Hill residents is that planners don't like quirky and crooked, they like logical and straight. In their nightmares they see the Hill being flattened, its streets being widened and its melange of buildings being torn down and replaced with sensible concrete high-rises. Their fears are not entirely misplaced, for this is exactly what happened to Boston's West End" (Keane, 1998).

5. The Boston Redevelopment Authority, formed in 1960, combined planning and urban renewal powers for the first time in the city's history. The agency prepared, funded, and implemented "sub area revitalization plans," emphasizing "neighborhood

planning, quality design (the staff exercised design review authority), building renovation and in-fill development, housing construction for all income levels, economic development, public infrastructure and facility construction and transportation" (Koff, 1998). The BRA is commonly viewed as being more focused on the downtown area than on the surrounding low income neighborhoods (author's interview with Thomas, 1996), which are the focus of the City's DND; also, since it is state-chartered it is not as well-controlled by local officials as is the DND. The BRA has extensive powers, including taking property via eminent domain (in November 1988 the BRA authorized the Dudley Street Neighborhood Initiative [DSNI] to also use this power), relocation of residents and businesses from designated urban renewal sites, demolition and rehab of structures, and participation in real estate development. It must gain the state Department of Housing and Community Development (DHCD) approval for its urban renewal project plans. In the 1970s and 1980s the agency gained admiration for its planning under director Ed Logue and its completion of projects such as Harborwalk (a seaside path that connects the North End with South Boston) and the Charlestown Navy Shipyard redevelopment. However, since Mayor Menino took office the agency has been decimated. "Today the BRA is a shadow of its former self, shrunk from 700 employees in the 1970s to 100, barely half of them planners. . . . In the last few years, the agency has taken on an increasingly fiscal orientation, even affixing EDIC—Economic Development and Industrial Corporation—to its name" (Kay, 1998).

6. The South End also includes Castle Square, a large "moderate-income housing project that was built in the 1960s under an urban renewal project. Castle Square is now a cooperative owned by the former tenants. It contains ground floor retail along Tremont Street with apartments above." There is extensive well-maintained landscaping, and even an oriental garden on one side (Hodges, 1998a).

7. The linkage program "requires developers to contribute toward new affordable housing, employment opportunities, child care facilities, transit systems, and the like, in return for the city's permission to build new commercial developments. . . . [Boston and several other cities] have linked project approval and/or funding assistance with the creation of employment opportunities for city residents and minorities. . . . As evidence of the political significance of linkage, every candidate for the office of Mayor of Boston endorsed some form of linkage program during the 1984 election campaign. . . . Linkage opponents in Boston have challenged that city's authority to adopt a linkage program. . . . Both the San Francisco and Boston linkage programs provide some opportunity for negotiation, and thus, potentially, are opening the door to equal protection challenges" (Andrew & Merriam, 1988). Establishment of such linkage programs may require amending state zoning and/or subdivision enabling legislation to allow such requirements.

8. The HouseBoston mortgage program (also known as BostonMORTGAGE), which is sponsored by the City Department of Neighborhood Development and Fannie Mae, provides homebuyers making less than $67,800 for a family of four (=120% of the median income of $61,560) a 97% loan for single family or condo purchase, a 95% loan plus 2% grant from the City (the BostonHOME Certificate Initiative, with the certificate obtained after completion of a Homebuyer Education program) for two-family building purchase, a 90% loan plus 5% grant from the same source for a three-family building purchase, a refinance program, and for "fixer-uppers" there is a single

loan for both purchase and rehab costs, with up to half the loan able to be used for rehab plus City grants of up to $5,000 for repairs to correct "essential health and safety items" (the Purchase Rehab Option, or HouseBoston-PRO) (Newberger, 1996). Any of these mortgages can be supplemented with $500–1,000 provided by the city for closing costs, and up to one-third of the cost of rehab ($3,000 maximum) from the Boston HomeWorks; more grant funds are available for deleading and exterior painting. They can also be paired with the soft second, MHFA, ACORN, 203k loans (a HUD program that allows the inclusion of repairs of over $5,000 in mortgages for owner-occupied 1–4 family homes) and other programs described in this note.

The DND, or Department of Neighborhood Development (in 1996 this was the Public Facilities Department), oversees many other programs. The Hidden Assets program, a collaboration with the Massachusetts Housing Partnership Fund, offers both long-term permanent loans, as well as gap financing (total project cost minus amount of permanent financing and cash equity available) of $20,000–30,000 per unit or $500,000 per project, to investors or developers of multifamily (5 or more units) housing in which at least 51% of the units are affordable to people making 80% of the median income or less. The gap financing is carried at zero interest, and payments deferred until the loan matures in 20–25 years. "Soft second" financing of up to $30,000 is offered to homebuyers through the Massachusetts Affordable Housing Alliance in which the city and state cover most of the payment costs for the first five years of the 30-year low interest loans. This can be used in conjunction with the closing cost and down payment subsidies described earlier, and is often part of the overall 5% down mortgage finance package described earlier. There are also four home rehabilitation/repair grant/loan programs for senior citizens, and a wide variety of programs for purchase and rehab of vacant homes and apartments, as well as new construction for low and moderate income buyers and a TeenWorks program that hires teenagers to paint the homes of low income residents.

9. There are a plethora of nonprofit agencies that offer many types of financial and technical assistance; some noteworthy ones are ACORN, the oldest grassroots organization of low and moderate income people in the U.S., which has grown to nearly 100,000 members since its inception in 1970 and is funded entirely by its $5 monthly member dues; ONE (Organization for a New Equality), a Boston-based national civil rights organization which, in cooperation with the BancBoston Mortgage Corporation, seeks first-time homebuyers to serve as caretakers of bank-foreclosed properties until they are rehabbed and sold; and NOAH (Neighborhood of Affordable Housing), which offers foreclosure prevention counseling in East Boston and is funded by the Pew Charitable Trust and the Boston Foundation. The Boston Building Materials Co-op is "a private, not-for-profit, consumer co-op. . . . Our purpose is to provide materials at low cost and teach people how to maintain and improve their homes." Members work one hour for every $200 they spend, with a 10-hour annual maximum. Annual membership ranges from $10 (tenants) to $30 (community organizations); anyone can shop there but members get lower prices. The co-op offers building materials, workshops, referrals to contractors, weatherization, and house calls, which are offered on a sliding hourly fee scale based on income and starting at $20/hour.

10. The Massachusetts State Housing Finance Agency (MHFA) has properties on which it has foreclosed due to nonpayment of loans, offers Mortgage Credit Certifi-

cates (MCCs, which give buyers federal income tax credits of up to $2,000 a year to buyers earning at least $25,000 a year), has a low-cost mortgage insurance program for low income buyers, and also offers many types of financial assistance including mortgages and rehab loans (for example, the Home Improvement Loan Program, which offers loans of up to $15,000 to low and moderate income borrowers with "a good credit record and a stable income" owning 1–4 family homes).

11. For abandoned city-owned properties, the Great Boston Yard Sale was begun in 1995 to make unbuildable city-owned lots available to adjacent property owners to expand their yard space. In its first year, over 300 lots were available. Auctions of city-owned tax-foreclosed property are also held, with all previous encumbrances being forgiven at the time of foreclosure and the former owner having no right of redemption after foreclosure either. Finally, the Residential Development Program (RDP) matches buyers of abandoned city-owned properties with project managers who help them through the process from financing through rehab and leasing. An income of at least $20,000, a good credit history, and savings of $5,000 are required, though.

Boston has a long history of inequitable tax appraisal and assessment procedures, as is so well documented in work as far back as that of Oldman, Oliver, and Aaron's 1972 article, which analyzed data on Boston properties from 1960–1964 and concluded, "How much and what kinds of unequal treatment exist in Boston? 'Plenty' and 'many' are the answers indicated by the study . . ." which found evidence of very high assessment—overassessment, in other words—in those parts of central Boston with the lowest property values. The result is financial taking of private property, producing a large inventory of tax-foreclosed city-owned property. Evidence from more recent studies (Bright, 1999) indicates that these policies may actively contribute to, and even precipitate, the decline of low-income neighborhoods such as Dudley. Although the Boston appraisal practices seem to have been improved, in many other communities overappraisal is still a major contributor to inner city abandonment and blight.

Much has been done to rectify the situation since Oldman et al.'s 1972 article. The city has established a Vacant Land Database on its Geographic Information System (GIS). The database is used "to determine how to use city-owned land and to plan for parcels which are tax delinquent and therefore likely to soon become city property. [It produces] maps for planners to use to market particular sites and assemble lists for public information." There is a priority system to get key properties back in use, with first priority being abandoned buildings, followed by vacant parcels that are either "desired by developers or have serious dumping problems." Owners of vacant properties have one year to redeem them, but the city "contests all attempts to regain property, since it brings no guarantees that the owner will develop or maintain the property." During the year-long redemption period, "the city searches for a developer who will build well-designed, affordable housing on the site." Under Project 747, the city first acquires a parcel; developers are then "chosen based on the quality of their design proposals, their track records, and the wishes of people in the neighborhood;" finally, developer financing is arranged using CDBG funds, local banks, the MHFA, and/or the Boston Linkage Program (Houston Planning Department, 1994).

As part of Mayor Thomas Menino's initiative to turn vacant properties into affordable homes, the DND's Real Estate Management Services Division offers "listings" similar to those used by real estate brokers in wealthier areas. It has sold more than 140 homes this way, with financing arranged through area lenders using one of the above-described mortgage products. "The Division has been very proactive for the past four years, acting like a real estate agency. It's so proactive that it sometimes disregards the community process—for example, a neighborhood may need a moratorium on sales and redevelopment of city-owned lots until the planning process is finished, but the Division is more interested in making a deal," one insider said (author's interview with anonymous insider, 1998). New construction prices range from $95,000 to 110,000 for single family, with higher prices for multifamily. Most of these homes are in the lowest income parts of town including Dorchester and Roxbury, yet to an outsider they seem far from what a truly low-income person needs. For example, a recent listing of 9 single family homes in the Woodward Park area of DSNI advertised a price of $99,000 for a 6-room, 1.5 bath house with no garage but a foyer, porch and 2-car driveway. "Total monthly costs run from $650 to $1,000 depending on the sales price and mortgage product. SO IF YOU CAN AFFORD TO RENT, YOU CAN AFFORD TO OWN!" a sales brochure proclaimed (DND, 1996), adding that buyers must have good credit and at least $2,000 saved as well as enough income to cover the monthly payment.

12. The nation's first citywide Main Street Program was established in Boston in 1995 by the City and the National Trust for Historic Preservation and is also run by the DND. "Over the course of the program, an estimated total of $4.2 million will be expended by the City of Boston and equally matched by the private sector." The DND is also charged with maintenance of city buildings, and this has led to DND involvement in several large historic building restoration projects including Fanueil Hall, the Old State House, and parts of the Public Library (Lipsey, 1998).

13. Other public housing projects have been undergoing renovation as well, beginning with the BURP (Boston Rehabilitation Program) program, which started in the late 60s, followed by Boston Housing Partnerships I and II (BHPI and BHPII) in the 1980s, and most recently under the Demo Dispo program, which was begun in 1994 (see Bratt, 1997, for details). For example, Columbia Point, once a rather infamous public housing development, has been redesigned—perhaps reinvented is more appropriately descriptive—into a mixed-use complex which has also succeeded in mixing incomes, even including some market-rate townhomes (author's interview with Thomas, 1996). The Commonwealth project in East Brighton "was transformed from a state of social and physical devastation into a nationally recognized model for public housing revitalization," mainly as the result of tenant activism (see Vale, 1997).

The Mission Hill public housing project (in the Jamaica Plain/Roxbury area near the Medical Center) used to be a nice place to live until drugs, especially crack, became widespread and "ruined the neighborhood. It's amazing what they can do," one resident said. Tenants got upset there, and at similar conditions in the adjacent Alice Taylor Apartments (also public housing); they organized, and obtained $20 million for renovation. Now the low-rise complex features individual apartment entrances, children's play areas, activities for children and teens, low chain link fences, landscaping, fresh paint, and pleasant urban design fixtures along with good ongoing maintenance (cleaning, removal of graffitti within 24 hours, control of junk cars, and so on), and law enforcement; for example, when undercover agents buy drugs from a tenant, the tenant is evicted within 24 hours. A social support network formed by tenants is credited with the turnaround; the tenant organization acts as the neighborhood's "eyes and ears," and often even confronts minor troublemakers, addicts, and drug dealers directly before calling the police. Lessons learned from this project include the following: Low rise, scattered site, income-mixed projects work best, especially if built or rehabbed by a CDC and/or nonprofit developer; defensible space and family-oriented design works best, including low see-through fences and private separate entries (rather than corridors) that create a sense of individual ownership and responsibility without cutting off visual surveillance by neighbors, placement of play areas in front of the entries, and so on; tenant management and even ownership works best if adequate funds are provided for maintenance; good maintenance is a must regardless of ownership, as is increased law enforcement; police must get out of their cars, meet the residents and walk the halls; and new, strong social networks among neighbors are important, so they can watch out for each other and provide services (for example, rides) which are otherwise offered by drug dealers. In general, "respect" of the residents and "creating a family-oriented environment" were cited as most important (American Planning Association [APA], 1994; also see van Vliet, 1997).

However, since one key element in successful public housing renovation appears to be more careful tenant selection (or, to put it more bluntly, displacement of "troublemakers," including those with serious drug, alcohol, and/or behavior problems) and another is limited income mixing, one must ask whether the assessment of the "success" of these renovated public housing developments should be linked in some way to assessing the fate of the displaced former tenants, too. Where do they live now? What are the effects of their rejection on the neighborhoods to which they move? Have programs been established to improve their lives, too (for example, renovating SRO buildings coupled with providing a wide range of social support programs for the residents—see Chapter 3 for an example).

14. The State Department of Housing and Community Development (DHCP, formerly the Executive Office of Communities and Development) supervises local redevelopment authorities including the BRA. "Massachusetts' cities and towns are taking a second look at the Commonwealth's Urban Renewal Program," a recent staff-written article proclaimed (MDHCD, 1998c). "Despite past criticism, urban renewal provides important tools for the revitalization of abandoned or underutilized urban areas that have been unable to attract private investment," the article continued, citing the ability of redevelopment authorities to assemble sites, handle environmental cleanup costs, secure financing and coordinate a wide range of agencies and specialists involved in remediation.

The DHCD also runs a great many other programs: It "makes state and federal funds and technical assistance available" for many activities including neighborhood revitalization, construction and management of public housing (including public housing modernization grants, and operating subsidies), demolition of abandoned structures, CDC-sponsored programs ranging from small business development to literacy, help for low income persons who need to pay for energy, sewer and/or water, crime prevention (including sponsorship of Neighborhood Watch), Neighborhood Housing Services state-funded housing rehabilitation loans, and encouragement of the provision of private sector affordable housing. The DHCD administers the state's public housing programs, lead paint removal, coordinates state antipoverty efforts, administers the federal food/nutrition and Community Services Block Grant programs (which are run by local Community Action Agencies and include several dozen activities including Head Start and substance abuse prevention) and allocates federal McKinney Act, HOME, and CDBG funds (MDHCD, 1998b). Since 1984, about $20 million in CDBG funds have been used to support a wide range of downtown development activities across the state (MDHCD, 1998d). MDHCD also taps into these funds to pay for residential rehabilitation, reclamation of abandoned and foreclosed properties, preservation of affordable housing units, and related acquisition, site preparation, infrastructure and demolition. For abandoned and foreclosed properties, the state supplements the CDBG funds with state-funded rehabilitation loans. The department also administers the Federal Section 8 housing programs, and supplements them with state-funded rental voucher programs.

MDHCD also offers a plethora of state-funded financial aid for low and moderate income housing. For example, the department offers below-market mortgage financing for buyers making less than 80% of the median family income, including a "soft second" mortgage that relieves buyers of the need for private mortgage insurance, waives most interest charges for the first five years and requires interest-only payments for the first ten years; it also sponsors a mortgage program designed to encourage income mixing in owner-occupied housing developments which, like DNI, includes deed restrictions on all resales to preserve affordability. The Rental Development Action Loan program offers 15-year operating cost subsidies especially for rentals to poor families, while the Housing Innovations Fund "was created to finance innovative housing needs" (MDHCD, 1998b) and offers loans and/or grants for SROs, housing for AIDS patients and recovering substance abusers, the mentally ill, and the physically disabled. The Housing Assistance for Rental Production program offers loans for mixed income (25% of the units must be "affordable") family housing production, and other programs provide grants for scattered-site low income housing for families and the elderly. These programs are funded with revenue from state housing bonds (MDHCD, 1998b).

One of the more innovative aspects of MDHCD's work is the Local Initiative Program (LIP) which, when combined with the enforcement provided by the Housing Appeals Committee, puts teeth in the usual lip service given to provision of affordable housing by the private sector. Basically, density bonuses are given to projects that meet MDHCD approval and reserve at least 25% of the proposed housing units (new or rehabbed) for low income residents, in cities or towns with less than 10% of housing units affordable to low or moderate income persons. After MDHCD approval, the developers, nonprofits or government agencies sponsoring the project must obtain a "comprehensive permit" from their local Zoning Board of Appeals (ZBA); this permit overrides local zoning and other regulations, according to state law (Chapter 40B Sections 20–23). If the local ZBA denies the permit or puts conditions on it that make it uneconomic, the developer can appeal to the MDHCD's Housing Appeals Committee. Thus, approval authority for low income housing development has been essentially removed from the local level (MDHCD, 1998b).

CHAPTER 5

Pittsburgh
Partnerships, Preservation, and the CRA

ROOTS OF DECLINE

Pittsburgh has been in decline for the past fifty years, mainly as a result of a massive loss of jobs. From 1958–1987 manufacturing employment plummeted by 69% (Barrett and Greene, 1993); approximately 100,000 jobs were lost in the 1980s alone (Brokaw and Lahvic, 1992), when the collapse of the already declining steel production industry (the mainstay of the city's economy) exacerbated the previous employment losses. The city still has a critical need for job creation: The current job market is characterized by high tech and medical jobs at one end of the spectrum, and low-wage dead-end jobs at the other (author's interview with Dowell and Smith, 1996).

Within the city itself people left at an accellerating pace from 1950 (676,806) to 1980, and continued leaving after 1980 albeit at a slower pace (see Table 5). More than 70,000 people, or 10.7% of the population, left the city from 1950–1960 (604,332), nearly 85,000 from 1960–1970 (520,089), more than 95,000 from 1970–1980 (423,959), and nearly 55,000 from 1980–1990 (369,879), which is a drop of close to 50% in forty years. Only Detroit and Newark, New Jersey, experienced greater population losses (U.S. Bureau of the Census 1950, 1960, 1970, 1980, 1990).

Although the majority of population losses occurred in the city, the suburbs have also experienced steady and severe population losses from 1970 to 1990. The population of the PMSA (which includes the cities of Pittsburgh and McKeesport as well as Allegheny County and parts of three other counties) swelled by 8.7%, adding nearly 200,000 new residents from 1950 (population 2,213,236) to 1960 (population 2,405,435), but has lost population ever since. From 1960 to 1970 almost 60,000 people left the PMSA; at least this shows that the suburbs were still growing, since this loss is smaller than that endured by the city alone. The huge losses in the city's population were

Table 5: Population Change in Pittsburgh Area, 1950 through 1990

	City of Pittsburgh	Allegheny County	Pittsburgh PMSA*	PMSA Area Outside Pittsburgh
1950	676,806	1,515,237	2,213,236	1,536,430
1960	604,332	1,628,587	2,405,435	1,801,103
1970	520,089	1,605,016	2,347,611	1,827,522
1980	423,959	1,405,085	2,218,870	1,794,911
1990	369,879	1,336,448	2,056,705	1,686,826

Source: U.S. Bureau of the Census, 1950–1990
*PMSA: Primary Metropolitan Statistical Area

finally joined by suburban losses from 1970 to 1980 when the PMSA lost nearly 130,000 people (the 1970 population was 2,347,611; the 1980 population was 2,218,870), including 35,000 from the suburbs. The suburban exodus became a hemorrhage from 1980 to 1990: The PMSA lost more than 160,000 residents (the 1990 PMSA population was 2,056,705), a "mere" 55,000 of whom lived in the city itself. It is interesting to note that well over half the PMSA population losses occurred during this decade, a decade in which the city's loss rate slowed considerably; perhaps the suburbs were hit harder by the steel industry's demise than was the city (U.S. Bureau of the Census 1950, 1960, 1970, 1980, 1990).

Area housing trends may illustrate the effects of delayed response to suburban population growth. During the decade of 1970–1980 nearly 100,000 units were added to the urban area's housing stock (which rose from 776,182 to 861,150); this indicates a real addition of more than 100,000 units to the suburban housing market, since the city actually lost more than 10,000 units during these years. Yet the population data cited above shows that during the same decade, suburban growth ceased and the suburbs actually began to lose population. Evidently builders got the message, since in the following decade fewer than 19,000 net units were added to the PMSA housing stock (total 1990 units was 879,811): Twenty-eight thousand units were built in the suburbs and 9,000 were lost in the city. The number of housing units in the city declined from 189,831 in 1970 to179,198 in 1980 and 170,159 in 1990.

The composition of Pittsburgh's population has also changed dramatically in the past 30 years. In 1960 there were 100,692 people identified as "Negroes" living in the city; by 1990 this number had dropped slightly to 95,362. However, the percentage of total population that fell in this category increased from 1/6 in 1960 to more than 1/4 in 1990, due to a tremendous exodus of whites from Pittsburgh: The 1990 white population of the city of Pittsburgh was 266,791, compared to a 1960 white population of 502,593.

(Other races and ethnic groupings make up very small portions of the population; for example, in 1990 less than 1% of the population identified itself as Hispanic.) It is interesting to note that population losses were so great that even the nonwhite population declined slightly, a situation which is atypical even of Snowbelt cities (U.S. Bureau of the Census, 1950, 1960, 1970, 1980, 1990).

Finally, in 1990 the city had the oldest average population of any metropolitan area in the nation, despite the fact that it was not attracting retirees. No wonder that the January 1996 issue of *Executive Report* (a local business magazine) featured a photo of a tombstone with the inscription "Pittsburgh, 1816–1996" and the headline, "Do or Die! Can We Resuscitate This Region?"

SIGNS OF CHANGE

Pittsburgh "provides a dramatic example of the coordinated and mutually reinforcing efforts of the public and private sectors. To its credit, Pittsburgh avoided the problem of wholesale urban renewal clearance that had haunted . . . many other American cities. Its revitalization efforts focused on both the neighborhoods of the city and on the downtown" (Levitt, 1987), and included attention to urban design, provision of amenities for the public, transportation improvements, and a marketing effort which has diversified the city's economic base by attracting high technology industries.

Downtown revitalization occurred well before the neighborhood problems were addressed. Starting in the 1950s, Pittsburgh made judicious use of the federal urban renewal program to make its downtown a showcase of revitalization, with the help of the city's corporate base—described as "the key to revitalizing Pittsburgh's downtown" (Levitt, 1987). Thirty years later corporate resources were again tapped, this time to revitalize the city's low income neighborhoods. But this time corporate participation came only after years of work by residents and the city, sometimes willingly but more often in response to political and legal pressure. "Pittsburgh has had remarkable success in maintaining its neighborhoods in the face of enormous obstacles," Barrett and Greene (1993) reported. This success has been achieved by focusing on resident-led initiatives, formation of public-private partnerships, and aggressive use of the Community Reinvestment Act (CRA).[1]

Resident-Led Initiatives

In response to the city's problems, many community-based organizations (CBOs) were formed: Seventeen of these evolved into community development corporations (CDCs), while the rest have remained less formal organizations staffed with volunteers. By far the best known of the CDCs is the Manchester Citizens Corporation (MCC); one could reasonably say that revitalization of the city's low income neighborhoods began with this organization. Further, the metamorphosis undergone by MCC in the 1960s and 1970s is reflective of changes in approaches to achieving successful revitalization that have occurred throughout the country.

The Manchester neighborhood is located on the city's lower north side. Built in the 19th century to house the city's elite, it is characterized by beautiful multistory wood-trimmed brick row houses interspersed with very large Victorian and Gothic-style brick or stone detached homes. In the 1950s the neighborhood was 80% white; as whites moved to the suburbs, blacks began to move from the smaller, plainer homes behind the mansions into the larger structures on the street (Gratz, 1995). By 1965 the area was still home to 15,000 people, but the population and job losses being incurred by the city coupled with the riots that occurred after the 1967 assassination of Dr. Martin Luther King, Jr., precipitated the neighborhood's decline: Eight years later the population had slipped to just 4,200 (Perlmutter, 1993). Today the area has a low income, predominantly African-American population of around 3,600. "Yet it was one of only three neighborhood communities in Pittsburgh that showed population growth in the 1990 Census, and city planners and historic preservationists from all over the United States now visit it as an example of historic preservation that does not displace low and moderate income residents" (in a telephone interview with the author, Brandon, 1992). The main reason for this population turnaround is the role played by the MCC in improving the neighborhood's quality of life.

Founded in 1965 and incorporated in 1971, the 1,500-member Manchester Citizens Corporation is the city's oldest CDC. Originally, the group advocated removal of the existing Victorian row houses and their replacement with suburban-style garden homes; residents succeeded in having the city's Urban Redevelopment Authority (URA) destroy 900 of these before reversing their approach in the 1970s. The reversal occurred after Arthur Ziegler, cofounder of the Pittsburgh History and Landmarks Foundation, took community activist Stanley Lowe (now widely considered the "father" of Pittsburgh's neighborhood revitalization) on a trip to Georgetown, a Washington D.C. neighborhood of restored 19th century brick row houses which was considered a slum in the 1950s but has since become the city's most prestigious and expensive neighborhood (Gratz, 1995).[2] "We had buildings as good, if not better, still standing in neighborhoods all over Pittsburgh. We started adding up the numbers we'd lost [from demolition of the row houses] and how few [new units] we'd gained. And it clicked. We only got six houses on a block," Lowe said, explaining the residents' decision to replace demolition and suburban-style construction with preservation and restoration (Gratz, 1995). By 1976 the demolition had been stopped and the neighborhood had become the largest National Register Historic District in the city (there are now several larger ones).[3]

During this period, neighborhood planning and resident participation also characterized the city's planning efforts. As early as 1970, the city assigned seven planners to work with community-based organizations in specific neighborhoods. As Bramhall (1974) explained, "The community planners helped the city to deliver improvements to residents and created a climate that made neighborhood groups more powerful." By the late 1970s relationships with some neighborhood groups were firm enough to allow more authority to be turned over to them. First was a contract in 1979 between the MCC and the Urban Rehabilitation Authority (URA), which called for the MCC to manage a renewal program for the Manchester neighborhood that focused on restoration of the area's numerous historic buildings. Shortly thereafter the city completed a revitalization plan for the Homewood neighborhood and provided funds for establishing a CDC to oversee its implementation; allocated a federal Urban Development Action Grant (UDAG) to six north side neighborhoods for housing rehabilitation; helped residents of the Oakland neighborhood to develop plans for improving their area; and funded an effort to promote business in the East Liberty commercial district (Lurcott and Downing, 1987).

This community-based planning extended to implementation, as capital budget funding was allocated to the neighborhoods based on six-year development programs; the city attempted to funnel funds to low and moderate income neighborhoods. For example, from 1977–1986 the city allocated $786 million for facilities, infrastructure and other revitalization efforts in Pittsburgh's 88 neighborhoods, a figure which accounts for 80% of the city's capital investment (City of Pittsburgh, 1986). But cuts in the 1980s in federal Community Development Block Grant (CDBG) funding reduced available CDBG funds from $26 million in 1980 to $17 million in 1986, a reduction that was passed on to the neighborhoods (Lurcott & Downing, 1987). Clearly, additional funds were needed from a new source, and the private sector seemed to be the only alternative. "It's acknowledged in Pittsburgh that public money is not going to solve the problems of the neighborhoods—there's not enough money in the world to do that. We have to get private leadership active. Then we can support it with public resources," said URA's Economic Development Department Director Evan Stoddard (Barrett & Greene, 1993).

Public-Private Partnerships

By 1983 the success of these "pilot" programs that turned project management, marketing, and planning over to CDCs was clear, so formation of larger public-private partnerships involving the corporate sector became feasible and, in view of the losses of CDBG funds, somewhat imperative. A major step was taken when the Ford Foundation, Howard Heinz Endowment, and the Mellon Bank Foundation, working with the URA and the city planning department, formed the Pittsburgh Partnership for Neighborhood Development (PPND) as a vehicle to provide support for resident-led revitalization efforts.[4] "Early on, public commitment to provide operating support for the five CDCs encouraged the Ford Foundation to make an initial commitment to a Pittsburgh program. Ford's commitment, in turn, was crucial to generating local foundation interest in the operating support program. These private commitments made it easier to obtain additional public funding . . ." former city planning director Robert Lurcott (Lurcott & Downing, 1987) explained.

Resident-led neighborhood revitalization is supported by the public and private sectors in three ways: providing funds for CDC operating costs, funds for projects, and technical assistance. In all three arenas, PPND is a major player. The organization "acts as an intermediary between foundations, banks, other corporations, and institutions (such as hospitals and universities) on one side, and community development corporations, technical assistance organizations, and special community development projects on the other. You can't talk for long about reinvestment efforts in Pittsburgh without hearing the name PPND. It's an unusual organization that often provides the much-needed glue holding together complicated, multi-layered projects," Lunt (1993) said.

In its first two years, PPND funnelled more than $1 million into the city's five largest CDCs (MCC, Oakland Planning and Development Corporation, North Side Civic Development Corporation—which had been active in the UDAG program mentioned earlier, East Liberty Development, Inc.—which took over the role played earlier by the chamber of commerce, and Homewood-Brushton Revitalization and Development Corporation) for operating and project expenses. These funds were augmented with money from Pittsburgh Local Initiatives Support Corporation (LISC) and the city's Neighborhood Fund, a nonprofit organization organized by the city in 1984 and run by a board composed of neighborhood representatives, city staff, and private agencies which allocates CDBG money to other CBOs (Lurcott & Downing, 1987). Now, PPND gives financial support to many more CDCs (Lunt, 1993).

Providing adequate operating funds is especially important. Former PPND executive director and director of the Pittsburgh branch of the Federal Reserve Bank of Cleveland Sandra Phillips said, "You need two kinds of money to make community development work—operating money and development money. On the operating side, it is necessary to provide money to the local CBOs (which are often staffed by volunteers and poorly funded) so they can hire people with the skills to properly manage real estate development. PPND's chairman, Donald Titzel of Mellon, agrees. 'Any group finds it easier to get project money rather than money for staff, lawyers, and other expenses'" (Lunt, 1993). All of the city's CDCs, and many community organizations that are in a more "fledgling" stage of development, have received small grants from the city's Neighborhood Fund. PPND has also been instrumental for many years in supporting the daily operation of the five CDCs mentioned in the previous paragraph. Each CDC involved receives about $100,000 each year for operating costs, an allocation which totalled over $2 million from 1983–1987 for the five CDCs. Since then, PPND has expanded its funding well beyond the original five.

Project finance is also important: As Lurcott (Lurcott & Downing, 1987) said, "Without development projects to point to, the program most likely would have foundered." Here too partnerships prevail, as foundations have covered gap financing needs; LISC has invested $14.5 million in short-term construction loans, market studies, interest rate subsidies and related items; and the city has provided a CDBG-funded venture capital fund for small businesses that are run by the CBOs, as well as gap financing (using UDAG and other funds) for vacant/underused property development and other CBO-based real estate ventures. This money has been more than matched by other sources: "Phillips said that on a typical project PPND works on, about 20% of the financing comes from banks, about 50–60% comes from the URA, and the rest comes from PPND and other sources. 'The bank loan is very important money, because it and our money leverage the public money. Banks often compete with each other to participate on deals, because a lot of these are good deals and they help them meet their CRA requirements.' No PPND-sponsored project has ever defaulted, though some have had to be refinanced" (Lunt, 1993).

Finally, training for community leaders and technical assistance in design, marketing, and management has been provided by PPND, using city-allocated CDBG money and other sources. A total of $13.26 million was spent on neighborhood technical support from 1980–1986, of which $7.1 million was city/federal funds and the remaining $6.16 million came from foundations (Lurcott & Downing, 1987).

Aggressive Use of the CRA

Although the city, the residents, and private foundations through PPND were heavily involved in revitalizing Pittsburgh's poor neighborhoods by the mid-1980s, lending institutions were minor players at best. Yet now, the city is widely acknowledged as home to some of the most involved lending institutions in the nation. Given the fact that lenders are reluctant to make loans in low income central city neighborhoods, how was this achieved? "Pittsburgh's leaders . . . played a little hardball," Barrett and Greene (1993) said, adding that the city told the banks it would deposit its own money in those lending institutions that had the best ratings on providing mortgages, repair loans, and business loans (especially to minority and women-owned businesses) in poor neighborhoods. Since city deposits are large, the strategy worked: Before the program the banks loaned about $6 million in these neighborhoods each year, but as of 1993 that figure had risen to $18.8 million.

But much of the credit for change goes to the city's low income residents, who have actively enforced the CRA's provisions since 1987. That year, neighborhood activism was precipitated by an announced proposal from Union National Bank (later Integra Bank/Pittsburgh and now National City Bank) to purchase Pennbancorp (another Pittburgh bank). The MCC analyzed Union Bank's Home Mortgage Disclosure Act (HMDA) data and discovered that the bank had made no loans in the Manchester area for the past six years. MCC former director Stanley Lowe then galvanized 16 other CBOs to form the Pittsburgh Community Reinvestment Group (PCRG) and mount a protest of the merger. The bank, under direction of its new vice president Donald Reed, withdrew its merger application and met with PCRG representatives; three days later, an agreement emerged that called for the bank to provide $109 million in community loans, the second largest CRA-based commitment ever made at the time (Lunt, 1993). In 1996, the bank's commitment was raised to $1.67 billion (Daniels, 1996). Thus PCRG became "one of the first CBOs in the U.S. to use the CRA as a leveraging tool to build relationships with financial institutions to finance neighborhood development" (PCRG, 1995c).

A Closer Look at the Parties Involved

The large number of low income neighborhoods (when compared to cities like Boston, Seattle, Portland and the Twin Cities) and the extensive level of neighborhood organization mean that revitalization in Pittsburgh has been a complex process, with many stakeholders. Activities of the main parties involved citywide are profiled here, as are some examples of the numerous CDCs and developers that are participating.

Manchester Citizens Corporation (MCC). Asked to describe the role of Pittsburgh's most famous CDC, MCC Executive Director Rhonda Brandon replied, "Any kind of problems that occur in this neighborhood, they come to this office!" She explained, "We do new infill construction, restoration, and are an advocate for the neighborhood." MCC also works with area homebuyers, prequalifying them and "handholding" through the loan approval process. Asked about how MCC overcame the dual loan approval hurdles[5] of buyer approval (many low income buyers have income from overtime and other sources that are usually discounted or not counted by lenders, and/or imperfect credit histories) and structural approval (older homes in need of rehabilitation and/or in changing neighborhoods are often disallowed by lenders), she replied, "PCRG got over all those reasons. Their CRA agreements opened a multitude of doors. Think about it: PCRG represents more than 30 neighborhood groups—that's a lot of people. When you put all those together, you've got strength!" (in an interview with the author, 1996).

The effort of MCC founder Stanley Lowe working through PCRG to develop CRA agreements with the banks means that lending institutions have been helpful. One example of the results is a $1 million line of credit given to MCC for many years by Northside Depository Bank. Another example is MCC's partnerships with Fidelity and Community Savings banks to offer the "Ain't I a Woman" housing initiative program, which encourages home own-ership for low income single women. The program offers low interest rates, a 50% discount on closing costs, no loan origination fees, a simplified applica-tion process and personal attention from the staff. "They had a big stick," Brandon (1996) said. "Before CRA, banks could care less about us. We weren't getting this kind of cooperation. The lenders are great now," she said.

There is still plenty of opportunity for renovation. Vacant lots in the area sell for $2,500–3,000; the cheapest lot with a dilapidated house would cost around $2,000. The most typical property includes a three-story, 5,000 square foot house and costs much more. When fixed, these houses are worth $80,000 but MCC can sell them for around $50,000, thanks to a subsidy from the URA (in an interview with the author, Brandon, 1996).

MCC's funding sources are diverse. The main source is PPND, along with CDBG funds and private foundations. "We ask for no money from resi-dents," Brandon said. In the mid-1990s MCC, the URA, the Housing Author-ity of the City of Pittsburgh (HACP) and several community groups received a large new funding source: a $7.5 million pilot HOPE VI Plus grant to con-duct a model public housing program. A total of only six cities were awarded funds under this federal HUD-sponsored program.

"We're doing total revitalization of 107 units of public housing, and we are leveraging it to $19 million with money from foundations and other sources" Brandon explained. First, a total of 107 dilapidated public housing units on seven sites scattered throughout the Manchester area were demol-ished. One of MCC's first priorities was the provision of new townhomes for the 60 former public housing tenants who lived in those units. Many residents own their new homes, which are integrated into the community via mixed income development: Besides the units for the displaced people, 83 addi-tional homes will be built and sold to owner-occupants. "The infill strategy integrates the neighborhood, both socially and economically. This project will change the nature of public housing as we know it. It will be privately owned and managed and indistinguishable from any other housing in the neighborhood," according to a 1995 MCC handout (MCC, 1996). Pointing out that it is unusual for a community group like MCC to be entering the busi-ness of providing and managing public housing, Brandon said, "Remember, this is a model pilot program!"

HOPE VI Plus involves more than bricks and mortar: More than $2 million is set aside for a Support Service Program. A wide range of social services will be provided under this program, including GED certification, computer literacy, life skills training, credit counseling, home ownership training, and so on.

The HOPE VI Plus program is one part of an overall ten-year neighborhood development strategy plan, the Manchester Plan, that was developed by MCC and area residents over a three-year period. "The plan identifies every nook and cranny of this neighborhood, ranking them in terms of opportunities versus risk," Brandon explained, describing how the microplanning approach was applied. Factors determining risk included public housing, Section 8, market rate housing, and prevalence of gang and drug activities.

The plan provides guidance for much more than public housing. It envisions specific commercial and industrial development to occur over the next three to five years, along with rehabilitation of more than 200 houses. A total of $40 million (mainly from banks and other private sector sources) is available to be spent on a four-phase implementation effort through the year 2001. Phase 1, completed in 1997, focused on major commercial and industrial projects plus creation of new and rehabbed housing units. Phase 2 focused exclusively on housing, with 40 new and rehabbed units offered for sale or rent. In phase 3, historic housing will be made available for rent, and in phase 4, about 40 homes will be finished. MCC established a new resident-run property management and marketing company, Manchester Action Corporation, to oversee much of this development (MCC, 1994). The plan calls for a total of 233 homes to be offered for sale (123 new and 110 historic rehabs), 86 public housing units to be replaced, 21 rental units to be provided for senior citizens and the disabled, and 15 other rental units to be provided. So far, production of homes for sale is falling short of the plans, but the overall housing goals may still be achieved over a longer time. One possible reason for the delay is the cost and complexity of funding: As University of Pittsburgh Assistant Professor Sabina Dietrick said, "The costs average over $140,000 for both rental and for-sale housing. A variety of other public, private, and nonprofit financing were used to leverage the HOPE VI funds, demonstrating both the costs of building this type of housing and the extensive funding arrangements needed" (Dietrick and Ellis, 1999).

"The Manchester Community Plan represents a tremendous strategic shift in ideology for neighborhood development, especially in Manchester, a neighborhood that once saw over 900 of its historic homes demolished to make way for the 'suburban dream' in the city," a neighborhood newsletter (MCC, 1994) said. The structure of MCC itself coupled with frequent public meetings has ensured that residents were involved early in the planning and development process, and thus consensus was achieved and the "strategic shift" took place. The MCC is run by a Board that meets once a month and consists of a dozen lifelong area residents; MCC also holds community meetings five times a year. All MCC development proposals are approved by these neighborhood residents before proceeding. The results are dramatic. "Through the preservation and reuse of historic resources, as well as the construction of new homes that resemble existing ones, MCC retained Manchester's existing residents and returned self-sufficiency to the neighborhood" (MCC, 1994).

Much of MCC's effort is directed at dealing with a problem that is really the responsibility of local government. "Our biggest roadblock to revitalizing this area is acquisition: the difficulty of acquiring tax-delinquent properties," Brandon (in an interview with the author, 1996) said. Due to the many barriers to acquiring properties that have already gone into the government tax sale process, Brandon explained, "We take a proactive approach—we raise our own money and acquire them ourselves directly from the owners" before they are sold to recover back taxes. She added that often a "straw buyer" makes the purchase, since owners tend to raise the price if the buyer is a corporation. MCC also tries to utilize properties that are being offered through the government tax sale: A Treasurer's List is issued from which MCC and others can select properties that they would like to buy, but since Pittsburgh doesn't foreclose on tax-delinquent properties unless there is a buyer, the foreclosure process begins only after MCC's offer is made—thus, acquisition is slow. "We gave the URA a list of 18 properties two years ago, and so far we have acquired just two," she said, adding that waiting just gives the properties time to become even more dilapidated. MCC often ends up hiring contractors to "shore them up" before taking ownership, in order to keep them from falling down. MCC also hires young people to clean them up, board up the windows and pick up trash in the vicinity, services which are supposed to be provided by city departments. Apparently the city is not very helpful in many ways; asked about obtaining city assistance for some of this, Brandon simply laughed. Even tracking tax-delinquent properties falls to the neighborhood groups: For example, PCRG has taken on the job of identifying all tax-delinquent properties in need of rehabilitation.

Urban Redevelopment Authority (URA). The URA has worked with lenders to implement several innovative loan programs designed by PCRG. For example, the URA designed a reinvestment strategy that involves an interest rate subsidy and a home improvement loan/purchase program. A group of banks and savings and loans throughout Pittsburgh agreed to make home improvement loans to low and moderate income home buyers, originally at rates not to exceed 8% to buyers with annual household income less than $25,000 and 3% to borrowers with less that $13,750 annual income. The authority purchases loans with the proceeds from the sale of revenue bonds, and Community Development Block Grant (CDBG) funds. Originating lenders service the loans on behalf of the Authority for a small monthly fee. The principal and interest due on bonds are secured by the loan repayments of the borrowers and a lien on the property being improved. The bonds are further secured by the FHA, which will reimburse the mortgage holder, or bondholder for 90% of the loan amount in case of borrower default. The participating financial institutions agreed to buy back from the Authority loans that have been in default for 180 days at 90% of the value.

The Authority has also established grant programs to stimulate new construction of single family homes in moderate income neighborhoods designated as urban renewal areas. In conjunction with Equibank and several developers, it has established a market for new housing opportunities among low and moderate income families. The city pays the difference between the actual cost of the unit and the amount the buyer pays through a value established by the city and the bank. In the program's early years the average subsidy per unit was $13,000 (Marino, Rosser, & Rozran, 1979).

Pittsburgh Community Reinvestment Group (PCRG). The Pittsburgh Community Reinvestment Group is a nonprofit organization now composed of 27 CDCs and other community organizations representing about 50 low and moderate income neighborhoods. It was formed in 1988 by the Manchester Citizens Corporation (MCC), with staff assistance from the Pittsburgh History and Landmarks Foundation, to "work with financial institutions toward equal lending patterns and practices for all Pittsburgh residents and neighborhoods" (PCRG, 1995a), "streamline the revitalization process by promoting reinvestment in the city's poorer areas," (author's interview with Dowell, 1996) or, to put it more bluntly, "promote neighborhood reinvestment by financial institutions under the CRA" (PCRG, 1995b). The CRA gives groups like PCRG power to meet with bank executives regularly to discuss how these institutions can help meet community needs for credit and a wide variety of other issues. "PCRG presents its comments and concerns to the financial institutions in advance of the regulatory review process, when bank examinations are being performed by the FDIC, Federal Reserve Board, Office of the Comptroller of the Currency, or Office of Thrift Supervision" (PCRG, 1995b). PCRG writes up CRA agreements and forges partnerships with a dozen "very dedicated" banks to try to ensure that all the city's neighborhoods have equal access to banking services. The first CRA agreement was signed in 1988 with Integra Bank; since then, agreements to lend more than $2.4 billion for projects in inner city neighborhoods have been successfully negotiated by PCRG (PCRG, 1995a).

PCRG also compiles the Annual Lending Study, an in-depth report on lending activity (in the aggregate and for each of the 12 Pittsburgh banks that are members of PCRG) by income, race, neighborhood and loan types, using data provided in the Loan Application Registers which lenders must prepare and disclose in accordance with HMDA. The figures in the 1995 report (PCRG, 1995a) give compelling evidence of the success of the PCRG-bank partnerships: For example, in 1994 the banks approved 62.5% of the 898 applications received from African Americans, which is the highest rate in the study period of 1991–1994 and is up from just 37.1% in 1991. Loans on properties in African American neighborhoods amounted to $13,324,000 for 503 loans in 1994, which was a large increase over the 1991 amount of $7,013,000 for just 298 loans and was even an increase from 1993 figures, despite the fact that Pittsburgh's overall loan volume decreased from 1993–1994. Both loan volume and approval rates were also the highest in the four-year study period for low and moderate income neighborhoods. "Indicators suggest that Pittsburgh lenders are aggressively seeking business in markets which have been historically underserved: African American neighborhoods," the report states. However, there are still problems: For example, the loan approval rate for people making more than $30,000 per year was 58% for whites but just 42.6% for African Americans, and two out of the 12 banks have not made a single loan to an African American in Pittsburgh in the past two years.

Other services offered by PCRG include the Community Lender Credit program (a credit counseling service for low income people),[6] audits of the annual HMDA data reported by lenders, training in the CRA for bank employees, neighborhood tours, needs assessment, marketing, minority business development, establishing linkages between PCRG community employment projects, the development of loan programs (mortgages and other) for the city's poorer neighborhoods, advocacy for more appropriate federal lending criteria, publication of a Community Mortgage Comparison Chart that lists details of mortgage programs for low and moderate income people, support and recognition of lenders for good CRA compliance and reinvestment records (including letters of recommendation to federal authorities for regulated lending institution activities, and hosting an awards luncheon), and obtaining more than $1 million in grants for community reinvestment activities (PCRG, 1995a). "Most importantly, PCRG has raised the awareness of the needs and concerns of Pittsburgh's neighborhoods in the public and private sectors" (PCRG, 1995b).

Raising awareness jumped to the federal level in 1995. The emergence of a Republican-led Congress in 1995 led not only to "federal housing funds and community development grants being slashed" (Wilke, 1996) but also to efforts to weaken the CRA, which was soon listed by a Congressional Committee as the tenth most burdensome regulatory act in the nation. "Community based organizations around the country knew they would be in for a fight. . . . Leading the charge was PCRG" (PCRG, 1995c). An extensive campaign that included letter-writing, meetings with senators, a "Save CRA Town Meeting" in the City Council chambers that drew 400 people, and Congressional Testimony by Stanley Lowe, who said, "Without CRA, the 11,672 Pittsburgh residents who received loans in our neighborhoods in just the last four years would view affordable homeownership as nothing more than a dream," adding that the proposed anti-CRA legislation would set PCRG's efforts back 50 years (PCRG, 1995c). As a result of all this effort, legislation to gut CRA was not successful and regulatory reforms to ease the CRA's paperwork burden were approved.

The Lenders. The result of all this CRA-related activity has been a wide variety of loan programs offered by many lenders in partnership with the City, the URA, and others. The programs are generally universal—that is, they are available throughout the city—but different income levels and funding amounts apply in the Target Areas (referred to as Program Areas), which are neighborhoods in greater need of reinvestment than is the rest of town. For example, under the city-sponsored Pittsburgh Home Ownership Program, PNC Bank and nine others offer low interest, low down payment mortgages for existing and new homes, with maximum buyer incomes of $51,380 in the Target Areas and $42,200 in the Program Areas, and maximum house sales prices of $178,726 in the Target Areas and $146,230 in the Program Areas. It appears that this program is designed both to encourage middle income people to relocate in the Target Areas and to encourage less wealthy people to relocate in the Program Areas. Many lenders offer programs that include such features as mortgaging 100% of the rehabbed value of homes in need of renovation; favorable terms for first-time buyers; inclusion of all closing costs in the mortgage; credit counseling; grants for closing costs; acceptance of gift money to cover equity; and so forth. A number of innovative loan programs have also been developed by PCRG and implemented within Community Development Advisory Groups (CDAGs) formed as partnerships between the URA's Housing Department and the lenders (PCRG, 1995a). These are described in more detail in the section in this chapter, "Urban Redevelopment Authority (URA)." The Pittsburgh History and Landmarks Foundation even has entered the lending business, offering low interest short-term (one year or less) loans of $1,000 to $100,000 to nonprofit groups for restoration of historic buildings through its revolving Preservation Loan Fund (Pittsburgh History and Landmarks Foundation, 1996). The History and Landmarks Foundation has also partnered with Mellon Bank to fund a Comprehensive Neighborhood Development Initiative (CNDI), which provides loans for "a significant portion of the capital needed to enhance a community-based organization's ability to undertake a major project froom inception to completion . . . a comprehensive program that primarily will be used to fund entire neighborhood projects" (Pittsburgh History and Landmarks Foundation, 1995) in low and moderate income neighborhoods, including working with a bank team on preplanning, acquisition, and other matters involving technical expertise.

A Typical Nonprofit Developer: ACTION-Housing, Inc. ACTION-Housing is a nonprofit developer which has used HUD funds to develop may new low income rental units and rehabilitation existing ones in low income areas throughout the Pittsburgh region. Their record is impressive: creation or improvement of 24,274 housing units worth more than $205 million since 1957, including everything from emergency shelters to single family homes for sale. The agency has also helped revitalize 20 declining neighborhoods, and has been particularly active in Pittsburgh's Homewood-Brushton neighborhood. ACTION-Housing offers six major programs: special needs housing, home repairs and weatherization, mortgage assistance (which focuses on helping long-term unemployed homeowners to save their homes from foreclosure, and to deal with health, social, and economic problems), homeless assistance, public housing improvement (which also focuses on help with social and economic problems of residents) and family self-sufficiency (which involves one-on-one work with a case manager to help very low income single parent families get and keep housing, as well as reaching other goals.)

Executive Director Jonathan Zimmer has seen firsthand the problems of working with a large government agency. "The HUD subsidies are not always large enough to house the very poor, so foreclosures and evictions occur. One solution is to change the ownership to cooperatives, a solution that has already been done for two buildings. The Allegheny Housing Rehabilitation Corporation also bought three buildings from HUD, so they were saved," he said (in an interview with the author, 1996). In the late 1990s, ACTION-Housing got a HOPE III grant to acquire vacant property for homebuilding; they also have a Nehemiah grant from HUD to provide about 20 units of housing for homeless women and their children, among other activities. "It was very tough for us to do, we were general contractors for the first time," Zimmer (in an interview with the author, 1996) said.

A Typical CDC: The Bloomfield-Garfield Corporation. This area is divided into 4 wards (so presumably gaining a political voice is not easy). The Corporation was begun over 20 years ago by Father Leo Henry, who retired only recently. At the beginning the Corporation hired a part-time organizer from the IAF (Industrial Areas Foundation), who trained them every Saturday, in "Saul Alinsky style." The organizer's salary was paid from funds received from a membership drive. Then the Corporation studied the city budget and found CDBG funds; they applied and were given $35,000, which allowed them to hire developer Richard Swartz as executive director. He started rehabbing large buildings near the neighborhood's downtown edge, to stop the spread of decay from downtown into the area. The PPND (Pittsburgh Partnership for Neighborhood Development) began funding the corporation in 1985–1986 and is still a very important funding source, the other one being membership dues (which provide about two months' worth of operating costs each year). Until two years ago, when "we lost our line," state legislative grants were also an important source of funds, Bloomfield-Garfield Corporation Deputy Director Aggie Brose explained (in an interview with the author, 1996).

Father Henry appointed the first Board. Today, the Board is community controlled, since the members elect the board; usually about 400 votes are received. Businesses can also join; now about 50–60% of the area's businesses are members and Brose would like to see that figure rise.

The Corporation still spends much time and effort fighting for neighborhood resources. Its members have lobbied for better police protection, loan programs, and building code enforcement, and have "held institutions, elected officials and property owners accountable to the community at large" (Bloomfield-Garfield Corporation, 1996).

RESULTS

Evidence of Success in Bloomfield-Garfield

Since its inception, this CDC has been involved in more tha $12 million worth of housing and business development projects. It has successfully lobbied the city for creation of loan programs, helped attract more than two dozen new businesses to the area, helped 24 students complete a college preparatory program, supported after-school programs, held a business fair, helped create a neighborhood health center, and even organized a community foot race (Bloomfield-Garfield Corporation, 1996). The Corporation has now built or rehabbed over 150 single and multifamily units, attracted $9.5 million to Penn Avenue in investment, and obtained grants from the United Way, foundations, and banks to establish a youth development center which will act as an advocate for neighborhood youth, bringing funds for youth to this Census tract (for health care, jobs, recreation, and so on).

Coordination with other groups has also produced some good results. For example, Corporation officials attended the early meetings of PCRG to help make sure that lending institutions would make funds available in the area. PCRG and the Corporation work with the banks to overcome the most common problem loan applicants face: poor credit. Also, PNC (Pittsburgh Neighborhood Coalition) brought in paid consultants and created the Community Lender Credit program to help repair or reestablish credit for buyers. They have four full-time staff members funded by lending institutions, and also do lease-purchases with $1,000 down, escrowing $100/month for a year so the buyers can have time to fix their credit and also build up equity funds.

Use of the CRA has been another source of progress, such as the opening (through PCRG) of a full-service bank in the neighborhood, which had not had even a bank branch in years despite its resident population of around 13,000 people in 5,600 households (including 600 apartments, many occupied by the elderly). They have also used HMDA as a tool to obtain lending institution records. But these laws have prodded lending institutions into doing much more than opening banks. "It's so important for healthy communities to have Christmas lights, block parties, all the 'warm chatter' stuff," Brose said (in an interview with the author, 1996), adding that she writes numerous small grant proposals to facilitate this aspect of community life, and the banks usually fund them. For example, the Corporation got Dollar Bank to hire nine low-income teenagers on their summer payroll; PNC provides funds to send area children to summer camp. The bank also sponsors a day at the ballpark for area children, providing T-shirts, hats, and game tickets. "The CRA is our SPINE, it's the reason why PCRG (which is bank-funded) exists. It's a mandate. We tell the lending institutions, 'We'll be your eyes and ears to comply,' " Bruce said.

Evidence of Success Elsewhere

Pittsburgh now has many more assets than was the case in the 1960s, 1970s, and 1980s. The city has succeeded in attracting medical and high tech industries to at least partly replace the loss of jobs in the steel industry. Pittsburgh's poorer neighborhoods, although still suffering, are organized and actively trying to improve their neighborhoods' quality of life. The effort even shows in neighborhood physical appearance, which has improved spottily: In many areas, new or rehabbed buildings now are found next to properties still waiting for attention.

Most of the city's neighborhood funding has been spent on residential real estate development and renovation. Perhaps the best-known example can be found in the Hill District. The area's problems escalated when parts were cleared in the 1950s to make space for the city's Civic Arena, along with hoped-for nearby new development. But the new development did not happen for a long time. In 1990 the area's median income was still $7,000–11,000, and 47% of its residents had incomes below the poverty line (the neighborhood is nearly all African-American, and 41% of its residents are elderly). Now, thanks in part to PPND assistance, the lower part of the Hill District is the site of Crawford Square, a "showcase development" spearheaded by Elbert Hatley of the Hill District CDC. Completed in 1993, it includes over 300 housing units and plans call for the construction of 100 more; some are subsidized, while others are rented or sold at market rates. Although several Pittsburgh banks cooperated through PPND, 203 units were financed by PNC Bank alone (Lunt, 1993).

The Dorothy Day Apartments, which were designed and built for poor single parents and include child care and job training on site, were the result of a collaboration between a congregation, which owned an abandoned Catholic school site, and the city, which arranged more than $1.2 million in financing for the building's conversion (Barrett & Greene, 1993). The physical design also provides opportunities for interaction to develop among the residents, and this improves the project's safety. The Oakland and South Side areas have very active revitalization efforts; the Lincoln area is just starting (author's interviews with Dowell and Smith, 1996).

In the Oakland neighborhood, the local CDC approached a major national homebuilder headquartered in Pittsburgh, NVRyan L.P., about helping the group to provide housing on a vacant school site. The company agreed, giving a $3 million mortgage to the Oakland Planning and Development Corporation. The school district agreed to sell the property for $1 if one fourth of the new units would be reserved for low income residents. This was supplemented with a second mortgage of $100,000 from LISC, a $75,000 construction grant from the URA, $182,000 in loans from local sources through the Oakland Development Fund, a $2.7 million commitment from the URA to cover first mortgages for buyers, and a $200,000 grant from the Mellon Foundation to lower the purchase price of the units reserved for low income people. The site now holds 64 new townhomes and garden condominium units, and is generally considered an example of using complex financing to achieve success in mixed income housing provision (McKenna, 1988).

Nonresidential revitalization has not been forgotten. The state created its own Enterprise Zone program in 1983, long before the federal program was approved. Both East Liberty Development, Inc. and the North Side Civic Development Council, under contract with the URA, have received close to $1 million apiece from the state to implement enterprise zones in their neighborhoods. Additionally, the city earmarked several million dollars from its capital budget to establish a Neighborhood Business District Revitalization Program, which awarded grants to 16 business districts in its first year (Lurcott & Downing, 1987). Since then, 67 properties have been renovated, using $3.4 million in city loans plus $11.3 million in funds from the businesses involved. Other programs offer city matching funds to businesses wishing to upgrade their facades, and provide expertise to businesses with problems in bookkeeping, marketing, or security (Barrett & Greene, 1993).

A case in point is City Pride Bakery, which was conceived in the late 1980s by a group of recently unemployed bakers. Three years later, with the help of more than 100 people and 23 investors, the bakery opened. Financing was the key: $3.2 million in equity was raised, $5 million in loans was obtained, and $300,000 grant funds completed the package. The money came from the employees, individual investors, venture capital firms, the gas company, the Lawrenceville Development Authority ($500,000), local and national church groups ($400,000 in loans), the PPND (four banks pledged a line of credit and loans if $2.1 million in equity could be raised), and $1.5 million in subsidized loans from the state, the county, and the URA, plus loan guarantees from foundations and the bakers union. "This is the most complicated capital structure I've run across," said investor Luc Beaubien. "What this project tells us is that it doesn't have to be a big project to make an impact, and that we should seek out more small projects for our neighborhoods," added PPND chair and Pittsburgh National Bank Officer Ned Randall (Brokaw and Lahvic, 1992).

Another interesting case is the Homewood mini-mall. "Many of the lower Hill residents who were forced out moved to Homewood. Right after Martin Luther King was assassinated, riots and fires left the neighborhood badly scarred. Today the population is about 13,000, the majority of whom are African-Americans and have low incomes. Many businesses left after the riots," explained Lunt (1993). The revitalization effort is a model of partnership between residents and lenders: It was spearheaded by the Homewood-Brushton Revitalization and Development Corp., one of the five CDCs originally supported with PPND funds, and funded by PNC Bank and Mellon Bank. PNC Bank had a branch in the neighborhood, and its manager Marlene Bey is on the Homewood-Brushton Board.

> Mellon and PNC were approached about the mini-mall idea around 1989, according to Mellon CDC's Senior Vice-President Rick Savido. At first, the community group asked only for advice. "It's always good to get involved from day one and help steer them in the right direction," said Savido. PNC Bank, Mellon Bank, and the PPND helped the community group come up with a business plan. The two banks each provided half the financing for a buildout loan and a construction loan that came to a total of $250,000. The PPND provided a $35,000 predevelopment grant used to study architectural feasibility and $250,000 in loans at 3% interest. Another $362,000 was provided by the city's URA, while $500,000 (almost half of the total $1,361,900) was provided by the U.S. Department of Health and Human Services. The Rite-Aid drugstore chain has a long-term lease on more than half of the 14,180-square-foot space. In fact, its rent covers much of the debt service. "Rite-Aid has a track record of being able to make a location like this successful in inner cities," says Keith Crytzer, vice-president and manager of small business banking at PNC. One of the requirements of the federal grant is that the other storefronts must be rented to local entrepreneurs. (Lunt, 1993)

Another example of a PCRG-sponsored, PPND-funded success is the historic preservation-based renewal of the Allegheny West neighborhood, an area full of Victorian homes and tree-lined streets which was sliding toward low income but has become a mixed income, vibrant neighborhood as a result of the efforts of the neighborhood-based Allegheny West Civic Council (especially volunteer member Mark T. Fatla), CRA-based mortgage provision by Integra Bank (especially Vice President Donald Reed), and the PCRG. With PCRG guidance, Fatla and Reed negotiated a package for the neighborhood which provides funds for "community development mortgages" that do not have an income cap, as do many low income neighborhood lending programs. Not surprisingly, middle and high income people have begun to invest in the area. "People who live in low income areas because it's all they can afford tend to move out when they become successful and make more money. Allegheny West has found a way to keep the people who succeed. We're still a low to moderate income community, but we've always strived for a mix," Fatla said (Lunt, 1993).

All of these successes owe much to the residents' aggressive enforcement of the CRA. "The success of CRA agreements has led to over $2.4 billion in reinvestment initiatives in Pittsburgh" (PCRG, 1995c). One illustration of the impact of CRA-based negotiation is Integra Bank (now National City) CRA officers' commitment of $109 million in reinvestment funds. Another is the case of Mellon Bank, which in 1995 alone made nearly $239 million in mortgage loans to low and moderate income individuals in the five-state region served by the corporation, committed more than $9 million to equity financing for low and moderate income housing development by tax shelter partnerships, and invested $4.045 million in the Mellon Bank CDC. It also gave grants in the Pittsburgh area to ACTION-Housing for development of affordable housing, The Housing Solution for technical assistance provision, the Pittsburgh History and Landmarks Foundation for its Comprehensive Neighborhood Development Initiative, and PPND for its support of CDCs, as well as to a variety of health, human services, education, and arts projects (Mellon Bank Corporation, 1995).

Remaining Problems

Although the city has become a showcase for CRA-catalyzed partnerships, there is still a long way to go. As Lowe said, "There are 54 lending institutions in the Pittsburgh area. We now have an excellent relationship with 13 banks. We had no relationship with the banks before the CRA. We had to confront them all" (Lunt, 1993). Further, despite its impressive track record, there are some criticisms of Pittsburgh's financial partnership approach. CBOs that do not receive PPND funds have felt left out of the process, since the Neighborhood Fund which is available is not nearly as large as the PPND funding pool. Some participants felt that the program has shifted away from capacity-building and advocacy in favor of real estate and economic development, and residents have complained that some CBOs are ignoring the wishes of neighborhood residents as they become immersed in land development (Lurcott & Downing, 1987). As one PCRG staffer said, "the bricks-and-mortar orientation of PPND and the CDCs does not do much for Pittsburgh's critical need for job creation."

Perhaps this orientation is one reason why income and racial mixing have not occurred widely. For example, within the Bloomfield-Garfield CDC the Garfield side is still very low income and predominantly African American, while the Bloomfield side is mainly white and higher income; not surprisingly, revitalization is easier in the wealthier part of the CDC.

The main roadblock in Pittsburgh was seen by PCRG staff to be the need to build the capacity of community groups to locate funds, organize, lobby, and so on. Turnover in staff needs to be lowered, and they should be "professionalized" more. The community groups also need more resources and they need to do more strategic planning. It was felt that HUD could help with the resource issue as well as the other aspects of capacity building.

Another difficulty mentioned by PCRG staff is "merger mania," which threatens the good relationships now in place with lenders as they are taken over by larger outside banks. From March to November 1995 alone, Pittsburgh banks were involved in nine major mergers and acquisitions. One of these was especially challenging: In late 1995, Cleveland-based National City Corporation announced its intent to acquire Integra Bank, "PCRG's first and probably strongest financial institution partner. . . . By November PCRG, Integra Bank, and Pittsburgh Mayor Tom Murphy signed the largest CRA deal in the United States, for $1.67 billion. The terms of the agreement, dubbed 'The Partnership for the Future,' were accepted by National City Corporation." Yet the sheer number and size of mergers makes it ever more difficult for PCRG to influence the huge national lenders that are emerging.

Other areas of concern were the need for more foundation support and for more regional cooperation. One PCRG staff member said, "Foundations are not too helpful in Pittsburgh, although some do funnel money through PPND." Large-scale solutions are also hampered by the fact that in Pennsylvania cities have limited annexation power, thus making coordination difficult on regional needs such as providing transit to the airport.

Although CDC activists have encountered many remaining problems, the most severe of all is the inability to reuse tax-delinquent properties for years. Tax-delinquent property is an enormous problem; there are thousands of delinquent lots. The nonprofit organizations have formed a Vacant Property Working Group to deal with this issue; the VPWG developed a plan for about 100 tax-delinquent homes and is lobbying for changes in state laws (which govern treasurer's sales in "second class" cities), city policies (which appear to be causing much trouble), and prevention. The city has a program to transfer delinquent lots to adjacent owners for around $125. However, other types of reuse are difficult because there is no database, and all charges remain on the properties until they have already been through the treasurer's sale and been foreclosed (at which point all debts are wiped out). Regarding prevention, "the city doesn't have the staff to keep all these properties clean or even board them up. The Treasurer's Sale has become a joke because they'll put hundreds of parcels in with no intention of taking them unless they have a buyer," Brose said.

"If we put our name down to acquire a property, sometimes it wouldn't be done until five years later. By then it's a demo—I've got an empty lot. Times have changed, and the laws need to change. We're looking at both the state legislation and the city policies, because we found out that a lot of [the acquisition proposal] is policies. It lays on one desk for a month then another one. And there is a lot of service on these: Twelve kids may have inherited one house," Brose said (in an interview with the author, 1996).

It seems that support from the city is also lacking in other ways: For example, there are many code violations that are not pursued. "Community groups have to make these people that are PAID, accountable to do their job!" Brose said. The city's zoning has proved ineffective in limiting unwanted land uses: Rhonda Brandon (in an interview with the author, 1996) suggested the city help MCC develop covenants (deed restrictions) to "keep bar conversions out and low-income residents in."[7] Additionally, the city's operating budget crisis has been translated into less service for poor areas; for example, funds for building demolition in 1996 ran out four months before the end of the year. University of Pittsburgh visiting professor John Metzger, who was also the PCRG's first coordinator, summed up the problem as follows. "The Murphy administration is under increasing pressure to shift city funds away from neighborhood-based housing and community development and into new middle-class housing, high profile real estate and economic development projects, and public safety" (Metzger, 1995–96).

Aggie Brose summed up the effect on her CDC's revitalization efforts: "It all starts to roll back on you. You are pushing this boulder uphill and suddenly you lose six hands. I don't know who's running the show."

Prospects

Despite these problems, there is reason for optimism. The Housing Authority is now headed by former CDC director Stanley Lowe (who started MCC and PCRG), the URA is overseen by a former CDC director, and even the mayor used to run a CDC, so the political connections needed for strong support of grassroots neighborhood revitalization efforts are in place. The funding stream is also good: Both the URA and the PPND now channel city, lender, foundation, and CDBG funds to CDCs for operations and rehabilitation.

The state has helped with the issue of how to redevelop brownfields (which are prevalent in inner city areas) by passing legislation streamlining redevelopment and by assisting with finance. Redeveloping these abandoned contaminated sites had tied up public agencies and developers in red tape, trying to resolve issues of liability, level of cleanup, and so on. In 1995, the Pennsylvania legislature tackled the problem by establishing the Pennsylvania Land Recycling Program. The program sets clear standards for cleanup; releases lenders, owners, and developers from liability once the cleanup standards have been met; establishes a uniform environmental review process with schedules for final approval; and offers grants to localities for assessments, grants to those conducting cleanups, and technical assistance to interested developers. Results have been spectacular: 103 Pennsylvania sites were cleaned in the program's first two years (as opposed to just 10 sites in the previous 16 years), 200 more cleanups are being planned, and cleanups were underway in 51 of the state's 67 counties, including multimillion dollar projects in Pittsburgh and several other cities. The program was a 1997 $100,000 winner in the Innovations in American Government Program competition, sponsored by Harvard's Kennedy School of Government and the Ford Foundation.

A new ad hoc organization (the Vacant Property Working Group, or VPWG) was formed in 1996 to examine the problem of tax-delinquent properties and find ways to streamline acquisition and reuse. There are many leftover properties from urban renewal, as well as more recent abandonment, but not at the level of Cleveland or Detroit (author's interview with Dowell and Smith, 1996). Hopefully, the VPWG will be able to overcome some of the state and local institutional barriers to acquisition and redevelopment of these properties.

On the whole, Pittsburgh's efforts appear to be a model of community capacity-building. In view of the increased political power now vested in the hands of people with a strong interest in redevelopment, much-needed changes in state laws regarding brownfields, and the focus on tax-delinquent properties, the future of the city's low income neighborhoods appears bright indeed.

CONCLUSIONS

Obtaining lender participation is the cornerstone of low income neighborhood revitalization in Pittsburgh. Pittsburgh is "one of the most outstanding examples of developing the financial relationship portion of community development," according to National Community Reinvestment Coalition Executive Director John Taylor (Lunt, 1993). But although lender participation has been the hallmark of success in Pittsburgh, it was not voluntary: Threats of filing protests against proposed bank mergers, closures, and so on, under provisions of the CRA using data required by HMDA were the impetus used to bring banks (who are the only profitmaking businesses participating significantly in inner city neighborhood revitalization) to the negotiating table. The banks have risen to the challenge in several ways which are both unique and replicable, the most notable being the formation and funding of the PPND.

Asked why Pittsburgh has been so successful in using CRA when many other cities have not, PCRG staff member Myron Dowell (in an interview with the author, 1996) explained, "Stanley [Lowe] has been instrumental in building relationships with the banks—and they weren't adversarial. He's a great leader. It's been unique here. It takes hard work to keep the relationships good in view of mergers, etc. in the industry." Other positive factors are the long-term nature of the relationship with the banks, many of which have been involved from the beginning, and Pittsburgh's role as a regional banking center. Finally, the dedication of the bank CRA officers, along with CDC leaders such as Aggie Brose and Rhonda Brandon, were also important in achieving success.

Two recommendations stem from this accomplishment. First, both the active use of HMDA data by CBOs (via PCRG) as a tool to apply the provisions of the CRA and the development of the PPND by the banks can provide powerful models for the many communities in which the CRA is still an underutilized tool. Information about these Pittsburgh approaches should be widely disseminated to lenders, neighborhood planners, and community activists elsewhere, who should be encouraged to take steps to expedite their adoption in their own locales. Second, vigilance is needed to ensure that the federal HMDA/CRA legislation is not weakened. Neighborhood planners, community activists, and federal officials should make sure that these pieces of legislation are improved rather than gutted in future years.

Resident-based planning and implementation is essential. Both the number and strength of Pittsburgh's CDCs are notable, as is the degree to which they have achieved autonomy in neighborhood planning, project construction, and program operation. The path through which this seems to have occurred began with a charismatic leader, Stanley Lowe, organizing the neighborhood and coordinating multineighborhood efforts such as the formation of the PCRG, a watchdog umbrella group which is truly unique. The MCC provides a model worthy of imitation by CBOs elsewhere, including its record of changing missions and organizational structure with time, forging relationships with the banks and government agencies such as the URA, focusing on the neighborhood's unique assets (historic buildings) and working closely with other CBOs by forming the PCRG network.

The period after the initial organization is one in which serious problems are likely to occur due to the need for capacity-building: It is difficult to find interim funding for the years it takes to get thoroughly organized and truly involve the residents, which is the next step along the path to success. Again, Pittsburgh revitalization owes its success at least in part to the fact that both financing and technical support for these crucial early years of neighborhood empowerment and capacity-building have been made available. For example, a faith-based organization—the Archdiocese—provided assistance in the Bloomfield-Garfield CDC's early days, and the city's Neighborhood Fund helped many fledgling CBOs. Once the CDC stage was reached, corporate foundations, financial institutions, and other groups filled the gap by forming a unique coalition, PPND. This organization then served as a catalyst and distributor of additional funds and expertise.

Providing adequate city services and supportive city regulations is important. The area's partial record of success shows that resident-led initiatives and CRA-enforced participation alone are not enough: Government policies must also support, not undermine, central city revitalization efforts. Supportive policies in Pittsburgh were evident especially in funding CDCs; however, more attention was needed to code enforcement, property cleanup and stabilization, creating appropriate zoning that limits bars, and especially to changing city policies that make it difficult to reuse tax-delinquent property.

Reusing tax-delinquent properties must be legally feasible and make economic sense. All CDC staff members interviewed cited the inability to reuse these properties as their biggest barrier to neighborhood revitalization. Clearly, the city should reexamine its procedures and fees in this area to reduce the barriers to reuse of these properties. A comprehensive database is another important step in the reform process, followed by commitment of staff to maintain the properties until their resale. In addition to changing city policies, it seems that some changes in state law will be needed if Pittsburgh's poor neighborhoods are to be empowered to facilitate reuse of their numerous tax-delinquent properties.

The MCC planning effort is a good illustration of the need for lot-by-lot microplanning. Residents and planners collected data on a wide range of neighborhood characteristics on a lot-by-lot basis, then synthesized and evaluated them according to the risks and opportunities they posed. This detailed knowledge of the neighborhood was important in the neighborhood's revitalization.

A wholistic approach is very helpful. All major strands of the urban "web" that determines quality of life in a neighborhood must be addressed if successful revitalization is to occur. Some projects in Pittsburgh illustrate this fact. One example is the Dorothy Day Apartments, mentioned earlier in this chapter, which attempts to improve all four major contributors to quality of life: safety, services, shelter, and social support. This project also illustrates the fact that all major players involved in a neighborhood must be included if a project is to succeed: The apartments were built in response to the needs of area residents by a church congregation using an abandoned school and a mixture of private and city funding, and are managed by a nonprofit corporation (Barrett & Greene, 1993). Another example is the Hope VI Plus public housing effort being led by MCC, which provides a wide range of social services in addition to housing.

NOTES

1. The Community Reinvestment Act of 1977 requires all federally chartered and insured financial institutions to meet the credit needs of the communities from which they take their deposits. Enforcement occurs mainly when a bank applies for a branch closure, branch opening, or merger. Community groups such as the Pittsburgh Community Reinvestment Group (PCRG) can comment on the proposal in advance of the

regulatory review process, when CRA examinations are performed by one of the four institutions assigned this task (PCRG, 1995b).

2. The Pittsburgh History and Landmarks Foundation was founded in the 1960s by Ziegler and others. "Its biggest accomplishment to date has been Station Square, the 52-acre waterfront office and shopping development that rivals Boston's Quincy Market as a national success story. (The centerpiece is the abandoned 1901 Pittsburgh and Lake Erie railroad station, with its lavishly ornamental interior intact.) Ziegler had been outraged by the destruction of neighborhoods like Manchester . . . his philosophy had always been that restoring historic housing need not displace low- and middle-income residents" (Gratz, 1995). Richard M. Scaife's foundations have been a leading source of Landmarks' funds since the 1960s. "Since its creation, Landmarks has directly or indirectly reclaimed some 500 apartments" (Gratz, 1995) as well as converting a historic convent on the city's North Side area (also low income) to a popular bed and breakfast, turning a 19th century abandoned factory into a restaurant/brewery, and assisting with the development of a housing cooperative by/for homeless single mothers. MCC founder Stanley Lowe served as assistant to the president of Landmarks and director of its Preservation Fund in the early 1980s (Gratz, 1995).

3. Chartered by Congress in 1949, the National Trust for Historic Preservation is a nonprofit organization funded by foundation and corporate grants, dues from its 250,000 members, merchandise sales, and endowments. The Trust provides education, technical, and financial aid to nonprofit and public agencies involved with preservation efforts, including management of the National Main Street Center for preservation and enhancement of historic business districts, issuance of the Eleven Most Endangered Historic Properties list, assistance in formation and operation of historic districts such as Manchester, and maintenance of the National Register of Historic Places.

4. Several other foundations have since joined PPND.

5. Underwriting guidelines for FHA and VA loans have had a significant effect on mortgage lending patterns. These guidelines include fairly strict limitations on lending on structures in need of repair, on buyer qualifications, and on lending in declining, or even simply changing, neighborhoods. Although "conventional" (that is, non-FHA or VA) loans are not subject to these underwriting criteria, in reality many lenders utilize very similar criteria in approving these loans.

6. This service, the Community/Lender Credit Program (CLCP), is funded by the Fannie Mae Foundation and 16 banks and has a staff of three, including Executive Director Louise R. Craighead, who said, "For banks, this is an alternative to a flat 'no' on a mortgage application. They can give the applicant a pamphlet about this service, and say, 'I can't help you at this time, but maybe later.' PNC Bank's Marva Harris, who is president of CLCP, says the program is intended to increase the number of mortgage applications from low-income and minority communities that can meet banks' credit standards. 'Over the past few years we've learned that poor credit history and lack of preparation for the process of buying a home are two of the biggest obstacles to achieving mortgage approvals. We are trying to show people who fear they may not qualify for a mortgage that they can turn possible rejections into approvals.' " The CLCP counsels people on improving their credit ratings and on finding their way through the homebuying process (Lunt, 1993).

7. Bars were also a major concern of Stanley Lowe, who advocates cooperative efforts between preservationists and neighborhood residents to buy and close bars and has helped to put 21 of them out of business. Since many bars in the area were also havens for drug dealing and other illegal activities, he has made enemies as a result: While working to close several of them, his own home was even firebombed (Gratz, 1995).

CHAPTER 6

Cleveland
A Promising, Multifaceted Approach

ROOTS OF DECLINE

Perhaps nowhere was a city more adversely affected by the federal policies and programs (described in Chapter 1) that devastated America's central cities than was Cleveland. Its history is an extreme example of their unintended destructive effects.

Like many of America's northern cities, the roots of Cleveland's troubles reach back to the early 1900s, when ethnic neighborhoods began to be replaced by racially segregated ones. But it was not until mid-century that the devastation, still prevalent today, took hold.

By the early 1950s Cleveland stood at a crossroads. Due largely to the availability of suburban mortgages and lots thanks to the FHA/VA programs, the city's central business district and its neighborhoods were deteriorating, crime was worsening, and thousands of city residents were leaving for new homes in the suburbs. During these years the city's fate was determined, as implementation of urban renewal and the construction of interstate highways (which displaced a total of 19,000 Clevelanders by 1975) "dramatically and permanently changed the face of the city, causing significant losses of both income and property taxes" (Keating, Krumholz, & Perry, 1995). The city used eminent domain to buy property, clear and improve it for redevelopment, then sell it at a low price to developers, with the U.S. government paying two-thirds of the bill. Nearly ten square miles—6060 acres—were involved, all on the city's east side where the African Americans lived. It was the biggest urban clearance effort in the United States.

The clearance was pushed by the Cleveland Development Foundation, which was "created by that purpose by members of the corporate elite;" the city government did not have the resources to execute or manage such large scale renewal. But even with CDF involvement, the results were poor: Private development was only attracted to a scant 160 acres, in Erieview near the lake. As a result, in 1967 HUD Secretary Robert Weaver "took unprecedented action in denying any new renewal funds to Cleveland as the city's vast program ground to a halt." Banker and planning commission member Tom Westropp said, "With respect to housing, the urban renewal program has been a disaster. I wish I could believe that all of this was accidental and brought about by the inefficiency of well-meaning people—but I just can't. The truth, it seems to me, is that it was planned that way." Part of the reason may have been the desire of President Lyndon Johnson to get Carl Stokes elected mayor, coupled with the business community's desire to get rid of Mayor Ralph Locher; their wishes came true when Stokes was elected in 1967, becoming America's first big-city black mayor (Keating, Krumholz, & Perry, 1995).

The displaced people went to the Hough, Mt. Pleasant, Glenview, and upper Central neighborhoods. Hough (an area roughly bounded by Superior and Euclid avenues and by East 55th and East 105th streets) got the greatest influx. Originally the home of the city's elite, in the 1940s Hough was solidly middle class. By 1950 it was becoming working class, and the mansions that lined Euclid Avenue began to be split into smaller apartment units, but still the neighborhood had 66,000 residents. Then the wave of displaced blacks arrived; between 1950 and 1960 the neighborhood changed from 95% European-American to 74% African-American (by contrast, the same Census showed that only 6.9% of the Cleveland urbanized area was African-American), and the neighborhood's population rose to 82,000 by mid-decade (Keating, Krumholz, & Star, 1996). "The most notorious [part of the city] . . . was the Hough neighborhood in the northeastern section of the city's East Side black community." As displaced people moved in, "Building code and sanitary violations became an accepted standard." Overcrowding, vandalism, and arson became prevalent, and tension grew. By 1964 one fourth of the city's welfare cases lived in Hough. The same year, residents picketed the Board of Education to protest the quality of the local schools, which were underfunded and running double half-day sessions. Whites then marched into black neighborhoods and overturned cars, broke windows, and beat people; blacks followed with sit-ins at schools. A barroom argument between a white bartender and a black customer led to four days of riots in Hough in 1966, leaving four blacks dead after 1,700 National Guard troops were called in (Keating, Krumholz, & Star, 1996). Stokes's 1969 reelection could not stem the tide of frustration and despair: In July 1968 riots broke out in nearby Glenville and there was a gun battle between black activists and police, known as the "Glenville shootout," in which three police officers and six others were killed (Keating, Krumholz, & Perry, 1995).

After the riots, civil rights laws were passed which began to open the suburbs to middle and upper class blacks. Over time those who could move out did, leaving the poor, the elderly homeowners, and the disabled behind in the riot-torn central city neighborhoods. The 1970s and 1980s also saw the globalization of industry and cutbacks in federal aid to cities, both of which hit Cleveland hard. By the mid-1970s Cleveland was in shambles: Businesses closed, schools declined, the landmark Playhouse Square theaters closed, downtown was dead, and even the Cuyahoga River caught fire. The city became known as "the mistake on the lake." The final blow occurred on December 14, 1978, when Cleveland became the first American city since the Depression to go bankrupt (Keating, Krumholz, & Perry, 1995).

Banking was dominated by a few institutions and was the most influential element in the area economy. As the massive job and population losses took a toll on city property and income tax revenues, city officials twice tried to raise revenues by asking the voters for an income tax increase but were turned down. Eventually, bond funds had to be tapped to cover operating expenses. These less-than-sound financing methods led the banks, which had already redlined much of the city, to extend this policy to city hall itself: They refused to finance the city's debt from May 1978 on, and when the city could not repay $14 million in short-term notes that was due on December 14, 1978, the banks again refused to refinance and the city went into default. Ironically, during the same time period banks diverted deposits from city residents, businesses, and even the city government itself to make high-interest loans in the suburbs. This was probably an effort to obtain higher rates of return so as to be able to pay the high interest that depositors expected during those years, but despite this financial justification, the practice was viewed as unethical by many—and with the passage of the Community Reinvestment Act, it became illegal as well. In 1981, community organizations challenged Cleveland Trust's application for mergers under the CRA, claiming that between 1977 and 1979 the bank pulled $156 million out of Cleveland and invested it elsewhere—for example, the bank loaned $40 million to a non-union steel mill in the South (Keating, Krumholz, & Perry, 1995).

Meanwhile, George Voinovich (who was mayor from 1979–1989 and did much to reverse the city's financial difficulties) offered heavy tax abatements to developers downtown, and advertised Cleveland as "the Comeback City." For example, Voinovich gave $250 million in city funds to two big bank office complexes on Public Square (AmeriTrust Center and Society Center offices), then used TIF on Tower City (a shopping complex on the same square) to get $42 million in tax revenues to build the Rock 'n' Roll Hall of Fame—a move that severely hurt the already strapped public schools, since the TIF diverted property tax revenues that normally would be available for school use (Keating, Krumholz, & Perry, 1995).

In short, largely as a result of federal policies (highway building, FHA/VA mortgage programs, urban renewal, antidiscrimination laws, failure to stop leakage of manufacturing jobs overseas, cuts in federal aid to cities—

Cleveland's CDBG funds dropped from $39.3 million in 1980–1981 to $22.9 million in 1988–1989 (Cleveland Department of Community Development, 1993)—and related policies discussed in Chapter 1, the city suffered huge job and population losses from 1950–1990. Local policies supported the trend: There was a lack of regional planning, virtually no suburban growth controls, alienation between some mayors and the urban business community, and funneling of city funds to downtown projects. New homes in the suburbs were available to all those who could afford them, and not surprisingly, soon only the poorest blacks remained in Hough. From 1967–1987, median home sales prices had fallen by 50–75% in Cleveland's inner city neighborhoods. By 1990, 70% of the housing stock was gone and the neighborhood was home to just 20,000 people, 75% of whom had incomes below the federal poverty line and 98% of whom were African-American (Keating, Krumholz, & Star, 1996). One longtime resident described the scene in the heart of Hough vividly when he said, "Ninety percent of the properties were vacant—you could ride wild horses through here!" (Quoted by Sweeney in interview with the author, 1996).

The results are illustrated clearly by Census data. In 1950, the city had 914,808 residents, but nearly 39,000 had left by 1960 (population 876,050). The trend escalated over the next decade as more than 110,000 people left town; the 1970 population was just 750,879. After that the pace of the exodus quickened, approaching 20,000 a year between 1970 and 1980; by the end of the decade the city had just 573,822 residents. From 1980 to 1990 the losses continued, reaching 505,616 in 1990, albeit at a much slower pace that was tempered by immigration of Asians, Latinos, and Poles. Thus, from 1950 to 1990 the city lost nearly 45% of its people. During that time the city's racial composition also changed; the 1990 Census showed that the city population was 49.6% European-American, 46.7% African-American, 2.7% "Other," and 1% Asian; 4.6% of the total population also considered themselves Hispanic.

During the same time period, suburban Cleveland experienced a population boom. In 1950, the SMSA population residing outside the city itself was 550,703; over the next ten years it nearly doubled to 920,545, gaining an incredible 36,980 people every year during that decade. 1970 figures showed that the suburban population had grown at an even faster pace, adding nearly 400,000 people over the previous decade (the 1970 suburban population was 1,312,850). These gains were more than enough to balance the city's losses; from 1950 to 1970 the SMSA/PMSA overall population grew (from 1,465,511 in 1950 to 1,796,595 in 1960 to 2,063,729 in 1970), as did that of surrounding Cuyahoga County (from 1,389,532 in 1950 to 1,647,895 in 1960 and 1,720,835 in 1970). But as the city population losses escalated over the next decade, suburban growth slowed and both the PMSA and the county population followed suit; in fact, the county actually lost nearly 40,000 more people than did Cleveland itself, losing more than 220,000 people from its

1970 peak to reach 1,498,400 by 1980. During this decade only the outlying suburban Lake, Medina, and Geauga counties experienced population growth; this growth made the overall PMSA population decline to a 1980 population of 1,898,825—a less severe decline than in the city and Cuyahoga county. Finally, from 1980–1990 it appeared that the area's population losses were slowing down: The PMSA losses paralleled those of the city, while the county lost 20,000 more people than did the city and the outlying counties experienced moderate growth (U.S. Bureau of the Census, 1950, 1960, 1970, 1980, 1990). See Table 6.

It appears that the city's loss of residents and the suburbs' exponential growth occurred in response to massive losses of city jobs and even larger job growth in the suburbs: From 1958 to 1977 Cleveland lost 130,000 jobs, while the suburbs gained 210,000. The economy also changed dramatically from manufacturing to service: For example, from 1970–1985 the Cleveland metropolitan area lost 86,000 manufacturing jobs but gained nearly 77,000 jobs in service industries (Keating, Krumholz, & Perry, 1995). This shift, which took place quite dramatically mainly from 1977–1983, hurt working class areas like Hough especially hard.

Not surprisingly, the exodus took a heavy toll on the local housing stock. From 1970–1990 the city actually lost 40,000 housing units, but its loss of 245,000 people makes it clear that vacancy rates must also have risen substantially. Meanwhile, the suburban PMSA gained 122,000 units over the same time period but gained less than 13,000 people, so clearly more than enough new homes were provided in the suburbs to accommodate the urban refugees. But the housing picture is more complex than those figures indicate because 67,000 of the new suburban units were built in Cuyahoga County outside the city of Cleveland—an area that had a net loss of 65,000 people

Table 6: Population Change in Cleveland Area, 1950 through 1990

	City of Cleveland	Cuyahoga County	Cleveland/ Akron/Loraine SMSA*	SMSA Area Outside Cleveland	Cleveland PMSA**
1950	914,808	1,389,532	1,465,511	550,703	1,383,599
1960	876,050	1,647,895	1,796,595	920,545	1,783,436
1970	750,879	1,720,835	2,063,729	1,312,850	1,959,880
1980	573,822	1,498,400	2,834,062	2,260,240	1,898,825
1990	505,616	1,412,140	2,759,823	2,254,207	1,831,122

Source: U.S. Bureau of the Census, 1950–1990
*Standard Metropolitan Statistical Area
**Primary Metropolitan Statistical Area

during the same time period. (The remaining 55,000 new suburban units were built in the three outlying counties, which added 76,000 people. Clearly, overcrowding of units was not a problem in those counties.) Thus overall, Cuyahoga County (including the city of Cleveland) lost 310,000 people (which equates to about 97,000 vacated units) and gained 27,000 more housing units. This equates to some 127,000 vacant housing units, which is more than one-fifth of the county's housing stock. As vacancy rates climbed, prices fell and people moved out of the worst quality housing in disproportionate numbers. Not surprisingly, by 1987, houses in the city's worst neighborhoods was worth less than $20,000 each—one-half to two-thirds of the "real sales value" in 1967. Most of this loss in value occurred during just four years, 1978–1982 (Keating, Krumholz, & Perry, 1995).

The result was massive central city property abandonment: By the early 1970s there were some 35,000 properties in Cuyahoga County on which $87 million was owed by the landowners in back taxes, penalties, interest, and fees. Approximately 16,000 of these vacant delinquent parcels were in the city, with $40 million owed on them. So in the late 1970s the state passed legislation enabling cities to establish a Land Reutilization Authority (LRA) and the city passed an ordinance to activate it, establishing the Cleveland Land Bank.[1] But the program got off to a slow start partly because the city really did not yet want to acquire large amounts of inner city land, but mainly because two lawsuits were filed that stopped the foreclosure process on 15,000 parcels for two years, and there were difficulties with the enabling legislation. For example, one provision called for continued accrual of taxes, penalties, and interest on the county's books even after the city took ownership, which created trouble for the county's bond rating, as over $4 million in unpaid debt owed to the county by the city built up. Neither the city nor other buyers actually paid these as they were waived later in the process, but the effect "on paper" was devastating. Another provision automatically reverted unsold parcels to their original owners after 15 years, so the foreclosure process had to be completed again if the government wanted to regain title (author's interviews with McNamara, Sidoti, & Sweeney, 1996).

SIGNS OF CHANGE

Action on TOADS

Local officials realized there was almost no chance of getting most of the tax money back, since the byzantine state law made reuse difficult. So, in the mid–1980s city officials met with the county prosecutor's office to try to develop a plan for reducing the problem. In response, HB603 was passed in 1988 by the state legislature. It changed the offending provisions so that now, the city (or whoever takes title) must pay the actual foreclosure costs—title, appraisal, deed fees, and so on—but all taxes, interest charges, and penalties are removed. The bill also streamlined procedures; for example, it reduced the minimum foreclosure time from 5–9 years to 9–12 months, although the foreclosure process can still take up to 2 years. Also, the bill reformed the LRA—commonly known as Land Bank—procedures to make city acquisition easier. Now the county must send the city a list of properties that are being foreclosed, and the city must return an affidavit showing each one as either "nonproductive" (for vacant land not desired by the city), on the "wish list" (vacant properties, with or without structures, that the city would like to acquire), or "other" (for occupied homes or businesses). For the "wish list" properties, the affidavit serves as the city's bid and the city will receive title if no higher bid is received (author's interviews with McNamara, Sidoti, & Sweeney, 1996).

After the sale, unsold properties are forfeited to the state and then go to an annual auditor's sale. A list of properties is also sent to the city before this sale, at which time the city has a chance to bid on the "other" parcels—many of which are now vacant, as it often takes several years for an unsold property to move from the county sale to the auditor's one. Here, the selection can be wide—for example, in 1996, 240 properties in Cleveland were offered—and the price can be as low as $10. This sale can create problems because speculators pick up properties, then lose them again for nonpayment of back taxes a few years later (author's interviews with McNamara, Sidoti, & Sweeney, 1996).

The city also holds events such as Amnesty Week, a week in which owners can give their property to the city and all debt is forgiven. More than 200 calls were received during this week in 1996 (author's interviews with McNamara, Sidoti, & Sweeney, 1996).

Once a property enters the land bank, the Government Action on Urban Land (GAUL) program is applicable (Greenberg & Popper, 1994). Under this program, which was established by the Cuyahoga County Treasurer's Office, a developer or other buyer may acquire a land bank property for $100; however, this does not really reflect the site cost, as buyers often face $1,400–1,500 in excavation costs to remove the remnants of homes, contaminated soil, and so on. Also, most city lots are 35x120 (and appraise at $1,200–1,400), or 4,200 square feet; but under current zoning regulations 4,800 square feet are needed in order to build, so two lots must be acquired. To deal with these issues as well as problems of poor parcel size, shape, or location, any lot can be sold to adjacent landowners for $1, and unbuildable lots with under 40 feet of frontage can also be sold to anyone for $1. This program has resulted in an increased stock of affordable housing being provided by developers (Greenberg & Popper, 1994). Dates for the beginning and end of residential construction are included in the deed itself, along with a provision that the developer must pay taxes for five years. If default on these conditions occurs, the city can easily take back title (author's interviews with McNamara, Sidoti, & Sweeney, 1996).

The revised law places importance on city planning as part of the TOADS reuse process. The city is authorized to study, analyze, and evaluate potential, present, and future uses for such land and to plan or dispose of vacant land as it deems appropriate to fulfill purposes of its land revitalization program. This provision has produced two important policies. First, some lots are kept by the city for later assembly into large tracts that can be offered to developers in accordance with the plans. Second, any proposed use of the lots must be in accordance with a detailed plan prepared by city neighborhood planners who are assigned to specific parts of the city, in conjunction with neighborhood residents and CDCs. The city plan has been updated, and serves as a guide for city land purchases and cooperation with lenders and developers. A "microplanning" approach is used, with planners assigned to each neighborhood who "learn all about them, lot by lot." The "wish list" (described previously in this section) is developed from these plans. "It's a proactive approach," Nora McNamara, who works on developing neighborhood plans using land bank properties, said.

Unlike many other cities with large numbers of TOADS, Cleveland also maintains the properties it acquires (all of which are vacant), despite the cost of $700–800 per lot on a 1999 inventory of around 4,000 lots. Use of these lots as community gardens is encouraged, as this cuts down on the city's maintenance costs. Under the CDBG-funded community gardens program the city provides seeds, fertilizer, rototillers, and so on, for use on vacant city-owned lots, while another CDBG-funded program hires low income residents to clean up other vacant lots. The city even goes so far as to maintain privately owned lots too, which puts them in the position of being liable without having title. Asked why the city would take such a risk, Mike Sweeney (Director, Delinquent Tax Department, office of the County Treasurer) said, "Otherwise people would complain!" This responsive, risk-taking, can-do attitude appears to be a unique attribute of those few cities that have achieved some measure of successful low-income neighborhood revitalization (author's interviews with McNamara, Sidoti, & Sweeney, 1996).

Other City Support

There are many other related programs that help make Hough and other poor Cleveland neighborhoods more attractive. Substandard homes can be bought and fixed through Afford-a-Home, a program in which first time buyers can put just 3% down for first bank mortgages with low interest rates as well as deferred, interest-free second mortgages, with funding provided by $1 million from CDBG allocations. The Paint Refund program gives refunds from a $500,000 CDBG allocation to low income owners or tenants who paint their homes. The Housing Emergency Loan Program (HELP) offers 0% deferred loans and grants to low income owner-occupants for home improvements. Repair-a-Home gives 3% loans (with a term of 15 years for loans under $10,000, 30 years for larger ones) for fixing code violations. Under the city-sponsored Home Weatherization program, free weatherization grants from U.S.DOE and HHS (U.S. Department of Energy and Department of Health and Human Services) are available for low income households. The Store-front Renovation program utilizes CDBG funds to provide both low interest loans and rebates to store owners who improve the facades of their properties. Cleveland Action to Support Housing (CASH), a partnership between the city and 13 local lenders, makes mortgage loans for new homes at low interest rates, with even lower interest loans to owners for housing rehabilitation. The low interest results from depositing CDBG funds in the banks that give the loans.

The city has also contracted with nonprofit organizations to redevelop properties, applied for HOPE and HOME funds, and perhaps most importantly, used CDBG funds as the main source of city investment in low income neighborhoods. CDBG allocations have provided infrastructure, services, and rehabilitation; unlike in most other large cities, CDBG grants are the largest funder of Cleveland's 33 CDCs and other related resident groups. It is interesting that major city investment of CDBG funds came before the banks were willing to invest in these communities; for example, from 1982–1987 the city allocated almost $9 million to support the city's nonprofit housing providers (Keating, Krumholz, & Metzger, 1991).

City-Supported Resident Efforts. Much of this city CDBG grant support for CDCs flows through the Cleveland Housing Network (CHN), an umbrella organization of more than a dozen neighborhood CDCs, formed in 1981, that is largely funded by the city. It could be viewed as the CDCs' "general partner" or production arm, providing administration, legal assistance, and organizational capital. CHN was formed mainly to expand the Famicos program (described later in this section), so its traditional focus has been on rehabilitation and lease-purchase of existing housing, but recently CHN is branching out into new construction (Kate Monter, 1996).

From 1988–1991 the city dedicated $4.7 million more CDBG dollars to the CDCs, and another $1.75 million to the Cleveland Housing Trust Fund (HTF). In 1993 alone HTF provided $4.4 million to local CDCs to build 720 housing units—half for new construction and the rest for rehab. Total CDBG allocations to the neighborhoods from 1993–1996 topped $8.2 million, with another $18.5 million given by the city to the HTF from 1994–1996 (Yin, 1998). Some of these funds were used to subsidize moderate income housing; for example, one study of city-subsidized projects built between 1990 and 1992 showed a median sales price of $105,000 and an average local government subsidy of $27,000 (Simon & Sharkey, 1997). This emphasis on subsidizing higher-priced homes illustrates a longstanding conflict between the city and NPI (Neighborhood Progress, Inc.—a major provider of funds and expertise to the city's CDCs, founded by the Cleveland Foundation, Enterprise Foundation, and LISC) on one side, and the CDCs on the other. The city and NPI have pushed the CDCs to consolidate, operate with more attention to efficiency, and provide housing for people with a mix of incomes, in hopes of raising area real estate values; the CDCs have emphasized neighborhood resident control over consolidation/efficiency, and provision of housing for the area's existing low income residents (Yin, 1998).

Community development corporations affiliated with CHN have also contributed to the revitalization of many urban neighborhoods in Cleveland using federal tax credits for provision of low income housing and HUD Section 8 rental assistance funds to promote low income home ownership through a lease-purchase program. Many of the homes are abandoned units, now owned by the city, that are purchased through the Cleveland land bank. Federal tax credits are now the "primary vehicle" for housing development; they provide the incentive for corporate investors to become limited partners in CHN projects (author's interview with Monter, 1996).

This widespread use of the low income tax credit can be traced back to the Famicos Foundation, an organization that has its roots in Hough during the post-riot years. Started by Sister Henrietta in 1970 as a vehicle to foster homeownership, Famicos became well known for its innovative sweat equity housing rehabilitation lease-purchase program developed by its first director, retired chemical engineer Bob Wolf. After the program was replicated by several other neighborhood groups, Wolf helped form CHN to share resources and expertise, including information on the lease-purchase program. With the help of British Petroleum, LISC, and the Cleveland Enterprise Foundations, CHN "used the Famicos model as the basis for the low-income housing tax credit" (Keating, Krumholz, & Star, 1996). The credit attracted nearly $4 million in corporate investment in rehabbing more than 400 Cleveland housing units between 1986 and 1989 (Yin, 1998).

Much of Cleveland's progress can also be attributed to Chris Warren, who is generally viewed as a prime mover behind Cleveland's success. He had 20 years of experience working with the CDCs, including CHN before serving as the city's community development director, and later as its economic development director. He used the CRA to negotiate contracts with lenders; now there are more than half a dozen of them in place. The role of mayoral support can be seen here too, where a "compensating balance" program has been developed: The city has agreed to deposit government funds in a bank under CRA scrutiny in exchange for low-interest loans being given by that bank to a targeted low income area. Before CRA agreements were completed, Mayor Voinovich, who was very supportive, held press conferences on the bank steps to dramatize lender noncompliance with the CRA. Bank reports are still closely monitored by the city.[2] Voinovich later became Governor, but his successor Michael White is also supportive of these programs, as are the city council and the public (author's interviews with Monter, McNamara, Sidoti, & Sweeney, 1996).

RESULTS

Evidence of Success

The results of the Land Bank program were dramatic. By 1993 the 16,000-lot inventory had dropped to 4,340, and it has hovered around that number ever since. In 1993 a record 403 parcels were sold from the land bank inventory, of which 101 were used for new homes, 276 for yard expansion, and 26 for parking lots. Also, there were 135 gifts of parcels in lieu of foreclosure. Two hundred and three lots were used as community gardens, with the help of $50,000 in CDBG funds. The construction value of structures built on sold land bank lots reached $19.5 million, and real estate taxes paid totaled $45,206. Abandoned home purchases totaled 108 (38 by individuals, 32 by nonprofits, 27 by companies, and 11 taken by the city). A total of 500 lots were sold from the inventory in 1994, which caused the inventory to fall to around 4,000 lots by April. In 1995, 453 were sold for new construction of homes, yard expansion and parking lots. The Land Bank program saw 483 parcels acquired; 4,200 parcels remained at year's end (unpublished material and interviews with McNamara, Sidati, & Sweeney, 1996).

In 1993, tax abatements for 10–15 years were granted to buyers of 118 new homes and developers of 196 rehabbed units; the total was nearly double that of 1992. The city also hired 140 low income people to clear 2,891 vacant lots and do related jobs. CDBG funds totalling $355,311 were used for renovation of 118 storefronts in 40 buildings, creating 396 temporary construction jobs and $1,523,308 in private investment (Cleveland Department of Community Development, 1993); in 1995, the Storefront Renovation program allowed 81 businesses to invest $3,763,000 in renovation and the city gave rebates of $1,458,934—the biggest amount in the program's 13-year history (City of Cleveland, 1995). One hundred twenty-two substandard homes were bought and fixed through Afford-a-Home; 2,643 dwelling units were painted under the Paint Refund program; HELP gave $5,003,727 for home improvement—half deferred loans and half grants—to 614 low income owner-occupants; Repair-a-Home gave to fix 98 units at a total cost of $3,356,156. Free weatherization grants from U.S.DOE and HHS were given to 1,309 low income households. CASH made $3,075,090 in mortgage loans for 35 new homes (28 more are in process) and processed $1,036,539 in 4.5–5.5% loans to 64 owners to fix 148 dwelling units; more than 100 applications were in process at the end of 1995. CDBG funds rose from a low of

$22.9 million in 1988–1989 to $30.3 million in 1993–1994 (Cleveland Department of Community Development, 1993). Not surprisingly, in 1993 the city won its fifth All America City award from the National Civic League.

The city's GAUL program was selected as one of 25 semifinalists out of 1,600 applicants in the 1992 Innovations in State and Local Government competition held by Harvard's Kennedy School of Government in cooperation with the Ford Foundation. Each semifinalist was awarded a $20,000 prize. In 1993 the city applied again and this time was selected as one of ten finalists, receiving $100,000. They then held a "mini-innovations" contest and gave three grants of $10,000 each to the neighborhoods, as well as buying equipment (for example, computers for CHN) (author's interviews with McNamara, Sidoti, & Sweeney, 1996).

CHN's member CDCs have amassed an impressive track record, having acquired and rehabbed nearly 1,000 houses through CHN's lease purchase and rental programs. The program targets families with a median income below 35% of the area median income; the program's "typical" participant is a single African-American mother with 2–3 children and an income of less than $8,000 annually. Lease purchase payments average just $200 per month, which is less than half the average rent in Cleveland. Besides coordinating more than 100 home renovations and purchases each year, CHN has a Family Development Program in which a trained "coach" works with a family over a period of years to help them gain the skills needed to retain ownership. This effort can include everything from helping a family member obtain a GED to counseling in budgeting skills. In sum, CHN has "created an opportunity of homeownership for a group of people [very low income families] who are totally underserved by America's housing finance system" (Cleveland Housing Network, Inc., 1996).

Cleveland is different from most other U.S. cities in that the city negotiated CRA agreements—usually, community groups do this. By the end of 1995, CRA agreements rose to $1.28 billion, "the best track record in the nation" (Schwartz, 1995). The agreements helped to spur several new developments; "What started as a phenomenon at the beginning of the decade became a commonplace reality in 1995 with 300 new homes built and 100 new housing starts" in the city. For example, Cleveland's 200th birthday saw the construction of Bicentennial Village in the Fairfax area. This development includes 33 market-rate homes ($96,400–128,500), 16 Habitat homes, and rehabilitation of 200 homes as well as storefronts, landscaping, and streetscapes. The rebuilding involved the Housing Trust Fund, Paint Refund, Storefront Renovation, and Land Bank programs; key players were the city, Habitat for Humanity, NPI (Neighborhood Progress, Inc.) and Fairfax Renaissance Development Corporation. Groundbreaking for the $30 million Mill Creek development is another example: With 217 homes, this project in the Warner-Turney neighborhood is the biggest subdivision built in the city in

50 years. On 58 acres next to Cleveland Metroparks, the development includes hiking trails, bike paths, and a 45-foot waterfall. In the early 1990s, homes cost $119,900 to $168,800. The city contributed $1.4 million for site preparation (City of Cleveland, 1995).

In Hough, a $1.2 million grant given to the city from HUD in 1995 provided 0% second mortgages for buyers of 60 Beacon Place townhomes and 32 single family homes on East 84th Street between Euclid and Chester, next to (and designed to complement) the $13 million retail development Shops at Church Square, which opened in 1993 and is the first mixed-use residential/commercial development in a Cleveland neighborhood. This was also the first full year of assigning housing inspectors to neighborhood beats so they could take the offensive instead of simply responding to complaints, doing street by street surveys to develop a roster of the worst offenders. In August 1995, the city signed a memo of understanding with HUD for a Supplemental Empowerment Zone, obtaining $90 million in grants and $87 million in Section 108 loans to set up loan programs for real estate, machinery, equipment, acquisition, and development; the first six loans totalled nearly $10 million. The Empowerment Zone includes several neighborhoods: the Glenville Development Corporation, Fairfax Renaissance Development Corporation, Hough Area Partners in Progress, and Midtown Corridor signed contracts for commercial and industrial projects to create jobs in the Empowerment Zone. Overall, in 1995 the city invested $23.3 million in its neighborhoods and $5.2 million in downtown to encourage economic development (City of Cleveland, 1995). Perhaps the best example of CHN's success is found in the Broadway Housing neighborhood, where in the 1980s a home could not be sold for $35,000–40,000 but by the late 1990s homes were selling for $70,000–80,000.

The Hough area provides many other good examples of the kind of revitalization taking place. In particular, Central Commons is an interesting case. A consortium of foundations formed Neighborhood Progress, Inc., then formed the New Village Corporation as a development arm which offered low-cost financing to buyers. Neotraditional architect Andres Duany was brought in for consultation, and gave suggestions. The lots were placed in the land bank and now a number of entities, including Habitat for Humanity, have developed homes on these lots. The Cuyahoga Metropolitan Housing Authority (a separate agency from the city or county) is redoing the Commons area's public housing to incorporate much better design. The new housing looks like single family dwellings whereas the old housing looked like apartment buildings. In 1997, the commons area was designated as one of six prototype Homeownership Zones, making it eligible for millions of dollars in federal grants and loans.

The Lexington complex is another interesting example. Spearheaded by Hough Area Partners in Progress (HAPP—a community group formed in

1981 to revive the neighborhood) and aided by the Famicos Foundation, the first phase of Lexington Village consisted of 277 rental units for low and moderate income residents and was finished in 1987. LISC and the lenders later gave low-interest loans, supplemented by two federal UDAG grants, which allowed the Famicos Foundation and St. Louis developer McCormack Baron to build and manage an addition to Lexington Village of 183 town-homes for moderate income buyers. An interesting example of the importance of community input is found here, where one owner who did not want to move when the complex was built was allowed to stay, and the complex design was modified to go around the property.

Recently, HAPP has turned its attention to attracting the black middle class back to the area; thus, it is now promoting large single family homes which would be valued at $90,000–$250,000 but have low payments due to tax abatements and subsidies (Keating, Krumholz, & Star, 1996). Evidence of success here is found across from the high school, where middle and high income African Americans have built impressive homes, and in the nearby Glenville area, where a block or two have been revitalized using Nehemiah grant funds. The financing used here is typical of what works in low income areas: The city sells the land from its land bank for $100, local banks provide low-interest first mortgages, the city's CASH program provides second and third mortgages but their repayment is deferred and, if the owner stays for eight years, waived. Taxes are abated 7–15 years on the building, and private foundations provide grants to further lower the cost. The end result for the owner is a total payment of $475 for a very nice home.

The LRA program served as a catalyst for other development, and "revitalization is now occurring everywhere." LRA lots are sold for $100, low-interest financing is available thanks to CRA-based agreements with banks along with the Housing Trust Fund, and tax abatements are also given which help "fuel the fire." "The program made people consider Cleveland as a place to live who would have previously rejected it. Tax dollars are up, and there is a domino effect that attracts for-profit developers and businesses. It is very important to attract these if long-term success is to be achieved" (the author's interviews with McNamara, Sidoti, & Sweeney, 1996).

From 1990–1996 about 2,400 new homes were built in the city, which is a significant increase from the 300 new homes begun during the previous decade (James W. Rouse Forum on the American City, 1997). From 1990–1995 more than $100 million was invested in Cleveland's poor neighborhoods (Yin, 1998). But perhaps a better indicator of the extent of the city's success is the fact that, when asked what the biggest roadblock is to achieving success, the answer was unanimously agreed to be multiple bidders on the delinquent properties. This means that the city is now having difficulty acquiring all the properties it would like, so plan implementation is suffering. But it is certainly a new phenomenon, and appears to be a measure of the increased demand.

Remaining Problems

The Hough area is "pocketed," with one street being revitalized while an adjacent one still harbors run-down businesses, boarded-up buildings and vacant lots. Commercial services are still a problem, with too much land zoned for this and not enough variety of goods and services offered. Crime is evidently also still prevalent; for example, the local grocery store has the employees and merchandise entirely behind bars and glass. Customers must ask for their items, which are brought by the clerk and money is exchanged through a slot much as one finds in a bank or gas station. Racially, the area did not appear integrated. Still, it seems to be much better off than any other low income area visited.

Brownfields are a problem in revitalizing these properties. "There is a clear need for regional and state planning, because now it is cheaper to put new industry in greenfields," McNamara (in an interview with the author, 1996) said. Recognizing this, in 1995 the Ohio legislature passed SB221, which provides incentives and assistance for industries to locate on existing brownfields. The incentives include "covenants not to sue" which protects the industry from pursuit by the Ohio EPA if the agency approves a cleanup plan. But since underground storage tank sites are not covered, some inner city lots cannot benefit from this. The city's Empowerment Zone also provides funds for brownfields reuse.

Despite the progress in Hough, Cleveland's future is far from assured. "Original poverty areas (including Hough) that still exist today housed almost 1/5 of the poor in 1970, but now [1990] account for less that 10% of the poor in Cuyahoga County." Early poverty areas (including Fairfax and part of Central) housed 8% of the poor from 1970–1990 but lost many wealthier people then, so the percent of residents living below the poverty level has risen. Emerging poverty areas (on the outskirts of the city) had the greatest increase in numbers of poor residents. They also lost wealthier residents, and so now have a larger percent below the poverty level than do original or early areas; indeed, most of Cleveland's poor live there. The only places that used to be poor but are not now are two tracts downtown: in sum, poverty is spreading outward toward the city's edges and suburbs. If the trend continues, nearly three-fourths of Cleveland Census tracts will have high rates of poverty in the near future (Keating, Krumholz, & Perry, 1995). Other than the admirable level of city-county cooperation needed for the Land Bank, examples of regional growth management are virtually nonexistent. Without regional controls, the outward spread of the city's wealthy residents—with the poor not far behind—can be expected to continue.

The biggest roadblock is the depth of Cleveland's problems—the city has a 40% poverty rate, which necessitates services and job programs in addition to physical rehabilitation. The indirect, convoluted funding mechanisms required by the federal government create another roadblock. For example, taking advantage of the low income housing tax credit is very complex, requiring accountants and attorneys, and provides only a portion of funds needed for a project. Corporate involvement is desirable, but tax credits are too convoluted a way to encourage it, and Section 8 rental certificates are not nearly enough to encourage provision of adequate low income rental housing. HUD should bring back direct subsidies to supplement these approaches, and also should allow greater flexibility in existing programs, including mixed use and mixed income (author's interview with Monter, 1996).

In sum, there is no doubt that Cleveland still has many problems to solve, particularly with respect to improving the quality of life of its poor residents (Knack, 1999). Also, the city's approach has been much less than perfect: Compared to a vision of what the city could, or at least should be, Cleveland is farther from that vision than it would be if different political and economic decisions had been made (Keating, Krumholz, & Perry, 1995). However, unlike many large American cities, at least in Cleveland's inner city neighborhoods, the dream of revitalization is becoming a reality.

Although not a perfect success, the city's efforts measure up well when compared to the list of factors that appear to be necessary for success (see Figure 1 in Chapter 1). For example, even though Cleveland spent much more money and effort downtown, the city has also allocated a lot of staff, funds, and infrastructure support to the neighborhoods. Shelter quality has risen, crime is still present but declining, and a sense of neighborhood is spreading as new residents join the community.

CONCLUSIONS

Obstructionist laws and policies must be changed so that TOADS can be reused. As Greenberg and Popper (1994) point out, "TOADS (temporarily obsolete abandoned derelict structures) often lie on potentially valuable inner city land." But some state laws and local policies regarding property appraisal and/or resale are simply blatantly discriminatory against low income areas. Cleveland certainly illustrates this point, as until the state laws regarding disposition of tax delinquent property were changed, revitalization did not get off the ground. Being able to reuse these properties was certainly the key to revitalization of the Hough area, and as the figures cited earlier show, the reuse is bringing in millions of tax dollars to the city.

Citywide and regionwide policies must support inner city revitalization efforts, not undermine them. Although downtown improvement is important, focusing all redevelopment resources there can hurt nearby neighborhoods. As Mayor Michael White said, "The downtown and the neighborhoods are in the same boat. Cities that pay all their attention to downtown and ignore the neighborhoods will inevitably suffer" (Barrett & Greene, 1993). Mechanisms that produce regional business/government participation in supplying financial resources for inner city revitalization should be fostered, similar to Cleveland's city-county cooperative Land Bank program. The city can also provide assistance with issues such as land assemblage and title transfer—for example, in Cleveland the city clears the title and assembles the land directly. "If the layers of government aren't working together you can't get anything done. Cooperation is a win-win situation for everyone," Sweeney said, adding that there are nine offices working with tax delinquency in the county alone. Sidoti, who has worked in "the real estate end" of Cleveland government since 1979, added, "Without cooperation you just won't solve the problem—and you can do it!"

A supportive mayor is needed. Cities have voluntarily become active when conditions became so bad that the voters were demanding something be done, and when a mayor with a strong interest in redevelopment was elected; both the resident pressure and the mayoral leadership were present, and an atmosphere of teamwork and cooperation was therefore fostered rather than an adversarial relationship which seemed to exist between the inner city neighborhoods and the local officials in less successful project areas. An example from Cleveland is the mayor's press conference on the bank steps in an effort to get more funds to be made available to the city's low income residents via the CRA.

Lender participation is essential. Lenders (who are the only profit-making businesses participating significantly in innercity neighborhood revitalization) have been essential revitalization partners in Cleveland, but it was far from voluntary: Without the provisions of the federal Community Reinvestment Act they would not have become involved. Clearly, the CRA should be retained or perhaps even strengthened.

Residents must be empowered. Successful revitalization necessitates extensive community involvement in planning efforts. "Development of a strong local strategy should occur. The community should have the first responsibility for deciding what's done," McNamara said. Cleveland's staff cited the fact that in many Northern cities, neighborhoods have a history of 20 years of community organizing. "First they pushed for decent city services to be provided, and now they are moving on," forming CDCs to improve business, housing, and so on (author's interviews with McNamara, Sidoti, & Sweeney, 1996). Resident participation was spearheaded by Chris Warren, a charismatic neighborhood activist who was later hired by the city.

Microplanning and funding for implementation are very important. This is evident, as the level of detail in Cleveland's neighborhood plans shows. The plans are specific enough that the city can pinpoint lots that it would like to acquire for unique kinds of development. "Emphasize detailed (lot and block level), proactive planning with extensive community input, and a multiyear program—more than three years—with funds for acquisition so they can make things happen within a reasonable [amount of] time. This is attractive to developers, too. HUD funds are absolutely critical. You must have community consensus, and you must get private dollars to kick in too," McNamara said (interview with author).

NOTES

1. The LRA idea did not originate in Cleveland; St. Louis was the first city in the nation to establish a land bank for government-owned property in 1971. Unlike Missouri, the Ohio statute allows all cities to establish LRAs; now many localities, including Dayton, Youngstown, Columbus, and Toledo, have them (Marino, Rosser, & Rozran, 1979).

2. According to Professor Alex Schwartz (in an interview with the author, 1998) Cleveland differs from many other cities in that the city government itself negotiated CRA agreements—a job usually left to community groups (such as PCRG in Pittsburgh) to do. Schwartz's description of the CRA as "regulation from below" agrees with the author's view that the CRA is similar to many of our environmental laws in that enforcement is essentially left to individuals and NGOs. However, interest groups with a nationwide membership play a large role in enforcement of environmental laws, whereas CRA actions typically originate with a neighborhood resident-based group such as a CDC. Perhaps more effective networking of CDCs could bring nationwide pressure for action on local CRA-related issues, just as now occurs with grassroots lobbying on environmental issues.

CHAPTER 7

Conclusions

COMPARISON OF SUBSTANTIVE EFFORTS

All the successful projects and programs addressed the major substantive elements of safety, services, shelter and social capital which were identified from the literature (and outlined in Figure 1, Chapter 1) as affecting low income residents' quality of life; they differ from one another in the specific elements that are emphasized. For example, in Boston DSNI members addressed drug dealing, other crime reduction measures, brownfields, exposure to lead, illegal dumping, lack of parks, dilapidated housing, vacant lots, poor urban design and landscaping, need for a community center, small business development, and many other things which directly affect neighborhood quality of life. Likewise in Cleveland the program addressed many aspects of neighborhood quality of life, with special attention being paid to finding ways to provide decent and affordable housing. Table 7 compares the relative extent to which each of the quality of life indicators listed in Figure 1 was addressed by each revitalization effort. The information stemmed directly from comparative analysis of the interviewees' evaluations of post-project conditions connected with each effort, along with the author's observations of post-project conditions during site visits. Interviewees were asked to assess the degree to which the area's quality of life factors listed in Figure 1 were affected by revitalization efforts. Responses were grouped as follows: "extensive improvement," "good improvement," "moderate improvement," "slight improvement," and "no change." These are shown as E, G, M, S, and N in Table 7. Originally a sixth score, W, was included for those factors that had worsened; however, in reality no areas were identified as having worsened after the effort began, so the category was dropped. Since most of the revitalization efforts are still in progress, the assessments should be viewed as "post-project inception" rather than post-completion.

The author also assessed those factors for which post-project evaluation could be made either from observations during site visits, or from printed material. In most cases the interviewees' assessments agreed with the data, but in some instances the interviewees' assessments were higher than those of the author based on her direct observations of the area. In these cases a category was selected that gives equal weight to the interviewees' assessment and that of the author.

Relative assessments of quality of life factors alone are insufficient measures of success, however, because they do not account for differences in the size of the revitalization effort. For example, Boston's Dudley Street effort appears to have the most comprehensive approach; the revitalization effort there addresses nearly all aspects of the urban web that affects neighborhood quality of life, as is evident in Table 7. But Cleveland's approach is not far behind in comprehensiveness, and it covers a more extensive geographic area with more residents than does Dudley's core area. The reader should refer to each chapter for details on the scope of each revitalization effort.

Finally, success depends in part upon the extent and severity of the underlying problem. For example, although Portland has made a commendable effort, its underlying problems were far less severe than those in Cleveland, Pittsburgh, and most other cities in this study. Table 8 was developed from the material collected from interviews and publications regarding city and neighborhood conditions before the revitalization effort began. Interviewees were asked to assess the pre-project quality of life factors in Figure 1 for the area in which their efforts were directed. Responses were grouped as follows: "excellent for high quality of life," "good," "moderate," "severe problem," or "very severe problem." The "excellent" category (E) was not used by anyone to describe any neighborhood quality of life factor before revitalization began; thus it does not appear in Table 8. The others are shown in Table 8 as G, M, S, and V respectively. The author also ranked those few factors for which pre-project data was available from published sources; in all cases, the interviewees' views agreed with the author's so no adjustments were necessary.

By examining the data in all the tables, the reader can obtain a picture of the dimensions of revitalization success in each city. However, readers should bear in mind that this information is merely a cross-sectional appraisal of evolving phenomena; since many of the revitalization programs are ongoing, the information will probably change in the future.

Another caveat should be borne in mind for Tables 7 and 8: They say nothing about the relative importance of each factor. For example, reductions in crime rates or drug dealing may be more important in achieving successful revitalization than is the provision of urban design elements that foster development of social capital—or the opposite might be true. Thus any temptation

Table 7: Degree to Which Quality of Life Determinants Were Affected

Quality of Life Determinant	Boston	Cleveland	Minneapolis/ St. Paul	Pittsburgh	Portland	Seattle
SAFETY						
Crime	E	G	N	M	M	M
Death, Toxins	G	G	N	E	M	M
Substance Abuse	E	G	M	M	E	S
Other	G	G	M	N	E	M
SERVICES						
Government	G	E	M	S	E	E
Business	E	G	M	E	E	E
Social Services	E	G	G	E	E	E
SHELTER						
Affordability	E	E	G	G	E	G
Ownership	E	E	E	E	N	G
Maintenance	M	E	G	G	E	G
TOADS	G	E	M	S	S	G
SOCIAL CAPITAL						
Network	E	G	N	E	G	E
Design	E	E	S	G	E	G
Political Power	G	E	M	G	G	G
Ethnic, Income Mix	G	G	G	S	G	E
Organized Groups	E	E	S	E	G	G

Key: E = extensive effect/results
     G = good effect/results
     M = moderate effect/results
     S = slight effect/results
     N = not available or not applicable

to add scores, develop means or medians, or perform other statistical operations on the rankings would be completely inappropriate. For this reason, nonnumerical ranking systems are used.

Readers can draw their own conclusions from the data in the tables. It does appear that all the successful efforts did focus on a wide spectrum of quality of life issues; perhaps this broad-based approach is needed to achieve

Table 8: Degree of Pre-Project Severity of Urban Problems

Quality of Life Determinant	Boston	Cleveland	Minneapolis/ St. Paul	Pittsburgh	Portland	Seattle
SAFETY						
Crime	V	V	N	V	M	M
Death, Toxins	V	V	N	S	G	M
Substance Abuse	V	V	M	V	S	M
Other	V	V	M	N	M	M
SERVICES						
Government	V	V	S	V	M	S
Business	S	V	M	S	S	G
Social Services	V	V	M	S	S	M
SHELTER						
Affordability	V	V	M	S	V	S
Ownership	V	V	S	V	N	N
Maintenance	V	V	S	S	S	M
TOADS	V	V	S	V	G	G
SOCIAL CAPITAL						
Network	S	S	M	M	M	G
Design	V	V	S	N	S	M
Political Power	V	V	S	V	S	M
Ethnic, Income Mix	S	V	M	V	M	M
Organized Groups	S	V	S	S	M	G

KEY: G = good for quality of life
     M = moderate for quality of life
     S = severe problem
     V = very severe problem
     N = not available or not applicable

success. Overall, Cleveland's effort seems to have had the greatest positive effect on the most quality of life factors for the most people; however, the clear superiority of Cleveland is unclear. Every effort was situated in a different physical, economic, and social milieu and focused on different aspects of revitalization, so there is great variation among the projects. Some ranked especially highly on a few factors, while others excelled on many.

COMPARISON OF PROCEDURAL APPROACHES

Beyond making efforts to address the substantive aspects of neighborhood quality of life, the experience of the cities reveals some very interesting procedural common ground. It appears that there may be some important procedural guidelines to follow if successful revitalization is to be achieved; in fact, it appears that these guidelines may be even more important in successful revitalization than are the types of substantive issues addressed. Further, although the list of substantive quality of life factors in Figure 1, Chapter 1 appears comprehensive, the relative importance of the factors varies among neighborhoods; but the procedural common ground revealed in these studies is applicable anywhere. Indeed, it appears that if these procedural guidelines are not followed then it would be less likely that the revitalization effort would address the unique mix of substantive factors that characterize each individual neighborhood. Perhaps the penchant for government programs to focus on a single substantive factor (or a small set of them) instead of focusing on the process used to develop solutions for whatever substantive factors these areas face, explains the programs' failure to improve the quality of life in these neighborhoods. The areas of procedural common ground are discussed below.

Allow Area Residents to Take Charge to the Fullest Possible Extent

Residents know what they need far better than anyone else, and they also have extensive knowledge of the local web of people, policies, and physical elements upon which revitalization plans, projects, and programs must be based. An extensive body of literature on the value of resident participation in neighborhood improvement efforts, documentation of the failure of programs (for example, urban renewal) that did not foster resident-led efforts, and the frequent failure of those in power to consult or involve low income people in decision-making that affects their lives, all support this recommendation; for example, Barrett and Greene (1993) refer to resident-led revitalization as "trickle-up."

The path through which residents seem to have taken charge of neighborhood improvement efforts in the most successful revitalization efforts (Boston, Cleveland, and so on) began with a charismatic leader—or several leaders—organizing the neighborhood, often with the assistance of a faith-based organization of some kind (for example, the Archdiocese in Pittsburgh). Soon, this organization became a CDC or similar entity. Here is where serious problems are likely to occur due to the need for capacity-building: It is difficult to find interim funding for the years it takes to get thoroughly organized and truly involve the residents, which is the next step along the path to success. As University of New Orleans Professor Bob Washington said,[1]

"Community-based organizations (CBOs) are short-lived in poor neighbor-hoods. They need good long-range capacity-building, not just charismatic leaders." In the successful efforts, corporate foundations (especially Riley, Casey, and LISC/Ford) usually filled the gap. The case studies show that sufficient resident involvement is nearly impossible to achieve without a strong CBO; thus a lack of this "gap" financing can doom the entire revitalization effort to failure, since the entire effort may be jeopardized due to lack of resident involvement when the CBO closes its doors.

Lurcott and Downing (1987) also indicate that capacity-building is no easy task: "Leaders in neighborhood development must also be accountable to neighborhood residents and business owners, a responsibility most private developers refuse to assume. It seems to take a minimum of five years of experience in planning, advocacy, and on-the-job training to enable its leaders to make a community development corporation effective. In neighbor-hoods with more complex problems, training may take longer. For all these reasons, professional staffing and development of competent leadership will be costly and will require multiyear commitments of operating funds." This problem is illustrated by the Minneapolis NRP program's problems, which were due not only to failure to truly place residents in charge of the program in their neighborhoods but also to the relatively weak neighborhood leader-ship capacity.

Careful selection of the CBOs to be nurtured is very important. "Development itself is a complex business, one that not every community group can or should undertake. The whole community economic development effort is still in an embryonic stage nationwide, and needs to be nurtured and evalu-ated carefully. . . . The demonstrated ability of CDCs to leverage private investment funds is particularly important because many partnerships have failed in this crucial area, and leveraging is the key to local economic devel-opment through public-private partnerships" (Lurcott & Downing 1987).

Policy Recommendation. City-initiated revitalization efforts should be based on the idea that neighborhood residents should be in charge of organiz-ing, planning, and implementing projects and programs to the fullest extent possible, with the city staff serving as sources of expertise. This recommen-dation necessitates transferring both money and decision-making power from the local government to the CBOs, as well as providing technical assistance for them. The MCC provides a model worthy of imitation by CBOs else-where, including its record of changing missions and organizational structure with time, forging relationships with the banks and government agencies such as the URA, and working closely with other CBOs by forming the PCRG network.

Policy Recommendation. A clear need is to make funding for this im-portant post-organizing growth period available to those CBOs which appear to have the leadership and organizational abilities needed to proceed further.

Any level of government, or the private sector, could make funding available. A model of local government involvement can be found in Cleveland, where the city finances numerous CBOs using its CDBG funds. A private sector model exists in Pittsburgh, where a coalition of lenders provides funds for numerous CBOs. The city of Pittsburgh's early funding of MCC, its support of 17 CBOs through the Neighborhood Fund, the assistance given by the Archdiocese to Bloomfield-Garfield Corporation, and the PPND funding all are successful approaches to meeting this need which could be applied elsewhere. The federal government should develop incentives for localities to utilize some CDBG funds in this manner, and for private corporations, lenders, and foundations to provide greater support. Federal and state agencies can also tie the awarding of grants to the degree to which the activity or project for which the grant is sought is resident-led. Even if the federal government does not offer incentives or mandates, however, local governments and foundations can take these steps.

Provide Adequate Local Government Services

If the government is unwilling to invest heavily in ensuring that trash collection, police protection, code enforcement, transit, child care, medical services, alcohol/drug treatment, and so on are available, then resident-led efforts will produce very limited revitalization success. As Professor Clarence Stone of the University of Maryland said,[2] "The future of the city depends on its public services. [For example] you can't restore the city's economic health without restoring its schools." This guideline is also in line with a large body of literature that documents the importance of adequate infrastructure in economic development, the value of investing in human capital to improve the lives of the poor, and the effects on business development, residential property values, and public attitudes about neighborhoods when the city improves litter control, hires police officers, or provides high quality urban design features and landscaping in an area that lacked them.

Although provision of adequate services was important in most of the cases, none of them illustrates this point better than does Boston's Dudley Street. The entire revitalization effort began as an effort to force the city to do something to stop the extensive illegal dumping that was occurring, and "Don't Dump on Us" became a neighborhood rallying cry. Later, when plans for neighborhood revitalization were drawn up, considerable attention was paid to urban design features, linkages with history, public art and landscaping; one mural painted on the side of a local grocery store has become a symbol that is recognized far beyond the neighborhood's borders. Conversely, there were problems in getting the city's public works department to provide street paving and other infrastructure even after new homes were completed.

Currently, the burden of providing these services in low income areas falls disproportionately on CDCs and other nongovernmental organizations; sometimes services are even withheld from these neighborhoods until residents become organized enough to demand the same levels of service that wealthier areas are given.

Policy Recommendation. Cities should pursue adapting the concepts underlying TIFs, PIDs, BIDs and MUDs to provide funds for service provision in low income neighborhoods. Mechanisms such as TIFs appear to have much greater potential than has so far been tapped, since present expenditures on neighborhood improvement are repaid via tax revenue generated by the improvements rather than by a fee imposed on the existing population. The Minneapolis Housing TIF for TOADS is an interesting model that might be transferrable.

Special mention should be made of the problem of regulations. Many cities have applied zoning that makes common, economically advantageous uses of property by low income residents illegal: For example, renting out an accessory apartment or having a home-based child care business. Perhaps these uses would be viewed as nuisances in a wealthier neighborhood; in poor areas, they are important sources of income. At the same time, in an effort to allow any nonhome based business that might be interested in the area, uses are permitted which would be opposed in most wealthier areas because they are at best incompatible with homes, and at worst noxious (Babcock, 1979). Other regulations can also stifle development: These range from expensive replatting requirements to building codes not designed for rehabilitation. Finally, state regulations regarding brownfields, child care licensing, transferring ownership of delinquent tax parcels, and so on, can pose formidable roadblocks in these neighborhoods.

Need for Further Research. Much work needs to be done to locate and change regulations that discriminate against these neighborhoods. In many cases—for example, in Pittsburgh—a few draconian regulations governing the disposal of TOADS can stymie the best revitalization program. Cities, states, and universities should work together to identify regulations that are blocking redevelopment.

In poor areas many basic services such as quality education, code enforcement, protection from incompatible uses, and trash pickup, which are routinely provided in wealthier neighborhoods, have to be demanded by residents, a situation whose unfairness is compounded by the fact that these people have less money and so must struggle harder—devote more of their time and energy—to the basic job of keeping a roof over their head and food on the table. Many are less knowledgeable regarding how to fight for basic local services and have less political power to back them up than is the case with their wealthier neighbors. Perhaps this is exactly why localities neglect these areas—because usually they can save money by cutting services here, without anyone protesting—so they get away with neglect that would never be tolerated in a wealthier area.

Although this may make economic sense for the city or the school district, it is ethically unconscionable. One can see the logic behind the approach to revitalization taken by groups such as ACORN and the Saul-Alinsky-inspired IAF, which emphasize training in political activism and neighborhood organizing as the first ingredient for success. Of course, this activist approach must be accompanied by the provision of many other ingredients for success, ranging from startup funding to enforcement of federal laws such as the CRA, if neighborhoods are to be successfully revitalized. But a strong case can be made that without an active well organized resident group, the other ingredients needed for success will not be provided by the city, the lenders, or the foundations. First and foremost, residents must get the city's attention and support, because achieving nearly every policy recommendation and action suggested in this chapter hinges on having an activist neighborhood organization to push the city, the lenders, and the foundations to act.

Policy Recommendation. Cities should commit to maintaining city infrastructure and to making the relatively small investments required for urban design improvements in low income areas, particularly low maintenance landscaping. Such minor investments are in the city's own interest, as they can play a large role in revitalizing neighborhoods, help to restore trust on the part of area residents, attract private investment, bring in tax revenues for the city, and reduce expenses for code enforcement, police, and so on. For example, both Portland and Seattle have made major infrastructure investments in their inner city neighborhoods immediately adjacent to downtown, and both areas have been rejuvenated without displacing the poor population, largely by attracting private developers and businesses.

In view of the cuts in CDBG and other federal funds over the past 20-odd years, making more federal funds available is also needed. However, local action must not hinge on increased federal funding. Other strategies, such as involving foundations, should be pursued at the same time that requests are made for a greater federal financial commitment to America's forgotten neighborhoods. As MCC Executive Director Rhonda Brandon put it, "Start putting money into neighborhoods. There are people there—we can't just let them go for naught."

Fully Support Resident-led Initiatives

The active support of local governments—school boards, tax assessor's offices, special districts, the city government, and especially the mayor—is another essential ingredient for success. This conclusion also concurs with the literature, which includes many works that document the importance of city support for central city improvement efforts (Frieden & Sagalyn, 1992;

Wagner, Joder, & Mumphrey, 1995). But what causes local governments to become active, supportive partners? Cities become active when conditions become so bad that the area residents demand that something be done (working through their CBOs, as is described above), and when a mayor with a strong interest in redevelopment is elected. A second push can come from the city as when Cleveland defaulted on its debt and the mayor searched for a variety of possible solutions. With both resident pressure and mayoral leadership present, an atmosphere of teamwork and cooperation is fostered rather than the adversarial relationship which seems to exist between the inner city neighborhoods and the local officials in less successful project areas.

In successful projects, the case studies and the related literature show that although low income residents must play the main role in designing neighborhood improvement programs (Ford Foundation, 1973; Glaser, Denhardt, & Grubbs, 1995; Taub, Taylor, & Dunham, 1984), the residents are not expected to raise themselves up solely by their own bootstraps. Cleveland and Seattle in particular illustrate the value of establishing an ongoing close and supportive relationship between the city and the CBOs; as Gordon, Ulberg, and Locke (1996) said, "Currently, Seattle seems to have attained the mix of activists, organizations, relationships, and publicly and privately supported vehicles which together provide the necessary infrastructure for healthy communities." Seattle's empowerment of neighborhood-based organizations, such as community councils and CDCs, by providing staff, decision-making authority, and funding was an important factor in the success of its revitalization efforts. Community councils, CDCs, and other resident-led organizations generally took the lead in preparing detailed, lot by lot microplans for their neighborhoods, with technical assistance from the city, and even in many cases took the lead in allocating capital improvement funds, recommending zoning changes, and conducting other specific implementation activities. In the Twin Cities, the McKnight foundation has given millions of dollars to upgrade neighborhoods; in Cleveland, the city actually funds CDCs. In Boston, the city gave its delinquent tax land to the CBO; although delinquent tax lands were not a factor in Seattle, the city's making other government-owned property (acquired through highway clearance, urban renewal, and military base closings) available for reuse is an important part of the revitalization effort.

Local officials and staff often express frustration at the lack of "interest" on the part of low income residents. This perceived lack of interest can have many causes, ranging from a deep mistrust of local government to a simple lack of time. What can local officials do to organize residents? Not much directly; government representatives cannot become neighborhood organizers. They can, however, support residents' efforts in other ways. Local government can build trust and foster resident interest in neighborhood improvement by letting the residents make important neighborhood decisions themselves, including taking charge of planning efforts; by providing technical expertise and funding for resident-led planning and other resident-initiated projects; by letting residents allocate funds for plan implementation; by providing adequate city services; and by providing funds for CBO operations. Neighborhood activists can foster city interest in their concerns by offering to cooperate with the city on any of its neighborhood plans or projects for which financial support is available.

Another factor that was important in Seattle, the Twin Cities, and Portland was obtaining wide voter support. In Seattle, local voters have repeatedly approved millions of dollars in citywide funding for low income housing and related improvements; this strategy reflects the city's commitment to avoid displacement of existing low income residents. The city has made significant efforts to attract middle and upper income residents of all ethnic groups back to central city neighborhoods, and has encouraged a wide variety of housing types and land uses in the "urban village" tradition. It is now taking rather strict measures to encourage dispersal of low income housing and income mixing in higher income neighborhoods, although the success of this approach cannot yet be evaluated.

This focus apparently stems from an underlying attitude held by area residents, that the entire community should bear responsibility for helping to improve the quality of life in the poorest neighborhoods; put another way, instead of viewing these neighborhoods merely as competitors for scarce resources, their improvement is seen by middle and upper class residents as beneficial, and thus in the public interest. Residents have chosen to tax themselves to provide financial support to these neighborhoods; they have supported high density mixed use zoning that includes low income housing, and regional growth management strategies that favor central cities at the expense of suburbs; and they have supported this approach "with their feet" by moving into areas that were previously in very poor condition and are still populated with significant numbers of poor and even homeless residents. The most recent evidence of this somewhat altruistic grassroots activism is the November 1997 passage of an initiative to extend downtown Seattle's one-mile monorail by 45 miles. The initiative, which was spearheaded by a disgruntled city bus driver, passed by a 54% margin despite lack of support from area newspapers and very little campaign activity. Similarly, in Minnesota the state supported neighborhood goals by establishing tax-base sharing and by modifying TIF to help the neighborhoods. In Portland, regional infrastructure provision and regionally funded transit are a fact of life; voters also supported the decision to invest considerable sums in urban design and other physical upgrading activities in the city's SRO hotel district.

Policy Recommendation. Neighborhood activists should enlist the help of private nonprofit agencies and other interest groups to become active in local politics, so that candidates sympathetic to their needs may be elected.

They should attempt to obtain publicity for the problems their neighborhood faces, in hopes of making neighborhood quality of life an issue and winning voter support. Finally, residents and local officials should work together to acquire significant support from private foundations.

Need for Further Research. Beyond changing the community's power within traditional larger levels of government (by organizing to elect responsive mayors, councilpersons, tax assessors, school board members and state representatives), more profound changes in local governance and resident empowerment may be needed. Such a change appears to be happening within Boston's DSNI neighborhood. At DSNI's 12th annual town meeting held in the last week of June 1997, it seemed as if DSNI had actually become a neighborhood governing body in the purest tradition of grassroots small-town democracy which stretches back to the New England town meetings held to govern communities in Revolutionary War times: As 41 candidates competed to be elected to 27 seats on the DSNI Board, speeches were given, neighborhood issues were discussed, and votes were cast to elect what was clearly perceived to be a slate of elected representatives of the people. It seems that the DSNI board had in fact become a mini-local government—making plans, enacting regulations, owning land, raising money, and allocating city resources. This model takes the concept of neighborhood input to an entirely different level; if adopted citywide, the city government would be little more than a provider of a few citywide services and a coordinator of the various neighborhood governments; power to zone, raise funds, and so on. This "town meeting" model is, of course, the one that America's founding fathers had in mind when they spoke of democracy; it elevates the term "resident empowerment" to new heights. Such a course of action has been followed to a lesser extent in cities like Seattle, which has delegated some planning and funding authority to the neighborhoods; indeed, the role of community councils, neighborhood CDCs, and other grassroots organizations in Seattle's poor neighborhoods cannot be overemphasized. Still, many research questions remain before a recommendation of widespread reform can be made: Would neighborhoods of all ethnicities and incomes benefit from adopting such a governance structure? Where would the local governing board come from: an election at a community meeting? a general neighborhood election? voting by members of an existing neighborhood association, planning advisory group, or CDC? Should board membership be structured to reflect neighborhood demographics, as it is in Dudley and also in the Manchester CDC? Who should be allowed to vote? In Dudley, for example, youth are encouraged to participate. If implemented, does citywide government make sense anymore or would it not be better to have neighborhood government and metropolitan government? Put another way, are city governments obsolete in big urban areas, as David Rusk (1993) contends, and if so, would the addition of this neighborhood government assuage many of the fears of those opposed to regional control and allow the abolition of the citywide governmental level?

Keep Track of TOADS and Streamline the Procedures for Their Reuse

Nowhere is local government cooperation more important than in helping to put surplus properties back into productive use. This is an activity which is of primary importance if successful revitalization is to be achieved, yet the instances in which other cities and residents have cooperated to successfully accomplish this mission (as they did on Dudley Street) are rare.

The first indication that the revitalization of very low income residential neighborhoods might not be a hopeless task stemmed from some database analysis which indicated that a large amount of land in many low income inner city residential neighborhoods is government-owned. This property ends up in government hands for a wide variety of reasons. The most common are failure of owners to pay their local property taxes, which results in ownership by some local governmental body; and acquisition for use in urban renewal or highway projects that never were completed, which results initially in ownership by the state or federal government, although transfer of ownership to a local government can occur if a redevelopment project is proposed. In slightly less poverty-stricken areas loan foreclosure by HUD or the VA, along with property acquired by the now-defunct RTC as a result of bank failure, also become important pathways for government ownership. Military base closings, school closings, unused roadways, and abandoned railroad rights of way also provide surplus land in some cities.

Evidence shows that owners may be failing to pay their taxes not simply because they are poor, but because some state laws and local policies regarding property appraisal and/or resale are blatantly discriminatory against low income areas. For example, appraisal techniques based on comparable sales can produce very high tax bills if applied to areas where the property is not listed with realtors and is ineligible for mortgages, while those based on replacement cost overestimate the value of poorly maintained older homes. Appraisal techniques based on averaging within a geographic area clearly subsidize the wealthy and penalize the poor. Laws requiring a minimum bid that approaches a property's market value make government-owned land unattractive to developers and nonprofits alike. As Marino, Rosser, and Rozran (1979) explain, "In many communities [the delinquent tax property disposition system] is a poor method for preventing neighborhood deterioration due to abandonment. First . . . property on sale for taxes is not very attractive to potential buyers since debts secured by the property [for example, mortgages and mechanic's liens] are transferred along with the title and become obligations of the new owner [and, I would add, since they are often conveyed by quit claim deed, the government makes no promises regarding existence of these liens—it is up to the buyer to obtain a title search]. Second, properties not sold early in the delinquency cycle become less likely to be purchased in successive years, since each year adds another year's worth of back taxes to the major rehabilitation . . ." Some cities (for example, Chicago) do not impose these requirements, and have also accomplished some successful revitalization with these properties. "In order to save properties from abandonment, planners should develop tax delinquency indicators to serve as early warning signals that certain . . . buildings are in trouble. To maintain a neighborhood's attractiveness, strategies should be developed by local governments to acquire tax-delinquent properties from owners who are maximizing short-term profit (by not paying taxes) at the expense of the surrounding neighborhood" (Marino, Rosser, & Rozran 1979).

Initial research revealed that in the vast majority of cases these properties are active contributors to neighborhood decline. Governments were often unaware of their ownership of these properties; Greenberg and Popper (1994), the authors of several recent surveys on the subject, concluded, "most cities lacked comprehensive data on the numbers and types of abandoned sites within their jurisdiction. In some instances, cities had reasonably good figures on one type of abandoned property—housing, for instance—but could only guess when asked about numbers of abandoned commercial and industrial structures. Some cities kept accurate records on vacant lots but were less certain about the numbers of properties with standing abandoned buildings."

Thus it is not surprising that often the properties continued to be ignored and neglected even after government acquisition. They became physically dilapidated; many were abandoned or became unofficial homeless shelters, and some were even used as havens for those engaging in illegal activities. As Marino, Rosser, and Rozran (1979) explain, "There is often a considerable quantity of tax delinquent property in deteriorated neighborhoods. Investigation of the relationship between housing abandonment and tax delinquency has indicated that there is a positive correlation between multifamily property which is tax delinquent for two or more years and property abandonment [within five years] [see Sternlieb, 1969] . . . abandonment rapidly reduces the marketability of a neighborhood and restricts residents' access to conventional credit." Greenberg and Popper (1994) make the point more strongly: "Abandoned properties produce no legal revenues. They lower nearby property values, create public costs, and are expensive to police. They often frighten residents and business owners into leaving the vicinity, producing more abandonment . . . they also mean a substantial loss to the municipality in foregone taxes."

The importance of being able to reuse TOADS has mainly been addressed in the revitalization literature only recently (Bright, 1995 and 1997; Frieden, 1990; Judd & Parkinson, 1990), yet the case studies show that reuse is of paramount importance if revitalization is to succeed. Ownership of this land by the government presents an invaluable opportunity to improve these neighborhoods. As Greenberg and Popper (1994) point out, "TOADS often lie on potentially valuable inner city land." The Boston and Cleveland case studies show what an asset this property can be. But in order to take advantage of the opportunity, the discriminatory state and local policies that prevent their reuse in many parts of the country must be changed. In Boston, these changes allowed the city to give eminent domain power to the residents' group in order to facilitate land assemblage, as well as to donate its own parcels; in Cleveland a huge inventory of TOADS was sold to new owners for $100 or less after obstructionist state and local regulations were streamlined.

It may appear that changes in tax policy would not be critical in addressing the underlying causes of inner city neighborhood decline—particularly if one views the main cause as poverty. However, as discussed in Chapter 1, the literature clearly shows that a major cause of poor quality of life in these neighborhoods is not poverty itself but its concentration (which is, in turn, the result of many other causal factors ranging from FHA loans to highways). The fact that every effort described in this book includes at least some program aimed at mixing incomes, is testimony to the importance of reducing the concentration of poverty if successful revitalization is to be achieved. Given that displacement is not a desirable option, vacant properties (with or without structures) must be available for development if mixing incomes is to occur. However, the vast majority of TOADS are not readily available for development due to problems with lot size or shape, title, and especially delinquent taxes (as the Pittsburgh case shows). Thus reform of these laws and regulations is an essential first step. The Boston and Cleveland cases illustrate the significant positive impact that reform of these laws and regulations can have; in both cases, mixed income development was pursued as a revitalization strategy after the hurdles to reuse of TOADS were reduced.

Policy Recommendations. Cities should carefully examine their property assessment, collection, sale, and resale policies and eliminate legal and financial barriers to the reuse of TOADS. This may require some changes in state laws as well, but as Cleveland's experience shows, even this obstacle can be overcome. One specific policy that should be eliminated everywhere is the requirement found in many states that the purchaser of a tax-delinquent property pay all delinquent taxes, interest, penalties, and fees on the property. These can be confiscatory, making development unfeasible and essentially taking the small remaining value of the property without compensation. Perhaps a change in state law to exempt from future taxes (along the lines of a homestead exemption) delinquent property that is purchased by a new owner should be considered. Cities should also take an inventory of TOADS, particularly those that are city-owned. A maintenance program should then be initiated, and plans for their reuse should be developed.

Need for Further Research. Financial incentives are needed to make inner city TOADS attractive to new residents and developers. Many of these are discussed in the section "Involve the Private Sector," in this chapter; however, the city may also have some little-used avenues open to it. First, most state laws allow multiyear tax abatement for corporations, and in many cases similar abatements have been given for new commercial or industrial construction in poor urban neighborhoods. The instances in which property tax abatements have been offered for single family homes should be studied, and recommendations for improving their attraction ability should be made.

Pursue Regional Coordination

Another important way the city can support resident-led efforts is through proactive regionwide policies and programs. These can range from regional provision and control of services (ranging from transit to sewer lines—as one finds in Ottawa and Toronto), to passage of low income housing revenue bond issues and affordable housing siting policies (as is found in Seattle), to regional finance (as is found in Minneapolis), to growth management (as is found in Seattle and Portland). There is ample literature on the value of regional urban management (Rusk, 1993; Goldsmith, 1999) to support this conclusion. The examples in this book give evidence that the states have an important role to play in neighborhood revitalization, by passing legislation that supports regional coordination instead of suburban political and economic fragmentation.

Yet surprisingly, this appears to be a desirable but not an essential factor in successful revitalization; the two most successful examples, Boston and Cleveland, both suffer from a lack of regional control over land development. Cleveland's effort succeeded in part because of unprecedented cooperation between the city and the county in getting TOADS recycled, but this is just a part of the regional cooperation that the literature recommends.

Policy Recommendation. A clear need is to provide incentives for greater regional cooperation in managing suburban growth and in supplying financial resources for inner city revitalization, using mechanisms such as the Twin Cities TIF program (which taxes business to help pay for the refurbishment of nearby neighborhoods), the Minnesota tax base sharing approach (which redistributes local taxes to poor communities), or strict growth control measures such as those in Canada, especially Ottawa, and to a lesser extent in Oregon, Washington, and California (which help preserve the value of inner city property by redirecting new development within the existing city boundaries and/or water/sewer service areas). In the Twin Cities, the impressive list of state legislation providing regionwide financial and other backing for local revitalization is a fine example of what a "champion" (Myron Orfield) working for regionwide support at the state level can do.

Without these programs, localities can make a case (albeit an ethically weak one) for neglect of infrastructure and services in poor areas based on a shortage of funds coupled with political pressure to respond to the needs of more politically powerful (and tax generating) neighborhoods. There has been much discussion of the value of regional governmental cooperation, but little has been written regarding what has caused this cooperation to take place and what incentives could be offered to encourage it in other locations. Although regional cooperation usually results from changes in state laws, it is doubtful that individual states will independently design and implement many programs to foster regional cooperation. Thus, the federal government is urged to design policies that will reward states for enacting incentives for local governments in large metropolitan areas to engage in significant regional cooperation.

Need for Further Research. The apparent success of the Dudley Street revitalization as well as other revitalization efforts in less poverty-stricken parts of Boston, raises some interesting research questions. There appear to be parallels in terms of the vitality of the downtown and the central city neighborhoods among Boston, New York, San Francisco, Portland, Washington D.C., and Seattle. Unlike cities such as Cleveland, Detroit, Los Angeles, Pittsburgh, and Minneapolis, all these cities have very high central city residential real estate prices and many thriving in-town neighborhoods (although areas in dire need of revitalization also exist)—one could say they have a reputation as being lively, entertaining cities—despite also having suburban sprawl and large commuting populations. Are density, a focus on multifamily housing, mixing of incomes, small city land areas, or other factors responsible? If the existence of restricted land areas/urban boundaries is the reason, does this not fly in the face of the idea that commuting (especially when workers live in a different political jurisdiction) is bad for the central city? Research is needed for more detailed investigations regarding what makes these cities thrive despite sprawl and, in most cases, political fragmentation.

Involve the Private Sector

The most glaring "missing player" in the case studies is the private for-profit business sector; for example, in Boston, DSNI had to take over the role of developer when the private one backed out, and without the CRA, an "insider" at the bank and the city's willingness to pledge its CDBG funds as collateral, bank financing would have been a dream. The reluctance on the part of the private sector is no doubt due to the perceived higher risk and lower probability of making a profit in inner city redevelopment or other business ventures, than is the case with business opportunities in wealthier areas. If business is to enter these neighborhoods, the risk must be lowered and/or the profits raised. Government can play a key role in finding ways to foster participation by profitmaking businesses (developers, corporations, and lenders) in inner city neighborhood redevelopment by shouldering some of the risk and/or by raising the private sector return on investment.

The literature is full of material on the importance of attracting business to revitalizing communities (Porter, 1994; Kotler, 1978; Ford Foundation,

1973). Likewise, the economic development literature provides ample examples of the principle of government action to reduce financial risk and/or raise profitability in order to attract business to communities (Blakely, 1994; Blair, 1995). In fact, one of the reasons that the suburbs thrived while the citied declined is found in the suburbs' aggressive use of financial incentives to attract business and industry—incentives that the cities, with their shrinking tax bases and grants, were unable to offer.

Boston's Dudley Street Triangle is a mere 64 acres in size; the larger area on which less intense redevelopment efforts have focused covers 507 acres. More than $100 million will need to be spent on the Dudley Street effort, which sits like a beacon in a sea of blight. Likewise, Cleveland's Hough district is aproximately two square miles in size and is surrounded by many other neighborhoods in need of assistance. How much of the cost of replicating these successful efforts will the American public agree to shoulder? Clearly, there is a need to tap private sector resources as well.

Policy Recommendations. Partnership techniques learned in successful downtown revitalization programs should be applied to the surrounding low income neighborhoods. City-developer financial partnerships for reuse of government-owned parcels could be established, using techniques such as those used to redevelop Fanueil Hall and Pike Place Market as models for structuring such arrangements. In all the successful case studies, partnerships have been formed along these lines; however, the business world is represented solely by the nonprofit housing developer and the corporate foundation. Even nonprofit developers must shift some risk via financial subsidies; for example, the federal tax credits offered to investors or the state and local "equity loans" to buyers that are used in many of the cases are a form of subsidy. If for-profit business is to be attracted, a clear need is to provide more direct financial risk shifting so the private sector will participate more fully.

Cities should also provide technical assistance, or even take the lead, in problem areas such as land assemblage and title transfer. For example, in Boston the city gave eminent domain power to the residents' group in order to facilitate land assemblage; in Cleveland and many other cities, the city clears the title and assembles the land directly.

At the federal level, the Community Reinvestment Act (CRA) should be retained or perhaps even strengthened. Lender participation has been an essential element of all successful programs, but it was far from voluntary: as the Pittsburgh case study in particular shows, the CRA was used to force participation by lenders (who are the only profit-making businesses participating significantly in inner city neighborhood revitalization). According to Professor Alex Schwartz,[3] about 300 agreements worth $80 billion nationwide have been signed due to this act. "One positive effect is that the CRA has allowed banks to see that money could be made in inner city areas," he said. Still, this CRA-enforced participation is not enough: Without access to credit, real estate becomes virtually worthless, and using the CRA "stick" will not provide enough credit access to revitalize these areas on a large scale. In order to accomplish that goal, more steps must be taken.

The federal government should also develop a major risk reduction program to encourage lenders to begin operating voluntarily in low income central city neighborhoods again. For example, after World War II lenders were reluctant to make loans to returning GIs to buy suburban homes, or to developers and builders to build those homes. The federal government stepped in to reduce private sector risk and increase potential profitability by providing FHA and VA loans and loan guarantees, along with government-sponsored secondary mortgage purchasers (Fannie Mae, Ginnie Mae, and Freddie Mac). The results were immediate and long-lasting. The suburbs developed rapidly and the cities were drained. The same principles used by the federal government to encourage postwar suburban single family housing for young families should be applied nationwide to encourage lender funding for provision of single and multifamily housing in inner city areas: insuring loans, setting standards for development, cutting equity requirements, reducing interest rates, and so on. In all of the successful case studies, some or all of these techniques were used; however, there is no current nationwide program addressing this issue as the postwar government programs did.

The "carrot" offered by such a program must be accompanied by a "stick": rules to ensure that truly disadvantaged people and properties are assisted. Thus barriers placed by local lenders (such as refusals to loan on properties valued at less than $25,000, or on properties in need of rehabilitation) and by federal or local underwriting guidelines (such as discounting nonsalary income, penalizing properties located in mixed-use or changing neighborhoods, and so on) should be changed.

Other obstructive federal regulations should also be rewritten. Often, federal laws written in hopes of enticing private sector participation by reducing risk or increasing profitability are translated into regulations and administered in ways that keep most of the risk on private shoulders; not surprisingly, the private sector fails to respond until it is forced to do so. For example, the shortage of Section 8 landlords in many parts of the country has been attributed to unrealistically low rent ceilings coupled with draconian inspection and repair policies; together these act to reduce the program's profit potential to the point at which the perceived cost of the low income tenant is not worth the relative security of Section 8 rental payments. A clear need exists to change regulations that gut well-intentioned laws by requiring that they be administered so as to minimize risk to the government and maximize the risk to the private sector. It is important for officials designing both low income rental assistance and homebuying/building programs to remember that lenders, developers, and corporations exist to make a profit, not to implement helpful social programs—that is the job of the nonprofits and the government.

Stockholders of private sector companies view low income people and properties as high risk (equaling low profit) investments, and they have many other locations in which to operate with less perceived risk; thus, any government program to involve them with the poor must offer real risk-reducing/profit-increasing incentives.

Need for Further Research. Universities, private "think tanks," and federal agencies should conduct research to assess the viability and effectiveness of providing more indirect financial aid to cities. For example, in addition to directly giving federal funds to cities for use in poor neighborhoods (which is politically unpopular), perhaps greater incentives could be developed to reward corporate foundations, private businesses, and wealthy individuals for investing in those areas instead of downtown and in the suburbs. Such incentives can have very large impacts, as shown by the effect of FHA/VA loan guarantees on private sector suburban investment as well as the overbuilding (overinvestment?) by the private sector in response to income tax benefits for downtown office construction that were included in the Tax Reform Act of 1986.

Insist on Microplanning

In Boston, Cleveland, Pittsburgh, and Seattle, among others, successful revitalization is based on "microplanning." This involves obtaining a thorough, detailed knowledge of the neighborhood itself and the complex web of people, institutions and substantive issues that affect it, then developing highly detailed programs or plans based on this information (as was done in the Triangle by DSNI, in Manchester by the Citizens Corporation, and in Cleveland by the city). This approach is so clearly necessary in the biological and physical sciences that it appears ridiculous to ignore it; would an engineer build a dam without detailed geologic and hydrologic study of the exact portion of the river to be dammed, followed by plans and specs for every inch of the project? Of course not, no matter how much she knew about dam building in general. Yet in inner city revitalization, obtaining this level of detailed knowledge is the exception rather than the rule.

Be Comprehensive

The experience of the neighborhoods described in this book shows that successful revitalization efforts address all major strands (which include both substantive problems and the paths by which people and institutions influence them) of the complex "civological" web that determines the quality of life in low income neighborhoods. The importance of addressing a wide variety of substantive issues was discussed earlier. Regarding paths of influence, often the city will not act to improve a forgotten neighborhood until resident and/or private sector initiatives have occurred, and the residents and businesspersons will not take the initiative until the city has acted. This approach could work in a linear system but not a web system, which is characterized by interdependent relationships that require concurrent action by government, the private sector, and residents; all major players involved in a neighborhood must be included if a project is to succeed. Waiting for someone else to make the first change dooms the process of change to failure because quality of life cannot be improved by one party's actions alone. Likewise, attempting to change just a few of the substantive problems affecting the neighborhood is not likely to produce lasting improvement. Just as waiting for someone else to make the first change dooms the process of change to failure, so does jumping in unilaterally to change one strand of the web in hopes of revitalizing the area.

Many examples of this multifaceted approach have already been given in this book. The Dorothy Day Apartments in Pittsburgh (which were designed and built by a church congregation for single parents in a vacant school building, in response to the needs of area residents, using a mixture of private and city funding, and are managed by a nonprofit corporation—see Barrett and Greene, 1993) are one previously cited example. Another example is the turnaround at Boston's Alice Taylor public housing project. Viewed widely as a success, the major aspects of the rehabilitation effort are listed below, with references (in parentheses) to the substantive and procedural success factors in Figure 1, Chapter 1.

- It is a low rise, scattered site, income-mixed project, built/rehabbed by a CDC and a nonprofit developer (substantive factor: shelter; procedural factor: resident involvement).
- Defensible space and family-oriented urban design are very important, including low see-through fences and private separate entries (rather than corridors) that create a sense of individual ownership and responsibility without cutting off visual surveillance by neighbors, placement of play areas in front of the entries, and so on (substantive factors: safety and social capital).
- Good maintenance is extremely important, and tenant management or ownership are the best ways to achieve this if sufficient outside funds are provided for maintenance (substantive factor: provision of services; procedural factors: provision of resident involvement and outside financial support).
- Increased law enforcement is provided—police get out of their cars, meet the residents, and walk the halls (substantive factor: safety; procedural factor: provision of adequate services).
- Strong social networks among neighbors are encouraged, so they can watch out for each other and provide services (for example, share or

give rides) previously provided by drug dealers (substantive factors: social capital, services, and safety).

- Residents were extensively involved in redesigning the project, and attention was paid to every detail of the physical and social environment (procedural factors: resident control, microplanning).
- In general, "respect" of the residents and "creating a family-oriented environment" were cited by the project's tenants as the most important factors in successful revitalization (substantive factor: social capital).

(National Institute of Justice, 1993)

Provide Federal Support

Direct federal funding of programs to revive our central city neighborhoods should be increased. This is justified on both ethical and practical grounds. As Chapter 1 points out, federal policies, projects, and programs are largely responsible for the ruination of these urban neighborhoods and the financial draining of the cities that contain them. Further, it is simply unrealistic to expect central cities to be able to offer anything like the incentives that can be offered by the (still federally-subsidized) suburbs. Yet given the current political climate in America and the widespread misconceptions held by the public concerning reasons for the existence of slums, significant direct financial aid along the lines outlined here will not easily be forthcoming. The difficulty of seeking more federal government support is compounded by the "drop-in-the-bucket" nature of these successful examples: So much time and money is needed to successfully revitalize one small neighborhood that achieving wider success appears prohibitively expensive. But one reason that the efforts described in this book were as time-consuming and expensive as they were lies in the fact that all the factors that caused these neighborhoods to decline (as outlined in Chapter 1) are still in force: Thus, neighborhood activists are fighting a difficult uphill battle.

Policy Recommendation. The federal government is perfectly capable of making policy changes that would greatly reduce the adverse effects of mortgage lending, highway building, infrastructure provision, drug dealing, and so on, on these neighborhoods. If policy changes such as those suggested earlier were made, then more forgotten neighborhoods could be revitalized for less money, and the investments would be more likely to produce longterm success. Experts and activists should continue lobbying for a coherent federal policy to revive our forgotten neighborhoods, with adequate funding. There is a window of opportunity now, since federal finances are relatively good and there is much interest in suburban policy changes (such as curbing sprawl and reducing commuter auto trips). These policy changes could be coupled with programs designed to revitalize inner city low income neighborhoods, to form a program of sweeping impact.

Conclusions

The list of procedural factors discussed previously that appear to foster success allows comparisons to be made among the cities studied. Table 9 summarizes these comparisons. Two caveats should be borne in mind for this table: first, it is based on the author's assessment, and second, it says nothing about the relative importance of each factor. Therefore, use great caution in attempting to interpret the meaning of the scores, totals, or means and use them as indicators of relative positions.

Why was New York not included in the analysis? The city is so much larger than all the others in so many ways—for example, the number of TOADS in New York in the mid-1990s exceeded those in all the other cities discussed in this book put together—that is is difficult to compare it with the others. For example, New York has rehabbed more TOADS than all the rest of the cities, and has bred more neighborhood champions; yet putting it first in those categories in Table 9 did not appear to reflect reality, since the city still has many neighborhoods in dire need of help and for which little is being done. Thus, although site visits were made, books were read and written, and material was analyzed, a chapter on New York was not included in this book simply because there were far too many projects and programs to cover: A

Table 9: Presence of Procedural Factors That Foster Success

Procedural Factors	Boston	Cleveland	Minneapolis/ St. Paul	Pittsburgh	Portland	Seattle
Residents/CSCs in charge	10	7	5	9	7	8
City infrastructure/ services	8	9	4	2	10	7
City support resident-led	8	10	6	3	6	9
Streamline TOAD use	10	9	5	3	8	7
Regional coordination	1	7	9	1	8	10
Private sector/CRA	7	9	6	10	1	1
Foundations/Church	9	7	10	8	3	5
Microplanning	8	10	5	9	6	7
Comprehensive/web	10	6	4	8	9	7

Note: 1 = the lowest level of use of the factor; 10 = the highest level of use of the factor book could be written containing case studies of successful revitalization from New York alone, and another one could be written about its failures. New York was the only city visited where we found more than one project or program cited in response to our inquiries about what project or program might be an example of successful low income neighborhood revitalization, with reference to producing improvements in the quality of life factors listed in Figure 1; in fact, around 30 projects and programs were cited. Thus it was clear that any selection among them would be arbitrary, and the most ethical course of action was to leave completion of the New York story for another day. However, it was clear from the data collected that in the efforts considered successful, the same procedural factors were found as were discovered in the other cities.

From this table, one can see that each project or program is especially strong in its own unique way. For example, Boston and Cleveland had the most effective programs to encourage TOADS reuse; in Pittsburgh, reuse was stymied (by restrictive state laws). Seattle and Portland were the most outspoken proponents of mixed income, mixed use development, with Cleveland and Boston also promoting these to a lesser degree (mixing incomes is an important part of Cleveland's approach, with mixed uses taking a less important position; in Boston, the two appear to be reversed). Boston and Pittsburgh clearly lead the rest in the level of resident control as well as having strong CDCs; the picture was less clear in Seattle, Portland, Minneapolis and Cleveland, where there still appeared to be more heavy-handed city control than the residents desired. Cleveland, Pittsburgh, and Boston did the best job of microplanning, while the cities of Seattle, Cleveland, and Boston allocated staff to the neighborhoods in ways that appeared to work well (for city funding, the positions of Cleveland and Seattle were reversed). For other city aid, Portland had to be ranked first due to the city's extrordinary investments in infrastructure in the low income neighborhood studied, but again Cleveland and Boston were not far behind. Foundation support was most important and noticeable in Minneapolis, where the McKnight Foundation played a bigger role even than did the Riley and Ford Foundations in the Dudley Street neighborhood. Pittsburgh is the acknowledged leader in soliciting lender participation, mainly through expert use of the CRA, but Cleveland also did a noteworthy job here. Seattle and Minneapolis set the standard for regional support, with Seattle leading mainly because it has not only regional financial support but also growth management. Only two other cities were notable at all with respect to this factor; all the rest received the lowest rating, a sad commentary on the state of regional initiatives in modern America. Finally, with respect to having strong community leadership, Boston's Che Madyun and Pittsburgh's Stanley Lowe have become nationally known for their revitalization efforts in their respective neighborhoods. Cleveland's Chris Warren is slightly less well known although he clearly is still a champion of the city's program.

The overall conclusion is that although no city is strong in every area, it seems that Cleveland comes the closest to meeting that ideal. There is some disagreement about this conclusion in the existing literature (Knack, 1999; Keating, Krumholz, & Perry, 1995), which points out many problems still faced by the city's poor residents. Krumholz (who, according to a recent article in *Planning* magazine, is frequently referred to as "the Grinch of Cleveland"—see Knack, 1999—in spite of his other widely cited moniker as "the father of the Land Bank"), Keating, and Perry (1995) compare Cleveland to a vision of what the city could, or at least should, be, and find it farther from that vision than it would be if different political and economic decisions had been made. Here, Cleveland's efforts are compared with those of other cities identified as having been, in reality, successful—and in that comparative framework, it looks very good. So perhaps the truth is along the lines of the famous quote (attributed to Harry Truman) regarding democracy being the worst form of government except for all the rest: Cleveland has the worst results . . . except for all the others. For example, even though Cleveland spent much more downtown than they did in the neighborhoods, this statement is true of the vast majority of American cities. So, relative to the others, Cleveland allocated significant staff, funds, and infrastructure support to the neighborhoods.

It is important to realize that none of the case studies presents anything close to an ideal model of actions necessary to achieve successful revitalization, which could be derived from the procedural recommendations discussed earlier in this chapter. On the other hand, the reader should also remember that the lowest rankings in the table above still represent a level of effort that far exceeds that found in most other forgotten inner city neighborhoods: These cities represent the most successful efforts. The improvements in these neighborhoods have been made in spite of the continuing existence of all the forces which created the urban devastation in the first place (as discussed in Chapter 1); many of them were done with little city support and even less corporate, lender, state, or federal help; and funds were scarce. In view of these obstacles, every one of the revitalization efforts profiled in this book deserves acclaim. Further, all offer lessons that could benefit those areas still struggling to overcome the formidable obstacles to inner city neighborhood revitalization that still exist in America today. With millions of people—including the elderly, single mothers, and children—living in these forgotten places, any success is grounds for celebration.

NOTES

1. Washington, Bob. 1996. Speech (Oct. 4). University of New Orleans library.
2. Stone, Clarence. 1996. Speech (Oct. 4). University of New Orleans library.
3. Schwartz, Alex. 1996. Speech (Oct. 4). University of New Orleans library.

All speeches were given at a research-in-progress seminar sponsored by the National Center for the Revitalization of Central Cities.

Bibliography

ACSP-AESOP Tours. (1996). Unpublished material distributed at the annual conference of the Association of Collegiate Schools of Planning-Association of European Schools of Planning, Toronto, Canada.

ACTION-Housing, Inc. (1997). *ACTION-Housing 1995-96 Annual Report.* Pittsburgh: ACTION-Housing, Inc.

―――. (July, 1996). *Status Report on Housing Development Activities 1986–1996.* Pittsburgh: Unpublished report (July).

Activist Women Explore Shelter Issues. (October 1986). *The Neighborhood Works.* Washington, DC: Neighborhood Reinvestment Corporation.

Adams, I., & van Drasek, B. (1993). *Minneapolis/St. Paul: People, Place, and Public Life.* Minneapolis: University of Minnesota Press.

Adler, William M. (1995). *Land of Opportunity: One Family's Quest for the American Dream in the Age of Crack.* New York: Atlantic Monthly Press.

Ahlburg, Dennis A. (September, 1998). Characteristics of Poverty in Minnesota. *CURA Reporter.* Minneapolis: University of Minnesota.

Allen, W., & Mckinnon, A. (October, 1979). Development Pays Off in Newark. Commentary. *National Council for Urban Economic Development, 8:* 3–6.

Alterman, Rachelle. (1995). A Comparative View of Neighborhood Regeneration Programs in Nine Countries: Are the Lessons Transferable? *Urban Affairs Review, 30*(5), 794–765.

Alterman, Rachelle, & Cars, Goran. (Ed.). (1991). *Neighbourhood Regeneration: An International Evaluation.* New York: Mansell.

American Public Health Association Committee on the Hygiene of Housing. (1947). *Planning the Neighborhood.* New Haven, CT: American Public Health Association Committee on the Hygiene of Housing.

Anand, Geeta. (1995, July 22). A Neighborhood Restored. *Boston Globe,* p. 17.

Anderson, Elijah. (1990). *Streetwise: Race, Class, and Change in an Urban Community.* Chicago: University of Chicago Press.

Anderson, Donnie, Hadawi, Dristin, & Shuroro, Alaeddin. (1995, Spring). *Healthy Communities Project: A Plan for Economic Health for the Near Northside*

Neighborhood. Center for Economic Development Research and Service Report, 95–6. Arlington, TX: School of Urban and Public Affairs, University of Texas at Arlington.

Andrew, Christine I., & Merriam, Dwight H. (1988, Spring). Defensible Linkage. *APA Journal, 54* (2), 199–209. Chicago: American Planning Association.

Andrews, James. (1997, April). Dudley Street Neighborhood Initiative/Winthrop Estates. *Planning.* Chicago: American Planning Association.

Apgar, W.C., Jr., & DiPasquale, D. (1991). *State of the Nation's Housing.* Cambridge, MA: Joint Center for Housing Studies of Harvard.

Babcock, Richard, & Bonta, John S. (1973). *New Zoning Techniques for Inner City Areas.* Chicago: Planners Press.

Babcock, Richard, & Weaver, Clifford. (1979). *City Zoning: The Once and Future Frontier.* Chicago: Planners Press.

Bailey, Laura. (1995). *Proposal for the City of Houston Planning Department.* Unpublished. Houston, TX: Planning & Development Department.

Baker, Keith. (1995). *Evaluating Small Scale Community Based Programs.* Washington, DC: The Milton S. Eisenhower Foundation.

Barrett, Katherine, & Greene, Richard. (1993). Pittsburgh: Trickling Up. *Financial World 162*(5), 54–62.

Baum, Alice S., & Burnes, Donald W. (1993). *A Nation in Denial: The Truth about Homelessness.* Boulder, CO: Westview Press.

Baumgartner, M. P. (1988). *The Moral Order of a Suburb.* New York: Oxford University Press.

Begovich, Ray. (1995). From Blight to Bright: The Transformation of an Entire Block. *Journal of Housing & Community Development, 52*(5), 21–23.

Bernick, Michael. (1996). Transit Villages: Tools for Revitalizing the Inner City. *Access.* Berkeley, CA: University of California Transportation Center.

Birch, Eugenie. (1996). Planning in a World City: New York and Its Communities. *Journal of the American Planning Association, 4.*

Blair, John. (1995). *Local Economic Development Analysis and Practice.* Thousand Oaks, CA: Sage.

Blakely, Edward J. (1994). *Planning Local Economic Development: Theory and Practice.* Thousand Oaks, CA: Sage.

Bloomfield-Garfield Corporation. (1996). *Fact Sheet.* Unpublished. Pittsburgh, PA: Bloomfield-Garfield Corporation.

Blue Hill Avenue Task Force. (1996). *Blue Hill Avenue . . . A Community Vision.* Boston: Blue Hill Avenue Task Force, City of Boston.

Bogdon, Amy S., & Follain, James R. (1996). Multifamily Housing: An Exploratory Analysis Using the 1991 Residential Finance Survey. *Journal of Housing Research, 7*(1).

Boston Department of Neighborhood Development (DND). (1996). *Home Sales General Information.* Unpublished. Boston: City of Boston.

Bramhall, Russell G. (1974). *Individual Environmental Perception: Selected Individual Characteristics and Their Relationship to Residential Locational Preference—Indiana, Pennsylvania.* Thesis (MA), Indiana University of Pennsylvania.

Bratt, Rachel. (1997). From BURP to BHP to Demo Dispo: Lessons from Affordable Multifamily Housing Rehabilitation Initiatives in Boston. In William van Vliet

(Ed.), *Affordable Housing and Urban Redevelopment in the United States* (pp. 27–51). Thousand Oaks CA: Sage.

Breitbart, Myrna Margulies. (1995). Banners for the Street: Reclaiming Space and Designing Change with Urban Youth. *Journal of Planning Education and Research, 15,* 35–49.

Bright, Elise M. (1996). *Economic Asset and Community Development Plan for the Near Southeast Neighborhood: Fort Worth, Texas.* Arlington, TX: School of Urban and Public Affairs, University of Texas at Arlington.

———. (1995). *Taking without Compensation in Low Income Areas: Turning Tragedy into Opportunity.* Center for Economic Development Research and Service Report, 95 (13). Arlington, TX: School of Urban and Public Affairs, University of Texas at Arlington.

———. (1997). *TOADS: Instruments of Urban Revitalization.* National Center for the Revitalization of Central Cities. New Orleans, LA: College of Urban and Public Affairs, University of New Orleans.

———. (1999). TOADS: Instruments of Urban Revitalization. In F. Wagner & A. Mumphrey (Eds.), *Managing Capital Resources for Central City Revitalization* (pp. 45–79). New York: Garland Press.

Bright, Elise, Cole, Richard L., & Wyman, Sherman M. (1995). Central-City Revitalization: The Fort Worth Experience. In *Urban Revitalization Policies and Programs* (pp. 128–162). Thousand Oaks, CA: Sage.

Brokaw, Leslie, & Lahvic, Ray. (1992). Fast Rising. *Inc., 14*(8), 64–73.

Burchell, Robert, & Listokin, David. (1981). *Adaptive Reuse Handbook.* Rutgers, Center for Urban Policy Research (CUPR).

Bureau of Governmental Research. (1992). *Inventory of Economic Development Programs in the City of New Orleans, 1970–1992.* Working Paper No. 2 (September). New Orleans, LA: National Center for the Revitalization of Central Cities.

Bursik, Robert J. Jr., & Grasmick, Harold G. (1993). *Neighborhoods and Crime: The Dimensions of Effective Community Control.* New York: Lexington Books.

Burton, Dorothy, Meador, Pete, & Warren, John. (1987). *Community Revitalization in South Dallas/Fair Park.* Arlington, TX: School of Urban and Public Affairs, University of Texas at Arlington.

Byrum, Oliver. (1992). *Old Problems in New Times: Urban Strategies for the 1990s.* Chicago: American Planning Association.

Caro, Robert. (1975). *The Power Broker: Robert Moses and the Fall of New York.* New York: Random House.

Carson, Rachel. (1962). *Silent Spring.* Boston: Houghton Mifflin.

Carter, Claire. (1991, May 12). Whatever Ought To Be, Can Be. *Parade.*

Carver, H. (1960). Planning in Canada. *Habitat 3*(5), 2–5.

Central Area Action Plan—Implementation Team (CAAP-IT). (1996a). *CAAP-IT Reports, 1*(1). Seattle, WA: Central Area Action Plan.

———. (1996b). *First Annual Report of the Central Area Action Plan Implementation Team, March 1995–December 1995.* Seattle: Central Area Action Plan.

Central Area Development Association. (1996a). *CADA Projects.* Seattle: CADA.

———. (1996b). *Good Neighbor Fund Guidelines.* Seattle: CADA.

Central Area Neighborhood Planning Teams. (1996). *On the Move! The Central Area Community.* Seattle: CAAP-IT.

Central Area Planning Committee. (1993). *Central Area Action Plan.* Seattle: City of Seattle Department of Neighborhoods.

Central Area Planning Team. (1996). *Columbia City Neighborhood Planning: Experiences and Lessons from Other Communities.* Seattle: City of Seattle.

Cervero, Robert. (1996). Jobs-Housing Balance Revisited: Trends and Impacts in the San Francisco Bay Area. *Journal of the American Planning Association, 4,* pp. 492–511.

Change, Decay, and Some Revival. *The Economist, 310*(7593), p. 61.

Chicago, City of. (1996). *Cityspace: An Open Space Plan for Chicago.* Chicago: City of Chicago.

Church, Albert M. (1976). *Statistics and Computers in the Appraisal Process.* Chicago: International Association of Assessing Officers.

Cisneros, Henry. (1995). *Regionalism: The New Geography of Opportunity.* Washington, DC: U.S. Department of Housing and Urban Development.

Clark, Thom. (1985). Housing after Section 8: Coping with the Cuts. *The Neighborhood Works, 8*(1). Washington, DC: Neighborhood Reinvestment Corp.

Clapp, James A. (1971). *New Towns and Urban Policy.* New York: Dunellen.

Cleveland, City of. (1995). *Citizens' Report.* Cleveland: Office of the Mayor.

Cleveland City Planning Commission. (1991). *Cleveland Civic Vision 2,000 Citywide Plan.* Cleveland: Cleveland City Planning Commission.

Cleveland Department of Community Development. (1993). *Annual Report.* Cleveland: City of Cleveland.

———. (1994). *Annual Report.* Cleveland: City of Cleveland.

———. (1995). *Cleveland's Field of Dreams.* Cleveland: City of Cleveland.

———. (1996). Division of Neighborhood Services. *Year 22 Block Grant Council Briefing Document.* Cleveland: City of Cleveland.

Cleveland Housing Network, Inc. (1996). *The Lease Purchase Program.* Unpublished. Cleveland.

Clinton, Hillary Rodham. (1996). *It Takes a Village: And Other Lessons Children Teach Us.* New York: Simon and Schuster.

Coffey, Brian, & Kleniewski, Nancy. (1988). New Houses on Old Lots. *Planning, 7.*

Cole, Richard L., Smith, Ann Crowley, & Taebel, Delbert A. (1984). *The Quality of Life in Texas Cities: A Ranking and Assessment of Living Conditions in Texas' Largest Communities.* Arlington, TX: Institute of Urban Studies.

Committee for Economic Development. (1982). *Public-Private Partnerships: An Opportunity for Urban Communities.* New York: Committee for Economic Development.

Community Action Program. (1967). *It's Your Neighborhood.* Washington, DC: U.S. Government Printing Office.

Cook, James. (1987). Priming the Urban Pump. *Forbes, 139*(6), 62, 64.

Cooney, Catherine. (October, 1986). Coalition Pushes State to Fill Housing Gap. *The Neighborhood Works.*

Craig, W. (1983). The Second Coming of Newark. *New Jersey Reporter,* 19–23.

Cronon, William. (1991). *Nature's Metropolis: Chicago and the Great West.* New York: W. W. Norton.

Cullingworth, J. Barry. (1993). *The Political Culture of Planning.* New York: Routledge.

Daniels, Diane. (1995). Partnership for the Future. *Pittsburgh Renaissance News,* 29(49), 1.

Davis, Tim. (1996). *Calling the Fenway Home* (brochure). Boston: Fenway CDC.

Dietrick, Sabine, & Ellis, Cliff. (1999). New Urbanism in the Inner City: Four Projects in Pittsburgh. Unpublished. Graduate School of Public and International Affairs, University of Pittsburgh.

Detroit City Planning Department. (1995). *Detroit Empowerment Zone.* Detroit City Planning Department.

Dillon, David. (1988, July 3). A Downtown Success Story: Kansas City Brings Housing Back to a Historic District. *The Dallas Morning News,* pp. 1c, 3c.

Dolbeare, C. N. (1991). *Out of Reach: Why Everyday People Can't Find Affordable Housing.* Washington, DC: Low Income Housing Information Service.

Dornbusch, David, & Company, & Kahn/Mortimer/Associates. (1982). *Rainier-Atlantic (I-90) Corridor Development Study, Final Report.* Seattle: City of Seattle Department of Community Development.

Downs, Anthony. (1991). The Advisory Commission on Regulatory Barriers to Affordable Housing: Its Behavior and Accomplishments. *Housing Policy Debate, 2,* 1095–1137.

Dudley Neighbors Incorporated (DNI). (October 1994). *Our Community Land Trust.* Unpublished. Boston: DNI.

Dudley Street Neighborhood Initiative (DSNI). (1996a, January). *Creating Our Urban Village* (brochure). Boston: DSNI.

————. (1996b, June). *Most Notable Accomplishments in DSNI's History.* Unpublished. Boston: DSNI.

————. (1996c, Summer). *Newsletter.* Boston: DSNI.

Dudley Town Common [Brochure]. Boston: Dudley Street Neighborhood Initiative.

Edmondson, Brad. (1986). The Midwest: St. Paul's American Beauty. *American Demographics, 8*(5), 44.

Elias, C. E. Jr., Gillies, James, & Riemer, Svend. (1966). *Metropolis: Values in Conflict.* Belmont, California: Wadsworth.

Enterprise Foundation. (1995). *A Time of Change: 1995 Annual Report.* Columbia, MD: The Enterprise Foundation.

Environmental Protection Agency (EPA) Office of Research and Monitoring Environmental Studies Division. (1973). *The Quality of Life Concept: A Potential New Tool for Decision-Makers.* Environmental Protection Agency. Washington, DC: U.S. GPO.

Everybody's Money. (1977, Summer). Sweat Equity Pays Off. *Everybody's Money.*

Fainstein, Susan S. (1994). *The City Builders.* Cambridge, MA: Blackwell.

Fainstein, Susan S., & Fainstein, Norman. (1991). *Public-Private Partnerships for Urban (Re)Development in the United States.* Working Paper no. 35A. Piscataway, NJ: Center for Urban Policy Research.

Fainstein, Susan S., & Hirst, Clifford. (1993). *Neighborhood Organizations and Community Planning: The Case and Context of the Minneapolis Experience.* Working Paper no. 77, Center for Urban Policy Research, Rutgers University, New Brunswick, NJ.

Feagin, Joe R. (1975). *Subordinating the Poor: Welfare and American Beliefs.* Englewood Cliffs, New Jersey: Prentice-Hall.

————. (1978). *Discrimination American Style: Institutional Racism and Sexism.* Englewood Cliffs, New Jersey: Prentice-Hall.

Feagin, Joe R., & Parker, Robert. (1990). *Building American Cities: The Urban Real Estate Game.* Englewood Cliffs, New Jersey: Prentice-Hall.

Federation of Tax Administrators. (1984). *The Discovery and Collection of Delinquent Taxes: A Compilation of State Programs and Procedures.* Research report no. 101.

Ferguson, Ronald F., & Dickens, William T. (Eds.) (1999). *Urban Problems and Community Development.* Washington, DC: The Brookings Institute.

Fitzpatrick, Dan. (1996, July 1). What Happened to . . . The Hill District? *Minority Business Times* Supplement to the Pittsburgh Business Times.

Fleming, Ronald Lee. (1994). Saving Face: How Corporate Franchise Design Can Respect Community Identity. *Planning Advisory Service Report* 452. Chicago: American Planning Association.

Ford Foundation. (1973). *Community Development Corporations: A Strategy for Depressed Urban and Rural Areas.* New York: Ford Foundation.

Frieden, Bernard J. (1990). Center City Transformed: Planners as Developers. *Journal of the American Planning Association, 56,* 423–428.

————. (1995). The Urban Policy Legacy. *Urban Affairs Review, 30*(5), 681–686.

Frieden, Bernard J., & Sagalyn, Lynne B. (1992). *Downtown, Inc.: How America Rebuilds Cities.* Cambridge, MA: The MIT Press.

Friedenberg, E. Z. (1980). *Deference to Authority: The Case of Canada.* White Plains, NY: M. E. Sharpe (Random House).

Fuller, Millard, & Fuller, Linda. (1990). *The Excitement Is Building: How Habitat for Humanity Is Putting Roofs over Heads and Hope in Hearts.* Dallas, TX: Word.

Gallagher, Patrick J. (1997). *Holding Ground: The Rebirth of Dudley Street Viewers Guide.* Bethesda, MD: TLCI.

Gans, Herbert J. (1962). *The Urban Villagers: Group and Class in the Life of Italian Americans.* New York: Free Press of Glencoe.

Garreau, Joel. (1991). *Edge City: Life on the New Frontier.* New York: Doubleday.

Gilderbloom, John I. (1993, August 19). A New Lease on Life for Rent Control. *The Wall Street Journal,* p. A11.

————. (1995). Rebuilding Russell: Rebirth of a Louisville Neighborhood. *CUP Report, 6*(3/4), 5.

Gilderbloom, John I., & Mullins, Jr., R. L. (1995, Winter). The University as a Partner for Rebuilding an Inner City Neighborhood. *Metropolitan Universities, 2,* pp. 79–95.

Gilderbloom, John I., & Wright, Mark T. (1993). Empowerment Strategies for a Low Income African American Neighborhood. *Harvard Journal of African American Public Policy,* pp. 77–95.

Gittell, Ross J., & Vidal, Avis. (1999). *Community Organizing: Building Social Capital as a Development Strategy.* Thousand Oaks, CA: Sage.

Glaser, Mark, Denhardt, Kathryn, & Grubbs, Joseph. (1995, May). *Critical Partnerships and Community Organization: Local Government Intervention and the Formation of a Community-based Organization.* Portland, OR: Urban Affairs Association paper.

Go Ask Alice. (1971). New York: Simon & Schuster.

Goetz, Edward. (1998). Race, Class, and Metropolitan Housing Strategies: A Look at the Minneapolis-St. Paul Region. Paper presented at the Urban Affairs Association annual conference, Fort Worth, TX.

Goetz, Edward, Lam, Hin Kim, & Heitlinger, Anne. (1996). "There Goes the Neighborhood? Subsidized Housing in Urban Neighborhoods." *Center for Urban and Regional Affairs Reporter, 23*(1), 1–6. Minneapolis, MN: University of Minnesota.

Goldberg, M. A., & Mercer, J. (1986). *The Myth of the North American City: Continentalism Challenged.* Vancouver: University of British Columbia Press.

Goldsmith, Stephen. (1999). *The Twenty-First Century City: Resurrecting Urban America.* Lanham, MD: Rowman and Littlefield.

Gordon, Andrew, Ulberg, Cy, & Locke, Hubert. (1996). *Draft: Ethnic Diversity in Southeast Seattle: Presentation of Materials and Initial Findings.* Unpublished paper. Seattle, WA: University of Washington.

Gould, Jay M. (1986). *Quality of Life in American Neighborhoods: Levels of Affluence, Toxic Waste, and Cancer Mortality in Residential Zip Code Areas.* Boulder, CO: Westview Press.

Gratz, Roberta Brandes. (1994). *The Living City: How America's Cities Are Being Revitalized by Thinking Small in a Big Way.* Washington, DC: The Preservation Press.

———. (1995, March). The Preservationist. *Town and Country.*

Greenberg, Michael R., & Popper, Frank J. (1994, April). Finding Treasure in TOADS. *Planning,* 24–27. Chicago: American Planning Association.

Gruen, Victor. (1964). *The Heart of Our Cities: The Urban Crisis Diagnosis and Cure.* New York: Simon and Schuster.

Gunsch, Dawn. (1993, March). Urban Renewal Is an Investment. *Personnel Journal, 72*(3), 53–55.

Hanson, Warren. (1996). Greater Minnesota Housing Fund Background Information. Unpublished material obtained from the McKnight Foundation, Minneapolis.

Harayda, Janice. (1995, October). Sober View of the City: Essays Say Cleveland Has Much Work Ahead. *CUPR Newsletter.* New Jersey: Rutgers University.

Hardin, Garrett. (1968, December). The Tragedy of the Commons. *Science, 162,* pp. 1243–1248. Washington, DC: American Association for the Advancement of Science (December).

Hare, Patrick H., Conner, Susan, & Merriam, Dwight. (1981, December). Accessory Apartments: Using Surplus Space in Single-Family Houses. *Planning Advisory Service Report, 365.* Chicago: American Planning Association.

Harris, Ian. (1986, January). New Owner Replaces Absentees. *The Neighborhood Works.*

Hart, John. (1991). *Farming on the Edge.* Berkeley, CA: University of California.

Henry, J. Marilyn. (1996a). NAHRO Awards of Excellence. *The Journal of Housing and Community Development, 53,* 1.

Hill, Lewis W., & Boylan, Frankie M. (1972, June). A Housing Rehabilitation Program. *Planners Notebook.* American Institute of Planners, 2(3).

Hindley, Barbara. (1992). *The Boston Foundation, Catalyst for Community: Mapping a Neighborhood's Assets* [brochure]. Boston: The Boston Foundation.

Hinshaw, Mark L. (1995, February). Design Review. *Planning Advisory Service Report, 454.* Chicago: American Planning Association.

————. (1999). *Citistate Seattle: Shaping a Modern Metropolis.* Chicago: American Planning Association.

Hodges, Allan A. (Ed.) (1998a, April). *Boston on Foot: City Planning Guide.* Boston: Massachusetts Chapter, American Planning Association.

————. (1998b, March). Big Dig, Big Results. *Planning.* Chicago: American Planning Association.

Hoffman, Alexander von. (1994). *Local Attachments: The Making of an American Urban Neighborhood 1850 to 1920.* Baltimore, MD: Johns Hopkins University Press.

Holding Ground Productions. (1997). *Holding Ground: The Rebirth of Dudley Street* (brochure). New York: Holding Ground Productions.

Homsy, George. (1998, March). Bouncing Back: Neighborhood Power in Boston and Its Suburbs. *Planning.* Chicago: American Planning Association.

Hornburg, Steve P., Managing Editor. *Housing Policy Debate* (private correspondence with author, 4/2/98).

Horowitz, Craig. (1994, November). South Bronx Renaissance. *New York.*

Housing and Neighborhood Development Division. (1992). *Erie-Ellington Neighborhood Partnership Initiative.* Boston: Public Facilities Department.

Houston Planning Department. (1994, July 24). *Foreclosures and Revitalization Programs in Selected U.S. Cities: Table F-2.* Unpublished. City of Houston.

Howe, Deborah A., Chapman, Nancy J., & Baggett, Sharon A. (1994, April). Planning for an Aging Society. *Planning Advisory Service Report* 451. Chicago: American Planning Association.

Howington, Patrick. (1993, August). Home Fair for First-Time Buyers Offers Hope, Draws a Crowd. *The Courier-Journal,* p. B3.

Hoyle, Cynthia L. (1995, July). Traffic Calming. *Planning Advisory Service Report,* 456. Chicago: American Planning Association.

Ian, Harris. (1986, January). New Owners Replace Absentees. *The Neighborhood Works,* pp. 27–28.

Imbroscio, David, Orr, Marion, Ross, Timothy, & Stone, Clarence. (1993, February). *Baltimore and the Human Investment Challenge.* Working Paper No. 5. New Orleans, LA: National Center for the Revitalization of Central Cities.

————. (1993). Baltimore and the Human Investment Challenge. In *Urban Revitalization Policies and Programs* (pp. 38–68). Thousand Oaks, CA: Sage.

Institute of Urban Studies. (1970). *The Texas Property Tax.* Arlington, TX: School of Urban and Public Affairs, University of Texas at Arlington.

International Association of Assessing Officers. (1977). *Analyzing Assessment Equity.* Chicago: International Association of Assessing Officers.

————. (1977). *Property Assessment Valuation.* Chicago: International Association of Assessing Officers.

Jackson, Derrick Z. (1997, July 6). Dudley Street's Vision for a Village. Boston: *Boston Globe,* p. A19.

Jacobs, Jane. (1961). *The Death and Life of Great American Cities.* New York: Random House.

————. (1969). *The Economy of Cities.* New York: Vintage Books.

Jain, R. K., Urban, L. V., Stacey, G. S., & Balbach, H. E. (1993). *Environmental Assessment.* New York: McGraw-Hill.

James W. Rouse Forum on the American City 1997: Executive Report. (1997). Washington, DC: Fannie Mae Foundation.

Jencks, Christopher, & Peterson, Paul. (Eds.). (1991). *The Urban Underclass.* Washington, DC: Brookings Institute.

Judd, Dennis, & Parkinson, Michael. (1990). *Leadership and Urban Regeneration: Cities in North America and Europe.* Newbury Park, CA: Sage.

Kaufman, Tracy. (1996). Poverty Housing Defeats Families. *Habitat World, 13*(1).

Kay, Jane Holtz. (1998, March). The Hub is Hot. *Planning.* Chicago: American Planning Association.

Keane, Thomas M., Jr. (1998, March/April). Good Plans. *New England Planning.*

Kearns, Gerry, & Philo, Chris. (Eds.). (1993). *Selling Places: The City as Cultural Capital, Past and Present.* New York: Pergamon Press.

Keating, W. Dennis, Krumholz, Norman, & Metzger, John. (1989). Cleveland: Post-Populist Public-Private Partnerships. In *Unequal Partnerships: The Political Economy of Urban Redevelopment in Postwar America* (pp. 121–133). Piscataway, NJ: Rutgers University Press.

Keating, W. Dennis, Krumholz, Norman, & Metzger, J. (1991). Post-populist Public-private Partnerships. In *Cleveland Development: A Dissenting View,* ed. A. Schorr. Cleveland: David Press.

Keating, W. Dennis, Krumholz, Norman, & Perry, David C. (Eds.). (1995). *Cleveland: A Metropolitan Reader.* Kent, OH: Kent State University Press.

Keating, W. Dennis, Krumholz, Norman, & Star, Philip. (Eds.). (1996). *Revitalizing Urban Neighborhoods.* Lawrence, KS: University of Kansas Press.

Kleniewski, Nancy. (1997). *Cities, Change, and Conflict: A Political Economy of Urban Life.* Belmont, CA: Wadsworth.

Knack, Ruth. (1999, January). Cleveland: The Morning After. *Planning.*

Knox, Paul L. (1995). Book Review—Breakthroughs: Re-Creating the American City. *Economic Geography, 71*(3), 335–336.

Koff, Larry. (1998, March/April). Planning: Boston Style. *New England Planning.*

Kotler, Neil G. (1978). *Neighborhood Economic Enterprises.* Washington, DC: Kettering Foundation.

Kupel, Jim. (1984, September). Portland, Maine, Grows through Cooperative Effort. *American City & County,* 74.

Labich, Kenneth. (1993, September). New Hopes for the Inner City. *Fortune,* 82–90.

Lake, Robert W. (1979). *Real Estate Tax Delinquency: Private Disinvestment & Public Response.* New Brunswick, New Jersey: The Center for Urban Policy Research.

Lang, Michael H. (1982). *Gentrification amid Urban Decline: Strategies for America's Older Cities.* Cambridge, MA: Ballinger.

Lane, Vincent. (1995). Best Management Practices in U.S. Public Housing. *Housing Policy Debate.* Washington, DC: Office of Housing Research, Fannie Mae.

Lapping, M. B. (1987). Peoples of Plenty: A Note on Agriculture as a Planning Metaphor and National Character in North America. *Journal of Canadian Studies, 22:*121–128.

Lauria, Mickey, Whelen, Robert K., & Young, Alma H. (1993). *Urban Revitalization Strategies and Plans in New Orleans, 1970–1993.* Working Paper No. 10 (April). New Orleans: National Center for the Revitalization of Central Cities.

———. (1995). The Revitalization of New Orleans. In *Urban Revitalization Policies and Programs* (pp. 102–127). Thousand Oaks, CA: Sage.

Levitt, Rachelle L. (Ed.). (1987). *Cities Reborn.* Washington, DC: Urban Land Institute.

Levy, John M. (1981). *Economic Development Programs for Cities, Counties, and Towns.* New York: Praeger.

Lewis, Sylvia. (1998, March). Up Close: Mayor Thomas Menino. *Planning.* Chicago: American Planning Association.

Lincoln Institute of Land Policy. (1982). *Land Taxation and Land Use.* Cambridge, MA: Lincoln Institute of Land Policy.

Linnen, Beth. (1989, February). "Hard-Headed Do-Gooders" Drive the Redevelopment of Chicago's South Side. *Savings Institutions.*

Lipsey, Ellen J. (1998, March/April). Preservation Planning: A Status Report from Boston. *New England Planning.*

Local Initiatives Support Corporation. (1996). *Celebrating the Campaign for Communities and Fifteen Years of Revitalizing America's Neighborhoods.* New York: Local Initiative Support Corporation.

Loukaitou-Sideris, Anastasia, & Banerjee, Tridib. (1996). There's No There There: Or Why Neighborhoods Don't Readily Develop near Light-Rail Transit Stations. *Access.* Berkeley, CA: University of California Transportation Center.

Lowertown Redevelopment Corporation. (1998). *Lowertown—Welcome to Lowertown: Saint Paul's Exciting New Urban Village.* St. Paul, MN: Lowertown Redevelopment Authority.

Lunt, Penny. (1993). Urban Allies on the Move. *ABA Banking Journal, 85*(8): 34–42.

Lurcott, Robert H., & Downing, Jane A. (1987, Autumn). A Public-Private Support System for Community-Based Organizations in Pittsburgh. *APA Journal,* 459–468.

Lynch, Kevin. (1974). *The Image of the City.* Cambridge, MA: MIT Press.

McFarling, Usha Lee. (1994, November 13). Turning Back a Toxic Tide on Dudley Street. *Boston Globe.*

McHarg, Ian. (1969). *Design with Nature.* Garden City: Doubleday/Natural History Press.

McKee, Bradford. (1995, April). South Bronx. *Architecture—The AIA Journal, 84*(4): 86–95.

McKenna, Linda. (1988, July). Working Partnership. *Mortgage Banking, 48*(10): 63, 65.

McKnight Foundation. (1995). *Annual Report.* Minneapolis: McKnight Foundation.

McNulty, R. J., Jacobson, Dorothy R., & Penne, R. Leo. (1985). *The Economics of Amenity: Community Futures and Quality of Life.* Washington, DC: Partners for Livable Places.

Manchester Citizens Corporation. (1994, Fall). Manchester Endangered: A Strategic Plan for Action. (Pittsburgh, PA) *Manchester News.*

———. 1996. HOPE VI Plus Narrative. (Pittsburgh, PA) *Inside Manchester.*

Marino, Dennis R., Rosser, Lawrence B., & Rozran, Andrea R. (1979, March). The Planner's Role in Facilitating Private Sector Reinvestment. *Planning Advisory Service Report, 340.*

Martin, Thomas J. (1978). *Adaptive Use.* Washington, DC: Urban Land Institute.

Martz, Wendelyn A. (1995, March). Neighborhood-Based Planning: Five Case Studies. *Planning Advisory Service Report, 455.*

Massachusetts Department of Housing and Community Development (MDHCD). (1998a, April). *Orchard Park: Revitalizing a Troubled Public Housing Development* [brochure]. Boston: MDHCD.

———. (1998b). *Program Summary.* Boston: MDHCD.

———. (1998c, April). *The Rebirth of Urban Renewal: Medical City and a Revitalized Worchester* [brochure]. Boston: MDHCD.

———. (1998d, April). *Revitalizing Massachusetts Downtowns: More Than Just a New Façade* [brochure]. Boston: MDHCD.

Matulef, Mark Lewis. (1986, September/October). Focus on Chicago. *Journal of Housing, 43*(5): 228–231.

Mead, Lawrence M. (1992). *The New Politics of Poverty.* New York: Basic Books

Medoff, Peter, & Sklar, Holly. (1994). *Streets of Hope: The Fall and Rise of an Urban Neighborhood.* Boston: South End Press.

Meyer, John, Kain, John, & Wohl, Martin. (1965). *The Urban Transportation Problem.* Cambridge, MA: Harvard University Press.

Mellon Bank Corporation. (1995). *1995 Community Report: Our Changing Communities.* Pittsburgh, PA: Mellon Bank.

Merritt, Mike, & Goldsmith, Steven. (1994a, July 13). HomeSight Helps Fulfill a Dream. *Seattle Post-Intelligencer,* A12.

———. (1994b, July 13). The Neighborhood That Time Forgot. *Seattle Post-Intelligencer, p.* A1.

METRO VOTES Makes Its Mark. (1995, February). *SPC News,* p. 3.

Metzger, John T. (1986). *The Community Reinvestment Act and Neighborhood Revitalization in Pittsburgh.* Albany: SUNY Press.

Metzger, John. (1995–1996, Winter). The Future of Community Development in Pittsburgh. (Pittsburgh Community Reinvestment Group) *PCRG News,* p. 15.

Mier, Robert. (1993). *Social Justice and Local Development Policy.* Newbury Park, CA: Sage.

Miller, Donald H. (1997). Urban Sustainability Benchmarking—An Emerging Strategy for Physical Planning. Unpublished Paper, University of Washington.

Mills, Steven. (1986, January). Bank Contributions to Community Investment Corporation Help Rejuvenate Run-Down Chicago Neighborhoods. *American Banker, 151.*

Millstein, David L., & Hopkins, John J. (1987, October). Hatching Opportunities. *Real Estate Today,* pp. 76–78.

Mimram, Wendy. (1995, May 6). Classes Help Put People into Homes. Boston: *Boston Globe.*

Minneapolis Community Development Agency (MCDA). (1995). *Year-in-Review.* Minneapolis: MCDA.

———. (1996). *The Minneapolis Community Development Agency.* Minneapolis: MCDA.

———. (1998). What Is the MCDA? Unpublished. Minneapolis: MCDA.

Morgenroth, Lynda. (1994, April 24). Following Dudley's "Streets of Hope." *Boston Globe.*

Muhammad, Lawrence. (1994, May). Applied Academics: Louisville Professor John Gilderbloom Takes His Theories of Social Activism to the Streets. *Planning,* pp. 16–19.

Mumford, Lewis. (1961). *The City in History: Its Transformations and Its Prospects.* New York: Harcourt, Brace and World, Inc.

National Institute of Justice. (1990). *Crime and Public Housing.* Video available from the City of Fort Worth Municipal Reference Center, Fort Worth, TX.

Myers, Dowell. (1988, Summer). Building Knowledge about Quality of Life for Urban Planning. *Journal of the American Planning Association, 54*(3): 347–358.

National Trust for Historic Preservation. (1992). *Using the Community Reinvestment Act in Low-Income Historic Neighborhoods.* Washington, DC: National Trust for Historic Preservation.

Neighborhoods Against Urban Pollution (NAUP). (n.d.). *Working for Clean and Healthy Cities* [brochure]. Roxbury, MA: NAUP.

Nelson, Arthur, & Milgroom, Jeffrey H. (1993, April). *The Role of Regional Development Management in Central City Revitalization: Case Studies and Comparisons of Development Patterns in Atlanta, Georgia, and Portland, Oregon.* Working Paper No. 6 (April). New Orleans: National Center for the Revitalization of Central Cities.

———. (1995). Regional Growth Management and Central-City Vitality: Comparing Development Patterns in Atlanta, Georgia, and Portland, Oregon. In *Urban Revitalization Policies and Programs* (pp. 1–38). Thousand Oaks, CA: Sage.

Netzer, Dick. (1972). *Economics of the Property Tax.* Washington, DC: The Brookings Institute.

New Day Films. (1996, Fall). Holding Ground: A Battle Cry for Hope. *New Day Newsletter.* Ho-ho-kus, NJ: New Day Films.

———. (1997). *Holding Ground: The Rebirth of Dudley Street* [film]. Ho-ho-kus, NJ: New Day Films.

Newark Struggles to Recreate Itself. (1998, December 28). *New York Times,* p. B1.

Newberger, M. H. (1996). *Calling Allston-Brighton "Home"* [brochure]. Allston, MA: Allston-Brighton CDC.

Newton, Patrina L. (1994). *Retail Potential in the Stop Six Neighborhood.* Arlington, TX: School of Urban and Public Affairs, University of Texas at Arlington.

Odum, Eugene Pleasants. (1975). *Ecology: The Link between the Natural and the Social Sciences.* New York: Holt, Rinehart and Winston.

Office of University Partnerships. (1995). *University-Community Partnerships: Current Practices.* Rockville, MD: U.S. Department of Housing and Urban Development.

Oldman, Oliver, & Aaron, Henry. (1965). Assessment—Sales Ratios under the Boston Property Tax. *National Tax Journal, XVIII,* 36–49.

Olsen, Susan, & Lachman, M. Leanne. (1976). *Tax Delinquency in the Inner City.* Lexington, MA: Lexington Books.

Olson, Christopher. (1985, February). St. Paul Revives an Urban Village. *Building Design & Construction, 26*(2): 63–66.

Orfield, Myron. (1997). *Metropolitics: A Regional Agenda for Community and Stability.* Washington, DC: Brookings Institute.

Orum, Anthony M. (1995). *City-Building in America.* Boulder, CO: Westview Press.

Osborne, David, & Gaebler, Ted. (1993). *Reinventing Government: How the Entre-preneurial Spirit Is Transforming the Public Sector.* New York: Plume.

Ottawa, City of. (1996). *Planning Our Region.* Unpublished. Ottawa, Canada: City of Ottawa.

Page, Clint. (1984, February 13). Corporate Leadership in Urban Development. *Nation's Cities Weekly, 7,* 3.

Paine, Sylvia. (1995). Treasured Island. *Minneapolis-St. Paul, 23*(10), 62–63.

The Partnership Cure for Cities. (1998, June 25). *The Economist, 307*(7556), 54.

Patton, Michael Q. (1993). *The Aid to Families in Poverty Program: A Synthesis of Themes, Patterns, and Lessons Learned.* St. Paul, MN: The McKnight Foundation.

Peattie, Lisa R. (1994, Winter). An Argument for Slums. *Journal of Planning Education and Research, 13*(12), 136–143.

Peirce, Neal. (1982, January 11). Urban Progress Depends on Grassroots Talent: Small Business Can Rise or Fall on Local Factors. *Nation's Cities Weekly, 5,* 3.

———. (1982, January 11). Urban Progress Depends on Grassroots Talent. Center Promotes New Policy for Neighborhoods. *Nation's Cities Weekly, 5,* 3.

———. (1983, August). How Women May Remake Face of American City. *Nation's Cities Weekly.*

———. (1985, July). Renewing an Inner City and Retaining Historic Character. *Nation's Cities Weekly, 8,* 4.

———. (1995, April). How a City Finally Found Its Way. *National Journal, 27*(13), 826.

———. (1995, September). Redeveloping a City—The Smart Way. *National Journal, 27*(37), 2304.

———. (1997, March 9). St. Paul's Lowertown Provides the Nation a Model for Urban Villages. *Saint Paul Pioneer Press,* 25A.

Peirce, Neal, & Guskind, Robert. (1993). *Breakthroughs: Re-Creating the American City.* New Brunswick, NJ: CUPR Press.

Perlmutter, Ellen M. (1993, February 20). Fire Consumes Part of Manchester History. *Pittsburgh Post-Gazette,* B4.

Perry, Stewart. (1987). *Communities on the Way: Rebuilding Local Economies in the United States and Canada.* Albany: SUNY Press.

Phillips, E. Barbara. (1996). *City Lights: Urban-Suburban Life in the Global Society.* New York: Oxford University Press.

Pittsburgh, City of. (1986). *Draft Six-Year Development Program.* Pittsburgh: City of Pittsburgh.

Pittsburgh Community Reinvestment Group (PCRG). (1995a). *Follow the Money: Neighborhood Lending Report 1991–1994.* Pittsburgh: PCRG.

———. (1995b). *The Pittsburgh Community Reinvestment Group.* Pittsburgh: PCRG.

———. (1995c). *Year End Report.* Pittsburgh: PCRG.

Pittsburgh History and Landmarks Foundation. (1995). CNDI [Program Description]. Unpublished. Pittsburgh: Pittsburgh History and Landmarks Foundation.

———. (1996). *Preservation Loan Fund* [brochure]. Pittsburgh: Pittsburgh History and Landmarks Foundation.

Podolefsky, Aaron, & Dubow, Frederick. (1981). *Strategies for Community Crime Prevention: Collective Responses to Crime in Urban America.* Springfield, IL: Charles C. Thomas.

Pogge, Jean. (1985). *From Obstacle to Opportunity: An Evaluation of the Multifamily Tax Reactivation Program.* Chicago: Woodstock Institute.

Porter, Michael. (1994). The Competitive Advantage of the Inner City. *Harvard Business School Review.* Cambridge, MA: Harvard University.

Portland Bureau of Planning. (1991). Unpublished handouts. Portland: City of Portland.

Powell, Stewart, Walsh, Maureen, & Healy, Melissa. (1986). One More Blow for America's Cities. *U.S. News and World Report, 101*(5), 31.

Pratt Institute Center for Community and Environmental Development. (1992). *Uprooting Poverty through Community Development.* Brooklyn: Pratt Institute Center for Community and Environmental Development.

Providence Plan Housing Corporation. (1995). *Rebuilding Providence.* Providence, RI: Providence Plan Housing Corporation.

———. (1996, January). *Rebuilding Providence: A Report to the Board of Directors for Calendar Year 1995 Activity.* Unpublished.

Reardon, Kenneth M. (1995). *Institutionalizing Community Service-Learning at a Major Research University: The Case of the East St. Louis Action Research Project.* Unpublished paper, University of Illinois at Urbana-Champaign.

Rogers, Mary Beth. (1990). *Cold Anger: A Story of Faith and Power Politics.* Denton, TX: University of North Texas Press.

Rogowsky, Edward T., & Berkman, Ronald. (1995). New York City's "Outer Borough" Development Strategy: Case Studies in Urban Revitalization. In *Urban Revitalization Policies and Programs* (pp. 69–101). Thousand Oaks, CA: Sage.

Rooney, Jim. (1995). *Organizing the South Bronx.* Albany: State University of New York Press.

Rosen, David. (1987, December). Housing Trust Funds. *Planning Advisory Service Report, 406.* Chicago: American Planning Association.

Rothschild, Jan. (1996). South Bronx Comprehensive Community Revitalization Program. *Planning, 62*(4) 6.

Roudebush, Janice, & Well, Leslie J. (1980, May). Low- and Moderate-Income Housing: Part I, Increasing the Supply and Accessibility. *Planning Advisory Service Report, 350.* Chicago: American Planning Association.

Roudebush, Janice, & Well, Leslie J. (1980, June). Low- and Moderate-Income Housing: Part II, Conserving What We Have. *Planning Advisory Service Report, 351* Chicago: American Planning Association.

Rubin, Debra K. (1989, May 4). Blighted Cities Rise from the Ruins. *ENR Market Focus, 222*(18), 40.

Rusk, David. (1993). *Cities without Suburbs.* Washington, DC: Johns Hopkins University Press.

Saffrin, Joni, & Goldberg, Alan. (1985, September). Cities Reclaim SRO Housing. *The Neighborhood Works.*

St. Paul Division of Housing. (1995, April). Presentation to the Residential and Economic Development Task Force of the Long-range Capital Improvement Budget Committee. St. Paul, MN: City Department of Planning and Economic Development.

Saltman, Juliet. (1990). *A Fragile Movement: The Struggle for Neighborhood Stabilization.* Westport, CT: Greenwood Press.

San Diego Homeless Finding Shelter in Doomed Building. (1983, March 28). *Nation's Cities Weekly, 6,* 8.

Sands, Gary. (1994). Community Lending and Appraisal Standards. *The Appraisal Journal, 62*(4), 553–557.

Savageau, David. (1993). *Places Rated Almanac: Your Guide to Finding the Best Places to Live in North America.* New York: Prentice Hall Travel.

Sawicki, David S., & Craig, William J. (1996, Autumn). The Democratization of Data: Bridging the Gap for Community Groups. *Journal of the American Planning Association, 4,* 512–523.

Schein, Virginia E. (1995). *Working from the Margins: Voices of Mothers in Poverty.* Ithaca: Cornell University.

Schill, Michael H., Nathan, Richard P., & Persaud, Harrichand. (1983). *Revitalizing America's Cities: Neighborhood Reinvestment and Displacement.* Albany: State University of New York Press.

Schulgasser, Daniel M. (1989, March). *Urban Revitalization in Newark, New Jersey: From the Core to the Periphery of the Issue.* Unpublished paper.

Schwartz, Alex. (1995). Rebuilding Downtown: A Case Study of Minneapolis. In *Urban Revitalization Policies and Programs* (pp. 163–202). Thousand Oaks, CA: Sage.

Schwartz, Alex, & Vidal, Avis. (1996, August). *Between a Rock and a Hard Place: The Impact of Federal and State Policy Changes on Housing in New York City.* Unpublished paper.

Scott, Mel. (1971). *American City Planning Since 1890.* Berkeley, CA: University of California Press.

Seattle City Council Legislative Department. (1996). *Mayor's Recommended Seattle Projects for the Proposed King County Park and Conservation Bond.* Seattle: City of Seattle.

Seattle, City of. (1980). *Ordinance 109163.* Seattle: City of Seattle.

Seattle, City of, & City of Mercer Island, City of Bellevue, King County, Metro, and the Washington State Highway Commission. (1976). *Memorandum Agreement.* Seattle: City of Seattle.

Seattle Department of Community Development. (1976). *Atlantic Neighborhood Improvement Plan.* Seattle: City of Seattle.

———. (1989). *Seattle's I-90 Area Development Policies.* Seattle: City of Seattle.

Seattle Department of Housing and Human Services. (n.d.) Unpublished. Seattle: City of Seattle.

———. (1996). *Notice of Funding Availability (NOFA): Low-Income Housing for Families and Individuals.* Seattle: City of Seattle.

Seattle Department of Neighborhoods. (1995). *City of Seattle Fifth Annual Response to the Southeast Seattle Action Plan.* Seattle: City of Seattle.

Seattle Department of Parks and Recreation. (1996a). *Central Park Trail News and Updates.* Seattle: City of Seattle.

———. (1996b). *Free Summer Concert Series* [brochure]. Seattle: City of Seattle.

———. (1994). *Waterfall Garden: Pioneer Square* [brochure]. Seattle: City of Seattle.

Seattle Planning Department. (1993a). *Community Preferred Reuse Plan for Sand Point.* Seattle: City of Seattle.

———. (1993b). *Toward a Sustainable Seattle: Seattle's Plan for Managing Growth.* Seattle: City of Seattle.

Sheehy, Sandy. (1991, December). Saving a Neighborhood. *Metropolitan Home,* 64–69.

Silver, Christopher. (1985, Spring). Neighborhood Planning in Historical Perspective. *APA Journal,* 161–174.

Simons, R., & Sharkey, D. (1997). Jump Starting Cleveland's New Urban Housing Markets: Do the Potential Fiscal Benefits Justify the Public Subsidy Costs? *Housing Policy Debate, 8*(1), 143–172.

Singer, Karen. (1989, January 16). A Reborn Providence Turns to Face a Bright Future. *Adweek's Marketing Week, 26.*

Sommerfeld, Meg. (1993, June). In Baltimore, Residents, Foundation Lift a "Sinking" Community. *Education Week, 12*(38), 10–11.

Southeast Effective Development, Inc. (1996, spring). SEED Announces Phase Two of Rainier Valley Square. *Spectra, 1*(1).

———. (1991). *Southeast Seattle Action Plan Executive Summary.* Seattle: Southeast Effective Development.

———. (1995). *Strategic Plan.* Seattle: Southeast Effective Development.

Spaid, Elizabeth L. (1994, June 21). A Neighborhood Starts to Recover from Decline. *The Christian Science Monitor,* 10.

Special Workshop to Examine Revitalizing Neighborhood. (1984, November 19). *Nation's Cities Weekly, 7,* 26.

Squires, Gregory D. (1994). *Capital and Communities in Black and White: The Intersections of Race, Class, and Uneven Development.* New York: State University of New York Press.

———. (Ed.). (1989). *Unequal Partnerships: The Political Economy of Urban Redevelopment in Postwar America.* Piscataway, NJ: Rutgers University Press.

State of Rhode Island and the City of Providence. (1994, June). *Nomination for Providence, Rhode Island Designation as an Enterprise Community.* Report.

Stern, Jennifer. (1989, May). Pratt to the Rescue: Advocacy Planning is Alive and Well in Brooklyn. *Planning, 55*(5), 26–28.

Sternlieb, George. (1969). *The Tenement Landlord.* New Brunswick, NJ: Rutgers State University.

Storer, John H. (1968). *Man in the Web of Life: Civilization, Science, and Natural Law.* New York: The New American Library/Signet Books.

Sutro, Suzanne. (1990, December). Reinventing the Village: Planning, Zoning, and Design Strategies. *Planning Advisory Service Report, 430* Chicago: American Planning Association.

Taub, Richard P., Taylor, D. Garth, & Dunham, Jan D. (1984). *Paths of Neighborhood Change: Race and Crime in Urban America.* Chicago: The University of Chicago Press.

Teitler, Andrea. (1995, May). Not in My Neighborhood: Urban Gentrification. *Crisis, 102*(4), 31–32.

Temkin, Kenneth, & Rohe, William. (1996, Spring). Neighborhood Change and Urban Policy. *Journal of Planning Education and Research, 3.*

Texas State Comptroller. (1994). *The Appraisal District Director's Manual.* Austin, TX: The State Comptroller.

———. (1994). *The Appraisal Review Board Manual.* Austin, TX: The State Comptroller.

———. (1991). *School and Appraisal Districts' Property Value Study.* Austin, TX: The State Comptroller.

Third Ward Redevelopment Council. (1995). *Greater Third Ward Community Plan.* Houston, TX: City of Houston.

Thomas, Carol J., Foster, Howard, Bowyer, Robert, Chester, Philip, & Southworth, Michael. (1998). *Boston: Revolutionary Ideas Affecting Planning* [information sheet]. Chicago: American Planning Association.

Tindal, C. R., & Tindal, S. N. (1990). *Local Government in Canada* (3rd ed.). Toronto: McGraw-Hill Ryerson.

Unified Community Economic Development Association (UCEDA). (1996). *Empowering the Community through Housing, Education and Economic Development.* Seattle: UCEDA.

Urban, Jim. (1996, January). Do or Die: Can We Resuscitate the Region? (Pittsburgh, PA) *Executive Report.*

U.S. Bureau of the Census. (1950, 1960, 1970, 1980, 1990). Census of Population and Housing. Washington, DC: Bureau of the Census.

U.S. Department of Education. (1994). *Youth and Tobacco: Preventing Tobacco Use among Young People.* Washington, DC: U.S. Department of Health and Human Services.

U.S. Department of Housing and Urban Development. (1995). *Empowerment: A New Covenant with America's Communities.* Washington, DC: U.S. Department of Housing and Urban Development.

U.S. General Accounting Office. (1990). *The Urban Underclass.* Washington, DC: The General Accounting Office.

Vale, Lawrence J. (1997). The Revitalization of Boston's Commonwealth Public Housing Development. In *Affordable Housing and Urban Redevelopment in the United States* (pp. 100–134). Thousand Oaks, CA: Sage.

Varady, David P. (1986). *Neighborhood Upgrading: A Realistic Assessment.* Albany: State University of New York Press.

Vardey, Lucinda. (1995). *Mother Teresa: A Simple Path.* New York: Ballantine Books.

Vergara, Camilo Jose. (1995, August). Downtown Detroit: An American Acropolis. *Planning, 61*(8), 18–19.

van Vliet, Willem, & van Weesep, Jan. (Eds.). (1990). *Government and Housing: Developments in Seven Countries.* Newbury Park, CA: Sage.

van Vliet, Willem. (Ed.). (1997). *Affordable Housing and Urban Redevelopment in the United States.* Thousand Oaks, CA: Sage.

Wagner, Fritz, & Mumphrey, Anthony J., Jr. (Eds.). (1999). *Managing Capital Resources for Central City Revitalization.* New York: Garland Press.

Wagner, Fritz, Joder, Timothy E., & Mumphrey, Anthony J., Jr. (Eds.). (1995). *Urban Revitalization Policies and Programs.* Thousand Oaks, CA: Sage.

Waldsmith, Lynn. (1995, October 20). 400 Homes for Detroit Part of $46-Million Plan. *The Detroit News,* 1A, 8A.

Wallace, James E. (1995). Financing Affordable Housing in the United States. *Housing Policy Debate.* Washington, DC: Office of Housing Research, Fannie Mae.

Walljasper, Jay. (1997, March 3). When Activists Win: The Renaissance of Dudley Street. Washington, DC: *The Nation, 264*(8); 11–17.

Ward 2/3 Community Project. (1995). Unpublished. Toronto, Canada: City of Toronto.

Waste, Robert. (1998). *Independent Cities: Rethinking U.S. Urban Policy.* New York: Oxford University Press.

Watson, Greg. (1995, July 22). Dudley Street Has Potential to Be Multicultural Version of Newbury Street. *Boston Globe.*

Weisman, Leslie Kanes. (1992). *Discrimination by Design: A Feminist Critique of the Man-made Environment.* Chicago, IL: University of Illinois Press.

Wekerle, Gerta, & Whitzman, Carolyn. (1996). *Safe Cities: Guidelines for Planning, Design, and Management.* New York: Van Nostrand Reinhold

Whelan, Robert K., Young, Alma H., & Lauria, Mickey. (1993, January). *Urban Regimes and Racial Politics: New Orleans during the Barthelemy Years.* Working Paper No. 7. New Orleans: National Center for the Revitalization of Central Cities.

Whyte, William Foote. (1966). *Street Corner Society: The Social Structure of an Italian Slum.* Chicago: University of Chicago Press.

Wilke, John R. (1996, February 13). Mortgage Lending to Minorities Shows a Sharp 1994 Increase. *Wall Street Journal,* A1, A4.

Wilson, David. (1987, January). Urban Revitalization on the Upper West Side of Manhattan: An Urban Managerialist Assessment. *Economic Geography, 63*(1), 35.

Wilson, William J. (1987). *The Truly Disadvantaged: The Inner City, the Underclass, and Public Policy.* Chicago: University of Chicago Press.

Woodhouse, Barbara. (1985, August 5). "So Damn Much Fun" Rebuilding "Broken Buildings and People." *Nation's Cities Weekly, 8,* 5.

Wurtzel, Elizabeth. (1995). *Prozac Nation.* New York: Riverhead Books.

X, Malcolm. (1966). *The Autobiography of Malcolm X.* New York: Grove Press.

Yin, Jordan S. (1998). The Community Development Industry System: A Case Study of Politics and Institutions in Cleveland, 1967–1997. *Journal of Urban Affairs, 20*(2), 137–157.

Young, John A. (1988, January 25). Richmond Study Focuses on Downtown Housing Needs. *Nation's Cities Weekly, 11*(4), 8.

Zimmer, Jonathan E. (1977). *From Rental to Cooperative: Improving Low and Moderate Income Housing.* Professional Paper. Beverly Hills, CA: Sage.

Index